# Business Government Interface in a Global Environment

# Business Government Interface in a Global Environment

Nitish Sengupta

HAR-ANAND
PUBLICATIONS PVT LTD

HAR-ANAND PUBLICATIONS PVT LTD
E-49/3, Okhla Industrial Area, Phase-II, New Delhi-110020
Tel.: 41603490 Fax: 011-41708607
E-mail: info@haranandpublications.com/haranand@rediffmail.com
Website: www.haranandpublications.com



First Published: 2013



Published by Ashok Gosain and Ashish Gosain for
Har-Anand Publications Pvt Ltd

Printed in India at Vinayak Offset

# Foreword

I must first of all give the credit for writing this book to Narendra Kumar, my old friend, who suggested that I should write a hand- book on this topic. The writing of this book coincided with the period of unexpected economic slow down in some sectors of our country's economy and the down grading of assessment of India by a number of international credit rating agencies like Standard and Poor. This has happened despite India's performance in various phases of our economic growth and the inherent strength of our economy which helped in the stepping up of the growth rate in the recent years. But the growth rate has come down from 7 per cent or 8 per cent to around 5 per cent this year. This unexpected turn down has affected not only our current growth rate, but also level of production, level of exports and the growth of foreign exchange reserves. Government has been accused of not taking enough bold decisions in the economic field which would have inspired the growth rate. I have been teaching Government and Business for over three decades principally in the Administrative Staff College of India at Hyderabad, University of Delhi's Faculty of Management Studies Management Development Institute and International Management Institute. I owe a deep debt of gratitude to Prof. A. Dasgupta, formerly Dean of the Faculty of Management Studies, Delhi University, and N. P. Sen, formerly Principal, Administrative Staff College of India, who encouraged me to develop Government and Business as a regular discipline within the curriculum of MBA programmes. I thank my colleagues in these Institutions and innumerable fellow professionals in the Governments, the academics and business for significantly contributing to my thoughts from time to time.

When I started developing this subject India was known for its proverbial License Permit mechanism through which all intending entrepreneurs had to pass. Thanks to the then Prime Minister of India, P. V. Narshima Rao (1991-96), and then Finance Minister, Dr. Manmohan

Singh, India said goodbye to the proverbial Licensing Permit Raj in 1991. This contributed to industrial and economic growth in a phenomenal manner during the next three decades.

For our present purposes, we need not go through the details of the extremely negative and conservative licensing policy of the Government during the seventies and eighties. With the spectacular deterioration of the Government's financial position in 1989-90, specially the intensification of the foreign exchange crisis and the need for Government is approach the International Monetary Fund for a bail out, there was inevitably a move towards dismantling of the costly Licensing Permit Raj. Licensing policy was relaxed as never before and import restrictions and foreign exchange restrictions were removed. The responsibility of entrepreneurial decisions was transferred to the entrepreneurs and managers after nearly three decades from the officials and ministers. This coincided with another key change. India's economy had been insulated from the world during the three decades through a variety of measures such as import control, foreign exchange control and regulation of foreign investment and foreign technological collaborations, and also control on exports. Now India became a part of the global economy. An Indian company was no longer under a compulsion to obtain raw materials and intermediate goods locally and could now get them from anywhere in the world. Similarly, it could sell its products to any other country wherever it could obtain the best price. In India's corporate landscape today, a number of Indian business houses have become global, e.g. Tatas, Birlas and Mittals while a number of companies which grew out of Indian entrepreneurship have passed on to foreign ownership, e.g. Ranbaxy, ACC and Ambuja cement.

Despite the down turn in recent months largely on account of deteriorating conditions in USA and EU and the withdrawal of funds by financial institutions from the Indian market to shore up their diminished capitals back home, Indian economy cannot be said to be beyond redemption. India's public sector has grown from strength to strength and is serving its role in sustaining the economy. There is no doubt the private sector will also follow suit. The point to remember is that there is no case for going back to the old days of Control and Permit Raj, but there is every case for continuing our reforms and deregulation while taking corrective steps to deal with the global situation and I have no doubt that India will once again resume its growth path.

I once again thank Narendra Kumar. I also thank the invaluable contributions made by innumerable friends and academicians, civil servants, students and industrialists and professional managers, discussion with whom spread over many days helped in no small measure in formulating the ideas presented here. I acknowledge the services rendered by Dipankar Nandi and Surinder Anand Kaur for stenographic assistance. I also thank my daughters, Mekhala Sengupta and Dr. Tamali Sengupta, for their understanding and suggestions.

**Nitish Sengupta**

# Contents

CHAPTER 1

# Business and Government: A Historical Survey

## WORLD VIEW

The globalizing of the world economy in the last three decades has in a way brought business and government much closer than ever before. This was all the more evident during the Wall Street crises from 2007 onwards when the spectacular collapse of all the major investment banks forced the U.S. government to take them over to protect employment and the interest of millions of bond holders. This public takeover of private debts would have startled U.S. presidents of the past generations. The same stand was taken by the European and Asian countries later on. The US government followed the same policies in several successive crises. The European Government also followed this policy in their own crises sometime later on. Currently with the deterioration of the Euro, the European community is also planning massive intervention to save the banking system in Greece, Italy, Portugal and Spain. Thus, it has come to be established that the government has a duty to intervene whenever any crisis occurs.

Germany and France have taken a saviour's rather than a service role in both rescuing the Euro and at the same time helping the beleaguered governments of Greece, Italy, Spain and Portugal out of the serious foreign exchange payment crises, created largely on account of improvidence and mismanagement of the currency. In Japan or in the ASEAN countries as well a fair degree of govt. regulation of business is prevalent. In India there has been a long spell of general deregulation in sharp contrast with the license-permit Raj of three decades. But government brought out an array of reliefs and concession to mitigate the effects of the Wall Street crises and also exercised the much needed fiscal and currency controls to contain price rise and inflation.

In the present day world no one will seriously dispute Government's power of regulation and intervention in economic life. This is so even in the few countries like Germany, which are formally wedded to free enterprise form or capitalism. Expanding role, and regulation of the private sector in some or other in the larger public interest as a part of national policy, In today's context one need not be a socialist in order to advocate, or accept greater Government regulation of private business. In the developing countries nearly all of which have embarked upon a declared policy of planned economic growth which allow some private enterprise in varying degrees. The role of Government is all the more important. Thus the question today is not whether there should be Government regulation of private business, but only to what extent it should be there. "The two most powerful institutions in society today; to quote Marshall Dimock, are business and government where they meet on common ground amicably or otherwise together they determine public policy both foreign and domestic for a nation." (Dimock, Marshall E – *Business and Government,* New York, Holt, Rhinemann and Winston Ine, 1960, p. 5).

Historically, there has always been close relationship of a very general kind between the established government and the economic system and institutions. Apart from the fact that it is the government alone which by the maintenance of public order in a community can create the basic conditions under which business and industry can flourish, the various policies followed by governments invariably cast decisive influence on the latter. Thus business and industry have always flourished in conditions of political stability in an area created or strong Emperor or king, and never in stages of political anarchy, or disintegration of a country into small principalities. In Europe the beginnings of modern capitalism were associated with the creation of strong monarchical governments which abolished all artificial economic barriers and established public order which made it possible for the mercantile classes to prosper. In our own country it was the political unification of the country in the early 19th century and the establishment of the strong British Raj which led to the growth of business and industry on modern lines.

However, it was only after the growth of industrial capitalism and the factory system in the eighteenth century that political science took serious notice of the ideal relationship between the State and private business. The periodic economic crisis through which the western world had passed, the two World Wars and the felt need for government intervention in the interest of planning and regulation have focused attention on this problem. Various theories have been advanced advocating State intervention varying forms to correct the imbalance created by utter planlessness, and to do away with such recurrent phenomena as over-production, violent fluctuations in prices, needless duplication, unemployment and poverty. All these theories are in reality variations of manifestations of various schools of political philosophy about the function of the State as applied to the economic milieu. They can be grouped under five broad schools of thought: anarchism, individualism, collectivism, socialism and communism. It is important to note that this classification is by no means watertight and that very often each group shades off so imperceptibly into another that it is almost impossible to draw a sharp distinction. Of them anarchism standing at one extreme advocated the total abolition of the State. Communism is at the order extreme, and seeks to place all property and all means of production and distribution under State ownership, and to subject the lives of individuals to very rigorous control and supervision. Between these two extremes lie individualism, collectivism and socialism. We can dismiss anarchism as just a matter of theoretical interest. Communism, on the other hand, is a form of socialism, the most extreme and complete one, in which private enterprise has no role. After the collapse of soviet communism China and Cuba remain the only countries formally wedded to Marxian communism, but in practice they have adopted market and free entities to the exclusion of Marxism-Stalinism. For our purposes we shall take brief notice of only individualism, collectivism and socialism which have a direct relevance for the subject of our study.

## INDIVIDUALISM

The prevailing climate of public opinion in Western Europe during the greater part of the 19th century has been characterized by the famous constitutional expert, Dicey, as 'individualism'. Briefly, it stood for government non-interference in business and the fullest possible scope for individual initiative unhindered by restrictions of the State. It proceeded from the simple assumption that every individual was the best judge of his interest, and therefore 'Legislation should aim at the removal of all these restrictions on the free action of an individual except those which are necessary for securing the like freedom on the part of his neighbor.' This freedom of enterprise and contract, it was held by individualists, would result in the greatest wealth and happiness of the greatest number, since, each individual would, unhampered by government regulation, act through the market mechanism in the consumers' or producers' interest whose sum total would be national interest. Normal laws of demand and supply would themselves lead to an 'equilibrium' and labour could from part of this 'invisible hand' as described by Adam Smith, the economist. The State's duties consisted only in defending itself against external enemies and, internally, in policing the community for which it could raise revenues. The French expression 'laissez faire' (let alone) summarizes excellently the spirit of individualism. "In general, individualists regard government only as a necessary evil shoes duty was merely to keep the ring' round the industry, to let men complete and fight it out, and only to ensure that they did not break the rules—especially their freely negotiated contractual obligations."

The economic aspects of individualism found their classic expression in the writings of Adam Smith, Jeremy Bentham, John Stuart Mill, Herbert Spencer, and the French Physiocrats. In his Wealth of Nations, Adam Smith advocated the principle of free competition. The same principle was also emphasized by the Physiocrats in France, one of whom, Francis Quesnay, wrote as follows: "Let absolute freedom of commerce be maintained; of the surest guardian of internal and external commerce, the most exact and profitable to the Nation and State, lies in the unlimited freedom of competition." The thoughts of Bentham and the writings of his disciples influenced State action in Britain to such an extent that Dicey has described the period from 1815 to 1870 as 'the period of Benthamism'. Bentham's thoughts were far from being purely negative. The aim of legislation was to promote 'the greatest happiness of the greatest number'. This positive aspect found expression not only in formulating the rules of the ring but also in innumerable positive actions like the Factory Acts, the Mines Acts, and the direct provision by the State of certain works of public utility such as roads, posts and other means of transport. Even an uncompromising opponent of State action like Adam Smith had conceded that the duty of the sovereign was 'that of erecting and maintaining those public institutions and these public works, which though they may be in the highest degree advantageous to a great society are, however, of such a nature, that the profit could never repay the expenses to any individual, or small number of individuals, and which it therefore cannot be expected that any individual or small number of individuals, should erect or maintain'.

In Herbert Spencer, the last of the great individualist philosophers, we find the most extreme type of individualism. Men, according to Spencer, wanted happiness above all, and could secure utmost happiness only by the unfettered exercise of his faculties. To achieve this end he must have a maximum of liberty. The only limitation on it should arise from the fact that there were also other human beings in the society thus each person could claim only that much liberty to exercise his faculties which was compatible with the possession of like liberty by others. The State was a necessary evil whose sole function should protect the individual against the wrongs of his neighbour or the violence of some foreign State, and thus to intervene only in the interest of a more equitable distribution of liberty. All other functions should be left to individuals or organizations. If the State went out of its way in these spheres it could not properly perform its true functions. "To each organ one function and only one" was his motto.

During the greater part of the 19th century, under the influence of these philosophers, the State's industrial policy in Western Europe and North America was reduced literally to *laissez faire*. The basic faith was that business should be left completely unfettered by governmental regulation. Such regulation or legislation interfered with the normal healthy growth of commerce and industry. Under the 'benevolent' influence of individualism the industrial revolution grew and the factory system developed with all its undesirable unhindered by any government control in the beginning. In the U.S.A. giant corporations acquire red monopolistic control with all its attendant evils.

It was the public outcry against these evils of unregulated industrial growth in England which first initiated the process of change in public opinion towards the acceptance of the need for State intervention, and eventually led to a reconsideration of these issues by the philosophers and the emergence of newer value judgments. First came an emotional reaction in Britain to the horrors disclosed by a series of official papers about trade and industry which the State had *let alone*. *The first revolt*, wrote Sidney Webb in his contribution to the Fabian Essays, "came from the artistic side. The first man, who really made a dent in the individualist shield was Carlyle, who knew how to compel men to listen to him." As early as 1843 Carlyle declared that "a government of the under classes by the upper classes on a principle of let alone is no longer possible in England in these days." This had its impact on the individualism of the age, and as we have seen, under Bentham's influence there was much talk of positive action by the State in several directions.

This line of thought culminated in John Stuart Mill who in his book, *Principles of Economy* came to the conclusion that while *laissez faire* was to be general rule, it was subject to "large exceptions". On the whole Mill had a conscientious objection to government interventions on several grounds: (i) "The compulsory character of the intervention itself, or of the levy of funds to support it"; (ii) the possibility of suppression of minority or individual rights; (iii) over-burdening of the State machinery which was inadequate to discharge even the existing duties; (iv) superior efficiency of a private agency owing of the stronger interest in the work; (v) "importance of cultivating habits of collective action in the people." As Mill emphatically states:

People among whom there is no habit of spontaneous action for a collective interests, who look habitually to their Government to commend or promote them in all members of joint concern—who expect to have everything done for them, have their faculties only half developed; their education is defective in one of its important branches.... There cannot be a combination of circumstances more dangerous to human welfare than that in which intelligence and talent are maintained at a high standard within a governing corporation, but starved and discouraged outside the pale.... It is therefore of supreme importance that all classes of the community, down to the lowest, should have much to do for themselves ... that the government should not only leave as much as possible to their own faculties the conduct of whatever concerns themselves alone, but should suffer them or encourage them to manage as many as possible of their joint concerns by voluntary co-operation.

Against these objections to State interference, Mill also put forward several exceptions favouring State action, e. g., (i) The incapacity of some people, notably children and the "uncultivated" to judge their own interest made it necessary for the State to intervene to protect their interests; (ii) Where individuals can judge their interest, but are 'unable to give effect to it except by concert which concert again cannot be effectual unless it receives validity and sanctions from the law'; (iii) Anything which it is desirable should be done for the general interests of mankind or of future generations, or for the present interests of those members of the community who require aid, but which is not of a nature to remunerate individuals or associations for undertaking it, is in itself a suitable thing to be undertaken by government." In many respects J.S. Mill was the bridge from the early 19th century absolute individualism to the full acceptance in the 20th century of the need for State action in all fields of economic life. Many of Mill's objections have lost force now. His exceptions, on the other hand, have become larger and larger under pressure of newer economic, social, industrial and political developments.

Laski in his *Grammar of Politics* (1925) declared that *laissez faire* as a systematic principle ended with the outbreak of war in 1914. Lord Keynes in 1926 published his lectures entitled *The End of Laissez Faire.* But as we have seen, the decline of *laissez faire* doctrine was not an event, but a long process which started even in the mid-19th century with the reaction against the horrors of unregulated industrialism. Even before the First World War absolute individualism had been discarded as a seriously argued philosophy, and the need for State action in a very wide economic area recognized. Among the intellectual influences shaping public opinion in Britain we can mention Charles Booth's *Survey of the Life and Labour of the People in London* (1891), *The Rowntree Survey at York* (1899), *The Fabian Essays* (1889), and the activities of Fabian socialists like Sidney and Beatrice Webb and Bernard Shaw who systematically preached not only the need for State interference in defence of the weaker sections and the labourers, but also for State participation in industry, State service for industry, and State insurance against risks of industry. The rise of trade unionism and the growth of the Labour Party in Britain and also cast decisive influence on the shaping of the public attitude.

The war of 1914-18 which inevitably led to near total governmental regulation and control of every aspect of economic life in nearly all Western countries accelerated this process. After the War there was no going back, but only progressive enlargement of the sphere of State action. The rise of totalitarian States—of the Communist variety in Soviet Union and of the Fascist variety in Germany and Italy which stood for everything opposed to *laissez faire*—had also its significance. The impact in particular of the experience of planned economic development in the Soviet Union was unmistakable. Not only the left-wing leaders and intellectuals in the West, but also leaders of freedom movements in colonial countries, notably Jawaharlal Nehru of India, drew their lessons from this.

Of equally wide implications were the lessons of the great world depression starting in 1929 which brought about unemployment and economic misery on an unprecedented scale in a large number of countries and led to vigorous political demands for State intervention. Close on its heels, with the publication in 1936 of J.M. Keynes' *General Theory of Employment, Interest and Money* began a general move for economic planning by government in countries like U.S.A. and Britain, although this planning unlike the Russian Five-Year Plans was confined to the prevention of unemployment and providing incentives and facilities for location of industries in backward areas. "The outstanding faults of the economic society in which we live," said Lord Keynes, "are its failure to provide for full employment, and its arbitrary and inequitable distribution of wealth and income." His recommendation was for "establishing certain central controls in matters which are now left in the main to individual initiative" in order to "exercise a guiding influence on the propensity to consume partly through its scheme of taxation, partly by fixing the rate of interest, and partly in other ways" and also in order to ensure "a somewhat comprehensive socialisation of investment" which, according to him, will prove "the only means of securing an approximation to full employment." The central controls necessary to ensure full employment will, of course involve a large extension of the traditional functions of government." His conclusion was "whilst, therefore, the enlargement of the function of government, involved in the task of adjusting to one another the propensity to consume and the inducement to invest, would seem to a 19th century publicist or to a contemporary American financier to be a terrific encroachment on individualism, I defend it, on the contrary, both as the only practicable means of avoiding the destruction of the existing economic forms in their entirety and as the condition of the successful functioning of individual initiative." The importance of Keynes' general equilibrium theory lies not only in its economic analysis of the self-deflationary process of contraction, the relationship between national income and investment - savings parity, between full employment equilibrium and arresting the deflationary process by increasing spending on consumers or producers goods. It also lies in his finding that the unregulated market economy may often lack reliable automatic powers to extricate itself from stagnation. "We should therefore substitute government action for the so-called automatic forces, for otherwise the economy having hit the rock bottom of the depression may stay there for an indefinite period waiting for profitable investment opportunities to arise naturally. Artificial inducements for saving and investment and for credit expansion so as to induce investment are therefore policies that government must apply." Keynes also commended these measures as a lasting solution to the problem of wars, for "if nations can learn to provide themselves with full employment by their domestic policy (and we must add if they can also attain equilibrium in the trend of their population) there need be no important economic forces calculated to set the interest of one country against that of its neighbour."

The Second World War further accelerated these trends towards greater State control over economy. After the War even in the Western democracies State control over industry and over distribution of its products, and planning in some form persisted. On the other hand the multiplication of the number of communist countries, the attainment of freedom by the Asian and African countries and their acceptance of the policy of centralized planning and management of their economics in order to attain higher rate of economic growth and income, changed the entire perspective in which individualism or *laissez faire* became purely a matter of academic interest. It is universally acknowledged that while individualism might have been valid in a bygone age of simple agricultural communities, it has no place in the industrial society of modern times. But it would not be correct to assume that individualism is altogether dead. It still survives in a very refined and limited form in the utterances made or attitudes taken sometimes by some industrialists, jurists, legislators and politicians on isolated issues on which government action is sought to be curtailed. But this surviving brand of individualism is not concerned with the freedom of the individual, but rather with the need for groups or corporate bodies to be free from undue governmental interference. Individualism survives today only in the slogans about free enterprise which are occasionally heard, or in the isolated activities of such groups as the Forum of Free Enterprise in our country or in the plea for self-regulation by industries to avoid the evils of *laissez faire* rather than accepting governmental regulation step.

## COLLECTIVISM

Collectivism arose as an inevitable reaction to the absolute play of individualism of the early 19th century. In the second half of the century it became quite clear both in the U.S.A. and Western Europe that whatever merits individualism might have had for a primitive society, it did not meet the needs of a complex highly industrialised society. There was consequently a change in public attitude and also philosophical thinking. This was the background of the rise of collectivism which treated the State, not as an evil, but as a desirable institution which was justified in interfering with the rights of the individual in the interest of the welfare of the society as a whole. Above all, collectivism stood for the authority and larger role of voluntary institutions (Trade Union etc.) and representative bodies rather than strengthening the direct coercive powers of the State.

The philosophical base for collectivism was provided by writers like Henry Sidgwick (*The Principles of Political Economy*) and Leon Duguit (*Law in the Modern State*). The latter believed that correlative with the power of the State to govern was a duty to provide public services. A public service is defined by Duguit as any activity which requires in the interest of social solidarity to be governmentally regulated and controlled. In a pioneer or non-industrial society a family was almost self-sustaining and had to depend on the State for almost nothing except security and public order. With the coming in of the industrial society people must depend on organizations to provide for such essential things as food, light, water and transport.

Whatever is essential to the smooth running of the society is a public service which it is the duty of the government to ensure.

Collectivism found expression both in U.S.A. and Western Europe in (i) various measures for governmental regulation of private business and (ii) various aids to private business and (iii) the creation of various institutions like cooperatives for providing public utility services. It is widely held in the U.S.A. That collectivism as represented by government aid and regulation of business (e.g. Sherman Antitrust Law, food laws, drug laws etc.) backed by a competent and impeccable government agency and active public cooperation can prevent many of the undesirable features of an unregulated industrial society, although it is also sometimes doubted if a political system with its doctrine of fundamental rights, judicial review, and separation of powers is well-suited to effective regulation. In recent times collectivism in the West has increasingly tended to come closer and closer to socialism, and the very name has also fallen into disuse.

## SOCIALISM

Despite the recent collapse of Marxism-led Socialism in Eastern Europe and Asia and the euphoric charade of private-sector led development nearly in every country, socialism in the broad sense of a social philosophy that accepts parliamentary democracy, but stands for the interests of the working class and the underprivileged, is still a powerful force.

Both collectivism and socialism stress the interest of the society rather than the rights of the individual. But whereas collectivism basically believes in a system of private ownership and private enterprise under over-all government regulation, socialism believes that all the means of production and distribution should be controlled and managed by the society, and that the interests of the society, as a whole cannot be secured so long as the capitalist system with its emphasis on the sanctity of private property remains. Thus the State plays a much greater role in socialism than in collectivism.

During the last one century and a quarter of its formal history, socialism has taken a great variety of forms. Utopian socialism of Robert Owen in England and Fourier and St. Simons in France in the early 19th century wanted to do away with the evils of unregulated industrialism through the welfare activities of model employers. Fabian socialism centring on a group of British intellectuals like Bernard Shaw, Graham Wallas, Harold Laski and Sidney and Beatrice Webb sought to eradicate poverty by educating public opinion about the need for socialist reforms and bringing about a series of reform measures not by any revolution, but through 'the inevitability of gradualness.' Guild socialism or syndicalism, as known on the Continent, viewed society as a combination of so many guilds or trade union bodies with the State or the "Commune", as they called it, as only the apex body. State socialism favours an extension of the state authority into the economic field through public ownership and operation of certain industries. Finally, Communism, or Marxian socialism, or scientific socialism as the Marxists themselves prefer to call it to distinguish it from other varieties of socialism, advocates the overthrow of the capitalist system by revolutionary working classes, the State take-over of all the means of production and distribution, the abolition of private property, eradication of all classes and the establishment of a classless society after a transitional phase of dictatorship of the proletariat. There is surprisingly little in Marxian literature about the socio-economic system that will follow capitalism in the long run. Essentially, Marx and his companion theoreticians concentrated on analysing the historical character of capitalism as a system that follows feudalism and precedes socialism, and in understanding the process of its disintegration and of the social revolution out of which socialism should emerge by necessity.

From the publication of Marx's *Communist Manifesto* in 1848 communism became a recognisable movement in the West side by side with the schools of thought and political parties generally called socialist. Despite their overlappings there is a conventionally accepted broad distinction between the two. The socialists like the communists believe in State control and ownership, as far as possible, of the means of production and distribution. Most of them lean heavily on Marxism in their analysis of the capitalist system, monopoly and unemployment and also liberally use Marxian concepts as tools of analysis. But, unlike the communists, they believe in the parliamentary democracy, party system, free press and freedom of thought and expression, and prefer to achieve their objectives through constitutional agitation and struggle, rather than violent revolution, though the latter is not ruled out in certain conditions. In the last one hundred and fifty years of its history Marxian communism took different shapes based on different interpretations of Marx's peculiar language and method of argument. Communism has taken different forms in the U.S.S.R., China and Yugoslavia. There was also vast difference between the State and Society that Marx and Engels envisaged in theory and the State and Society that emerged under Stalin's Marxism-Leninism, or Mao's Chinese Peoples Republic. In post-war Western Europe, notably France and Italy, communist parties have been functioning within the scope of parliamentary democracy and this has somewhat obliterated the traditional distinction between them and the socialists. The earlier monolithic character of international communism based on the concept of purity of ideology has been transformed into the acceptance of different roads to socialist society or its post-war theoretical variant, the people's democracy followed by different countries. But until the spectacular and traumatic collapse of Communism during the years 1989-91, Marxism-Leninism still remained the predominant doctrine in the countries from East Germany and Albania in the West to Vietnam and North Korea in the East with isolated pockets like Cube outside this block. The doctrines of Karl Marx remained the central point of all Marxist socialists.

Marxism, as developed by Karl Marx and Frederick Engels, and afterwards amplified and enlarged by Lenin, has now come to occupy a central place in socialism, not only because of its direct impact through international communism but also because of its indirect influence on the policies and programmes of socialist parties everywhere. The first of Marx's more important doctrine is dialectical materialism, also called historical materialism. In it Marx combined 'dialectics' as propounded by the 18th century German idealist philosopher Hegel, with materialism into an integrated philosophy of action. According to Hegel's theory the development of thought, or social development, takes place through contradictions or clashes between opposites that emerge in the thought or society respectively. Applying this to society Hegel viewed the bourgeois society as a system of different opposing classes which eventually turns itself into a form of State with its laws and policies. But Hegel's dialectics was conceived on a background of 'idealistic' philosophy which believed in the primacy of mind over matter. Marx transplanted it from this 'idealist' matrix to the environment created by the pervasive materialism of the age which believed in the primacy of matter/the physical nature/over mind, and not in any supernatural force or phenomenon. Dialectical materialism as evolved by him is based on the new discoveries in natural sciences important among which were the laws of transformation of energy, the discovery of cells and Darwin's Theory of the Origin of Species'. It, therefore, becomes a theory of social development consistent with the laws governing the physical universe, which believes in man's ability to transform the society by his own effort in accordance with certain natural laws of social development unaided by any supernatural force. Just as Marxism regards human consciousness as a product of 'matter' that exists independent of our mind, similarly, according to Marx, our society, politics, our religion, and attitudes are in general conditioned by economic factors which Marx calls the ultimate determining factor.

From dialectical materialism comes the second important concept, viz., materialist or economic interpretation of history. Applying the principles of dialectical materialism to the study of history Marx refused to agree with the orthodox economists that the capitalist system was part of the eternal order of nature. On the contrary, he regarded it as a passing phase in the transition from the feudal economy of the past to the socialist economy of the future. For Max the institutions or production, distribution and exchange which constitute the economic structure of the society are the real base on which the political, legal, moral or cultural superstructure rest. Those who control this economic structure necessarily control all other superstructures. Social change, according to Marx, arises out of a conflict between the changing forces of production and the existing and unyielding relations of production. The latter along with the accompanying legal and political superstructure do not change while basic changes have taken place in the material forces of production. This brings about a contradiction between the two which is resolved only when the former structure is changed in keeping with the changes in the latter.

The third important principle is the doctrine of class struggle. Society throughout history has been split into classes depending on the control over the means of production and distribution, and history, therefore, is the history of the struggle between these classes. Just as the slave society of ancient times was replaced through the struggle between classes by feudalism, and feudalism by capitalism, so the struggle of the present age is between the capitalist class on the one hand and the proletariat or the industrial working class on the other. Unlike the classical economists who argued in terms of the harmony of interest between various sections of the community, Marx saw economic life in terms of a conflict of interest between owners of property who do not work and workers who own no property.

Fourthly, there is the doctrine of surplus value of labour which emphasises that labour is the source of all value and should therefore be entitled to the profits of production in proportion to the value it contributes. But in the capitalist system the workers are getting much less than what they contribute in terms of their productive power. All the benefits of production accrue to the capitalists, for the efficiency of large scale enterprise breaks down the competition of the peasants and craftsmen and reduces all who have no property to joining the ranks of workers who sell their labour for existence.

Karl Marx saw the capitalist system as fulfilling a historic mission to draw out the productive power of labour. From its birthplace in Europe it stretched out all over the world, accumulated capital and developed new production techniques and by these means it raised the wealth of mankind to heights not attained under the peasant, feudal or slave economies. But in revolutionising the relations of production capitalism also started a development which will eventually bring about its own downfall. Marx saw the present age as a struggle between the capitalist class (or the bourgeoisie) and the proletariat whose interests are fundamentally antagonistic to each other. Again, the capitalist system, according to Marx, contains within itself contradictions which will evidently lead to its end. We saw the periodic crises of the trade cycles faced by the capitalist economy as symptoms of a deep-seated and progressive malady in the system.

In this treatment of the crisis there were three other distinct concepts. There is the theory of the reserve army of unemployed labour which shows how unemployment tends to fluctuate with the relationship between the stock of capital offering employment to labours and the supply of labour available to be employed. This reserve army goes on increasing further with the development of industry. Not only does the proletariat increase in number but it becomes better organised and to that extent also stronger. Secondly, there is the theory of the falling rate of profit which shows that the capitalists' greed for accumulation negates itself by reducing the average rate of return on capital. And thirdly, there is the theory of the relationship of capital goods industries to consumer goods industries which shows the ever-growing productive power of society knocking against the limitations upon the power to consume which are set by the poverty of the workers. Through these contradictions, the re-appearance of economic crises each time more threateningly, and through the struggle of the proletarian class, capitalism will ultimately be overthrown. Marx views society as essentially evolutionary under the logic of which capitalism will disappear. According to him so long as the society remains divided into classes, class conflicts are inevitable. The ultimate remedy lies in utilizing the growing proletarian movement as a vanguard for bringing about a classless society through a short-lived phase of dictatorship of the proletariat. In other words Marx envisaged the inevitable triumph of the proletarian movement in its struggle with the capitalist order. But having been successful, the proletariat should set on itself the task of abolishing all classes and bringing about a classless society. The period of proletarian dictatorship is viewed as a transitional stage at the end of which the state will wither away. In Marxian view mere extension of government ownership in the bourgeois state without changing the class relationship can only mean more oppression for the working classes. For the State is itself an instrument of oppression of lower classes and to increase its power without changing its class character is no remedy.

But cracks appeared in the solid Marxian edifice from late 1970s and became larger and larger as the 80s wore on. With snow-balling non-performance in the economies, rising dissatisfaction among large sections of population clamouring for higher standard of living, growing political dissent and consumerism and increasing burden of military expenditure, most of the countries took slow steps towards privatising and market economy starting with China. Soviet Union under President Gorbachev introduced Glassnost (openness) and/ Perestroika (restructuring) which led to decentralised decision-making in economic and politics, multi-party democracy and aspects of market-economy and private entrepreneurship. The trickles that started in the early 1980s led on to a gigantic tidal wave by 1989-90 that swept Communism off Eastern Europe and eventually Soviet Union which by the end of 1991 disintegrated with the 15 republics declaring independence. Nine of them formed a loose Union called the Commonwealth of Independence States (CIS) with a common military set up, but with separate international identities and separate memberships of the U.N. The spectre of international communism that dominated world political and economic scenario from 1917 to 1990 is as good as dead. China, Vietnam and Cube still profess communism. However in practice they have moved away from it and are openly encouraging free enterprise, market economy, foreign investment, export oriented developments and in general the freeing of the economy from pervasive bureaucratic control. But socialism in a broader sense still dominates political and economic thinking and governmental practices in many countries today. This has been the inevitable outcome of our experience with the working of unregulated capitalism—over-production and needless duplication, the manifest inequality of wealth and consumption, the growth of monopoly and concentration of industry in large groups and corporations, and above all, the recurrence of economic depressions and unemployment which seem to be inevitable in a system of unregulated competitive capitalism. The character of some essential and key industries also forces the State in the direction of State control. The general trend all over the world since the Second World War was in the direction of more and more government regulation of private industry. That phase is passing out. Nearly all countries including the former Socialist Countries are turning to market economy. The fact remains however that there cannot be a return to old style capitalism or *laissez faire.* Government control will have to remain in the areas of macro-economic management, infrastructure and special ameliorative measures for deprived and poorer sections of the population. But even in the U.S.A. and Canada government regulations are playing an increasingly larger role in the economy, not to speak of the valuable promotional role the government has traditionally been playing. In the last two decades or so the U.S. Government created a large number of regulatory agencies such as the Occupational Safety and Health Administration, the Environmental Protection Agency, the Consumer Product Safety Commission and the Equal Employment Opportunity Commission. There are also the traditional anti-trust or anti-monopoly state machinery and the numerous interventions in the form of regulation for advertising, food and drug safety or truth-in-lending. There are recent instances where the U.S. Federal Government in unprecedented moves came to the rescue of recession-hit giant automobile plant or several sinking investment banks with massive soft loans. Also of overwhelming importance in the Western countries is the State's growing concern for social justice and redistribution of incomes. Clearly we must accept the crucial role government must play in relation to business free from the usual political prejudices. As W.A. Lewis observes:

> On the one side are those who distrust individual initiative, and are anxious to magnify the role of government. On the other side are those who distrust governments, and are anxious to magnify the role of individual initiative. Both sides can appeal to history. No country has made economic progress without positive stimulus from intelligent governments, least of all England, the foundations of whose greatness as an industrial power were laid by a series of intelligent rulers from Edward III onwards, or the United States, whose governments, state and federal, have always played a large part in shaping economic activity. On the other hand, there are so many examples of the mischief done to economic life by governments that it is easy to fill one's page with warnings against government participation in economic life. Sensible people do not get involved in arguments about whether economic progress is due to government activity or to individual initiative: they know that it is due to both, and they concern themselves only with asking what is the proper contribution of each. (Theory of Economic Growth)

The overwhelming weight of public opinion in to-day's world is clearly in favour of the welfare state, macro-economic managements by the government, a growing role for the market forces with government's power of intervention whenever necessary in larger national interest and egalitarian pattern of society. As John Maurice Clark has said, 'Whether one believes government control to be desirable or undesirable it appears fairly obvious that the increasing interdependence of all parts of the economic system and such unsolved problems as the business cycles and unemployment will force more control in future than has been attempted in the past.'

The 1970s and 1980s had seen kaleidoscopic changes in the perception of Government role, both in the communist countries and the so-called free enterprise countries. Leaving out the earliest heresy of Yugoslavia, several socialist countries of Eastern Europe, notably Hungary, Czechoslovakia and Romania took steps in those years in the direction of relaxing state control and permitting private enterprise in a limited way, with very good results. But the most dramatic example has been the big cracks which have appeared in the policy frame and organization of Red China, professedly a citadel of Marxian orthodoxy until now. Under the leadership of Deng China from 1980 onwards made a small beginning with permitting foreign enterprises in several specially created economic zones, and followed it up by permitting small scale private enterprises in industry and agriculture in setting up joint venture between Chinese Government and foreign private corporations and in welcoming foreign initial investment in her special economic zones. There are open admissions that orthodox Marxism of the 19th century is not capable of finding solution to the problems of the late 20th century created by new unforeseen factors such as technology. Also, there are systematic efforts to inject into the Chinese public sectors an unambiguous emphasis on higher productivity and profitability and generation of surplus for further investment. The adoption by the 10th party congress of the motto "socialist market economy" marks the coup de grace for Marxism-Leninism-Maoism. There is avowed acceptance of market economy in replacement of the Marxist system of state-owned centrally planned economy in all the former communist countries with the lone exception of North Korea. All of them are encouraging private sector entrepreneurships and aggressively wooing foreign capital. At the other end, we see even the United States Government seeking to help several giant private sector corporation in crisis with a multi-billion dollar soft loan. France went in for nationalisation of the major chunk of its private sector economy and is now trying to retrace her steps in a massive exercise in denationalization. Indeed everywhere one sees evidence of Government policies combining features of both public and private ownership. The economic miracle achieved by some of these countries, such as Thailand, Singapore, Malaysia, Taiwan, Indonesia, Hungary and South

Korea would testify to their pragmatic policies away from doctrinaire application of any single school of thought such as State ownership or market economy. This mixture will possibly be the pervasive trend in Government—industry relationships in the coming years. There is increasing emphasis on private-sector led economic development and privatizing government's commercial enterprises with the state playing a facilitating and supportive role. Also, there is an unmistakable trend towards globalization of the economy with countries vying with one another in pursuing outward looking economic policies.

## INDIAN PERSPECTIVE

During India's colonial period except for the last three decades or so, government policy towards industry and business was, on the whole, indifferent, at times hostile. The first century of British rule, viz., the period of the East India Company, saw the decline of nearly all the indigenous industries. There are many reasons, technological, economic and political. By far the most important reason was the conscious policy followed by the imperial authorities of shutting out the British and latter also the European market from the Indian cotton and silk goods by direct prohibition or by creating very high tariff barrier and thereby destroying India's existing export market. On the other hand, official policy allowed an open door in India vis-à-vis goods produced in Britain. To take an example, British silk goods imported into India during the 19th century paid a duty of only 3½ per cent while a duty of 20 per cent was charged on Indian silk goods imported into Britain. In the case of woollen goods the disparity was even greater, the duties in 1831 being 2 per cent and 30 per cent respectively. Another key factor was the release of new technological forces in Britain by the Industrial Revolution and the competitive efficiency they gave to the industry there. The effects of this policy were compounded by the opening of the Suez Canal, improvements in the mode of ocean transport, construction of railways in India, and the introduction of uniform currency. With the political unification of India, and abolition of internal transit duties by 1856, the foundation of a national market was laid, and the sub-continent was opened up to unrestricted flow of goods of all variety made in Britain.

Until 1833 when the East India Company lost its monopoly trade, the Company had some sort of a vested interest in maintaining some of the existing industries in India in which it had a stake. To that extent the company's interests sometimes clashes with the interests of British industrial capitalism. But with the abolition of this monopoly there was now a new class of British traders who, unlike their predecessors in the

Company's days, did not come to this country to exchange British-made goods for Indian-made goods. They came essentially to secure market for goods manufactured in Britain. By the middle of the nineteenth century, therefore, India acquired the classic look of a colonial economy which was not thought suitable for manufacture, but only for production of raw materials which were to be exchanged for goods manufactured in England. Thus a doctrinaire adoption of the philosophy of *laissez faire* or free trade and practical selfish considerations of British industrial capitalism combined to lay down a government policy under which the efforts of the State were concentrated on the improvement of communications and on facilitating the flow of trade which consisted mainly of export of Indian raw materials and import of foreign manufactured goods.

This might not have happened if India had also been simultaneously affected by the Industrial Revolution. But in the prevailing situation, with British industry rapidly gaining unassailable competitive efficiency and the existing industries of India gradually becoming uncompetitive, India rapidly fell behind the West in the matter of industrial development. This process has been stated in picturesque details in the pages of Ramesh Chandra Dutt, in his classic *Economic History of India under Early British Rule* and also by Karl Marx in his writings on India. According to R.C. Dutt, the export of Indian cotton piece-goods to America declined from 13,633 bales in 1801 to 258 bales in 1829; Denmark which took 1457 bales in 1800 never took more than 150 bales after 1820; Portugal which took 9714 bales in 1799, never took over a thousand bales after 1825; and the exports to the Arabian and Persian Gulfs, which rose between four and seven thousand bales between 1810 and 1820, never exceeded two thousand after 1825.

"From 1818 to 1836 the export of twist from Great Britain to India rose in the proportion of 1 to 52,000. In 1824, the exports of British muslins to India hardly amounted to 60,00,000 yards, while in 1837 it surpassed 64,000,000 yards. But at the same time the population of Dacca decreased from 1,50,000 inhabitants to 20,000. This decline of Indian towns celebrated for their fabrics was by no means the worst consequence. British steam and science uprooted, over the whole surface of Hindustan, the union between agricultural and manufacturing industry." (British Rule in India, *Daily Tribune,* New York, June 10, 1853).

The English cotton machinery produced an adverse effect in India. The Governor-General reported in 1834-35: "The misery hardly finds a parallel in the history of commerce. The bones of the cotton weavers are bleaching the plains of India." (Marx *Capital*, Vol. I, Chapter 5).

Talking of Surat, an important textile manufacturing centre of yester-years, Bishop Heber in his Indian Journal says, 'The trade of Surat is now of very trifling consequence consisting of little but raw cotton, which is shipped in boats for Bombay. All the manufactured goods of the country are understood by the English except kinkobs and shawls for which there is very little demand; a dismal decay has consequently taken place in the circumstances of the native merchants.... There is a small congregation of Armenians (the principal merchants of the East) in a state of decay and general poverty.'

Equally forceful in his statement regarding Dhaka which was once described as the Manchester of the East—'Its trade is reduced to the sixteenth part of what it was, and all its splendid buildings ... are sunk into ruin, and overgrown with jungle!' All this was a direct consequence of Britain's refusal to levy protective duties on imports into India, and her deliberate policy on the other hand, of discouraging the flow of Indian goods to Britain and the west.

From time to time educated public opinion in India criticized this policy of free trade vigorously pursued by the government on the ground that an open door was favoured by the British to protect the narrow commercial interests of Britain. The following passage from a petition by some wealthy inhabitants of Bengal, quoted in R.M. Martin's *Anglo-Eastern Empire* (1832) illustrates this:

> "The petitioners and more especially the labouring and manufacturing classes of native are already suffering grievous hard-ships in consequences of these principles in trade and commerce which the petitioners are told are now actuating the English Councils, not being extended to the produce of that country. while every encouragement is held out to the exportation from England to that country of the growth and produce of foreign as well as English industry, while many thousands of the native of that country, who a short time ago derived a livelihood from the growth of cotton and the manufacture of cotton goods, are without bread in consequence of the facilities afforded to the produce of America, and the manufacturing industry of England; and the article of sugar, to the production of which the lands of the Petitioners might be turned is loaded with such heavy duties in England as effectively to shut the market against the industry of the East Indians when turned to his particular commodity."

The way in which Lancashire was allowed to meddle frequently in British Indian Government's fiscal policy and industrial policy strengthened this attitude of suspicion. The memories of bygone days when India was famous for the products of her industry added a touch of piquancy to the natural regret felt by patriotic Indians who demanded protection for Indian industry. It was pointed out that countries like United States, Germany and Japan appeared to have proposed industrially only after adopting the policy of protecting their infant industries and that Britain herself had discarded protection and gone all-out for free trade only after her pre-eminence in industry was established. But all these murmurs failed to create any impact on official policy until well after the twentieth century had begun. Industrially and commercially backward India was made to compete with the vast resources of technical skill imperial Britain which had also become the most advanced industrial country in the world.

The only area where organized industry made significant strides was plantation industry, e.g. jute, tea and coffee, where Europeans became interested very early, as these provided easy and high return on the investment. But this was due to private initiative rather than governmental action.

Modern industrial enterprise in India developed only after 1850. Its earliest manifestations came in the wake of the construction of railways which made it essential to have modern workshops for repair and maintenance of the rolling stock. The effects of the introduction of railways vis-à-vis industry are described by Marx in the following words:

> I know that the English millocracy intend to endow India with railways with the exclusive view of extracting at diminished expenses the cotton and other raw materials for their manufactures. But when you have once introduced machinery into the locomotion of a country, which possesses iron and coal, you are unable to withhold it from its fabrication. You cannot maintain a net of railways over an immense country without introducing all those industrial processes necessary to meet the immediate and current wants of railway locomotion, and out of which there must grow the application of machinery to those branches of industry not immediately connected with the railways. The railway system will, therefore, become in India truly the forerunner of modern industry.... Modern industry resulting from the railway system, will dissolve the hereditary divisions of labour, upon which rest the Indian castes, those decisive impediments of Indian progress and Indian power. (Marx, *The Future Results of British Rule in India*).

The development of railways broke down the isolation of the village, made the world market available to the Indian producer, facilitated both foreign and domestic trade and created the necessary condition for the growth of large-scale factory industry. It was no coincidence that this was followed in the later decades of the century by the establishment and quick growth of jute, cotton textile and coal-mining industries, and also of new forms of business organization in the shape of joint-stock companies and managing agency. Jute industry started, after the Crimean War had interrupted the supply of hemp and flax from Russia, at first in competition with the Dundee mill-owners who protested vigorously against allowing the growth of manufacturing industry in a colony suitable only for commercial exploitation. But the natural advantage offered by India were immense, and from the opening of the first jute mill at Rishra near Calcutta in 1855 the industry rapidly grew until it became the most important export industry of undivided India. While jute industry was started by British businessmen with the aid of British capital, the growth of cotton textile industry was very largely the result of Indian entrepreneurship with Indian capital. The first modern mill was set up in Bombay in 1851. After the American Civil War created the cotton boom for Indian cotton, there was no going back, and the industry rapidly grew. By 1870 Bombay had five spinning mills and eight weaving mills. Between 1870 and 1875 fifteen new mills were established. Although considerable technical expertise flowed from Britain this industry was exclusively the result of private efforts and initiative and the government was a silent spectator. Similarly the government had little or no role to play in the spectacular growth of coal mining in the 1960s and 1870s after the introduction of railways and steamers and increased used of iron had created a market for Indian coal. All early efforts at establishing an iron and steel plant in the late 19th century failed, thanks largely to governmental apathy and lack of support. The efforts of Jamshedji Tata, that prince among Indian entrepreneurs, after much initial failures, succeeded only when under Curzon there was a brief change in the attitude of the Government of India towards industry, and Tata could revive his old dream of a great Indian Steel Works with Indian capital.

The first open emphasis on the need for a conscious industrial policy to be pursued by the Government was made by the report of the Famine Commission in 1880. It took the view that in order to ward off famine which lifted its head from time to time government should foster the inception of new industries and introduce scientific methods of production in existing industries. Government was also urged to carry out experiments to guide and educate private trade and to assist persons desiring to develop new industry by obtaining for them technical advice and information. Finally, the Commission also advised the government to buy its own requirements from India rather than from Europe wherever possible. But beyond these points the Commission's report once again swung back to the *laissez faire* doctrine.

Even this fear was not justified. For in the prevailing all-pervasive *laissez faire* culture even the modest recommendations of the commission were not taken note of. As Vera Anstey sums up in her Economic Development of India.

> After the assumption of direct rule by the Crown in 1858, the doctrine *laissez faire* policy of the Home Government was extended to India, and even when it became apparent that certain exceptions must be made (for instance, as regards famine relief and public works), the policy was not retained in the industrial sphere. It was thought inevitable that India should remain predominantly agricultural, whilst the Government wished to avoid both the active encouragement of industries that (like the cotton mill industry) competed with powerful English interests, and increased State Expenditure. Hence, even at the end of the 19th century all that the Government did to assist industry was to provide a certain amount of technical and industrial education, and to attempt to collect and disseminate commercial and industrial information.

To quote the assessment of Percival Griffiths:

> The true charge against the British Government is that the policy of *laissez fare* was carried too far and too long in a country to which it was not suited. Such a policy may produce excellent results in a land where capitalists are venture-some and technical skill abundant. In 19th century India, moneyed men of the country—with the exception of a small Bombay Group—seemed to lack initiative, and technicians were almost entirely non-existent. Under such conditions the policy of *laissez faire* meant stagnation and continued poverty. (Griffiths – The British Impact on India).

On the other hand, under pressure from Lancashire, a tariff policy which, according to the same author, provided "the one shameful example of the sacrifice of Indians to British interests" was vigorously applied. Lord Lytton, under instructions from Home authorities overruled his Executive Council to abolish import duty on coarse cotton goods. Other import duties were also abolished, and from 1882 to 1914 India was, except for an export duty on rice, virtually a land of free trade. Again, in 1896, the import duty on cotton piece goods was lowered to 30 per cent while an excise duty at the same rate was levied on all Indian mill-woven clothes, coarse or fine. At the same time, the import duties on cotton yarn were removed.

The first isolated attempt at officially encouraging the growth of large-scale industry took place around 1900. The Madras Government under the guidance of Sir Alfred Chatterton, started a bold policy of surveying industrial possibilities, assisting private enterprises, improving technical education, and starting pioneer industries with State resources. Steps were taken for the improvement of handloom weaving, well boring, the introduction of oil-engines and centrifugal pumps for lift irrigation, the establishment of·the aluminium industry by utilizing the surplus water power of the Periyar Dam, and chrome-tanning. This policy received encouragement from Lord Curzon who had an Imperial Commerce and Industry Department set up in the Government of India in 1905. Next year the Madras Government had its own separate Department of Industries. Curzon's policy received a half hearted endorsement from the Home Government subject to the condition that pioneer industries established under Government auspices should be handed over to private enterprise as soon as their commercial success was secured.

During these years industrial development was also stimulated by changes in the Rules for the purchase of Government stores which had from 1883 onwards encouraged purchase of goods made in India whenever such goods of a suitable quality and at not 'unduly burden-some' price were available. This policy with the declared object of promoting the development of Indian industries was outlined in 1904, 1909 and again very drastically during the First World War. Other promotional steps taken were the Patents and Designs Act (1911) protecting both the inventors and the public on the lines of the English Patents Act (1909); the Tea Cess Act of 1903 providing for a cess on sale or export for assisting the industry; the Mines Act (1901); the Government report on the prospects of iron and steel industry (1899) and the guarantee of purchasing 20000 tons of still rails per annum for ten years from the Tata Steel Works; encouraging the setting up of cooperative societies with industrial objects; and the extension of facilities for industrial and technical education. We may have a few words on the last-mentioned step.

After the Educational conference at Simla in 1901 at which Lord Curzon presided attempts were made to grapple with the defects of the existing educational system, which (it was recognized) suffered in particular from being predominantly literary, rather than scientific or practical. Thus in 1903, a system of State technical scholarships, tenable abroad, was instituted, and the number of institutions giving education of his type was increased. Progress remained disappointing, as it was difficult to gain the confidence of employers, the cost of training was too great for artisans, the right types of students were not easily attracted, and those that came expected responsible posts with high pay as soon as they completed their courses. However, several first-class institutions giving advanced technical training (such as the Indian Institute of Science at Bangalore, the Cawnpore Technical Institute and the Victoria Jubilee Technical Institute, Bombay), a large number of both State-aided and voluntary institutions for training mechanical and railway engineers, and a still larger number of technical and industrial schools came into being directly in consequence of the move towards technical education initiated by Curzon. As Vera Anstey observes: 'We can say that a although the constructive work of the Government was still extremely limited the way had been prepared for the more drastic measures that were adopted when the events of the Great War demonstrated the urgent necessity for a more progressive policy.' (pp. 221-25)

But the general policy towards industrialization came up against deep prejudices and hostility entrenched in European business circles and the establishment at home where this was viewed as 'a serious menace to private enterprise and an unwarrantable intervention on the part of the State in matters beyond the sphere of Government.' Lord Morley, the Secretary of State for India, threw his weight behind this school and negatived the establishment of a separate Department of Industries and of setting up pioneer industries on commercial lines by the Madras Government and merely allowed educational work and the dissemination of information. Thus the provincial department of industry was abolished, most of the industrial units closed, and Chatterton, after his transfer to the Education Department, resigned and took service with the Mysore State. Although, after 1910, faced with opposition, the government appointed Directors of Industries in the provinces (not departments), their working was confined to collecting and disseminating training and advising government on technical matters.

Meanwhile Indian political leaders were clamouring for action by the Government to develop industry. The Swadeshi Movement (1905-11) in which political and economic motives were combined led to the establishment of many small and medium factories in consumers' articles many of which failed. As a result of these failures the public opinion became more vocal in pressing for state assistance, and for tariff barrier against foreign imports.

A significant area where government's regulatory policy operated was company law by which government sought to regulate the incorporation, management and operation of joint-stock companies. Beginning with an embryonic legislation as far back as 1850, the Indian Companies Act, 1913 sought to extend the provisions of the English Companies Act of 1909 to the Indian corporate scene. By 1913-14 there were joint-stock companies registered in India. A legislative attempt was made during the passage of the Companies Act in 1913-14 to extend the scope of the Act to the Managing Agents and bring the activities of these controversial elements under some kind of government control and regulation. But this was foiled by strong opposition from British business interests in the Bengal Chamber of Commerce, and the government was forced to withdraw the proposed restrictions from the Central Assembly. The institution of Managing Agency was left unregulated until the companies Act of 1956.

## INDUSTRIAL POLICY AFTER 1914

The outbreak of the First World War brought about the end of the policy of hostility and forced on the government a more progressive policy that included selective encouragement of some industries and protective tariff in order to meet the war demands, and also to fill the vacuum caused by the complete elimination of a whole range of imported goods from the Indian market. A Munitions Board was set up to control the purchase and manufacture of stores and munition of war. But this also brought out in bold relief some very major bottlenecks in the way of India industrializing herself fast, e.g., India's dangerous dependence on imports for some fundamental necessities of industrial life including fuel and skilled man-power, the absence of necessary infrastructure including internal and external transport facilities, uncertainty of the likely duration of the official policy of encouraging local manufacture after the War. 'Hence there was urgent need for a new constructive economic policy in the forefront of which should be industrial stimulation, and in particular the establishment of industries to produce machinery and other necessities of industrial production in general.' This led to the appointment of the famous Indian Industrial Commission in 1916, its terms of reference being to examine and report upon the possibilities of further industrial development in India and submit recommendations for a permanent policy of industrial stimulation.

The Commission's report. (1918). The recommended that 'in future Government must play an active part in the industrial development of the country, with the aim of making India more self-contained in respect of men and material; and that if is impossible for Government to undertake that part, unless provided with adequate administrative equipment and fore-armed with reliable scientific and technical advice.' The report showed how little the march of modern industry had affected the great bulk of the Indian population, which remained rooted in agriculture, winning a bare subsistence from the soil by antiquated method of cultivation, and concluded that the changed which had already, taken place in rural areas were due to 'economic' rather than to 'industrial' developments; that is, to changes in prices and marketing conditions, rather than to any marked tendency towards industrialization.

First, it proposed improved departmental organization for the encouragement and control of industries. This was to take the from of the creation of Imperial and Provincial Department of Industries and of an Imperial Industrial Service. Most of the actual administrative work was to be decentralized and placed in the hands of the Provincial Department of Industries under a Director of Industries aided by a Provincial Board of Industries. This was in consonance with the political reforms of 1919 which classed 'industries' as a transferred subject. In addition, It was proposed that an Imperial Department of Stores should be established at Calcutta, with a branch in each province, to control the placing of all Government orders and contracts.

Secondly, suggestions were made with regard to the improvement of technical training and education (including a scheme of apprenticeship foreman) and the improvement of conditions in factories and industrial centres (by improved housing, welfare work, sanitation, and other public health work).

Thirdly, there were proposals for the reorganization of the scientific staff of the industrial Departments.

Fourthly, recommendations were made for technical and financial aid to industries, the encouragement of industrial cooperative and provision of improved transport and freight facilities.

These recommendations were accepted in principle by the Government of India, but little could be done immediately owing to the war and post-war problems of reorganization, and also the difficulty of coordinating industrial policy with the political reforms of 1919 and with the recommendations of the Fiscal Commission (1921-22). Under the Montagu-Chelmsford

Reforms of 1919, 'industry' became a provincial subject, and although some of the provincial departments of industries set up after 1919 did good promotional work, central policy swung back to apathy and indifference until the Second World War intervened.

## SECOND WORLD WAR

A significant land mark was the setting up of a National Planning Commission in 1938 by congress President Subhash Bose. This body headed by Jawaharlal Nehru made several reports suggested industrialization of the country. The Second World War was a major water-shed in the development of Government-business interface in India. For one thing, India having become the main supply base for Allied War efforts in the Far Eastern and Middle eastern Fronts, her industrial development received a tremendous boost-up through substantial order for locally manufactured goods, and through the setting up of a large number of new industrial units in fields hitherto inconceivable, For another, in response to the needs of war- time economy the government in a bid to conserve and control the resources of the country and under the provisions of the Defence of India rules brought about a series of controls affecting various aspects of the economy, e.g. import, export, capital investment, foreign exchange, These controls became a permanent picture of the economic landscape, as these were found useful weapons by the government not only after the War, but even after independence to meet the needs of planned development.

We may now proceed to analyse the phenomenal industrial expansion more concretely. In the first place the existing units increased their output manifold by measures such as working extra shifts, adding extra plants, technical improvements and organizational changes and generally by improvised methods. Secondly, many new important industries were started during the war, e.g., mechanical industries, like diesel engines, pumps, bicycles and sewing machines; machine tools and cutting tools; chemical like caustic soda, chlorine, superphosphates; ferroalloys like ferro-silicon and ferro-manganese; non-ferrous metals and metal fabricating industries like cables; new items of textile, tea and oil processing machinery.

Government's pragmatism was shown in the fact that Walchand Hirachand was encouraged to pioneer ship-building, aircraft building, and automobile manufacture. Also, during this period, the production of a whole range of consumer goods like hydrogenated oil, electrical goods, plastics and resin started properly for the first time. Sir A. Ramaswami Mudaliar gave assurance on behalf of the Government of India: 'In case we in any form encourage the development of industries for our war needs, those entrepreneurs who had come to the assistance of the State would not be left high and dry to take care of themselves.'

Thirdly, the industrial upsurge found expression in a burgeoning of corporate activity. The number of joint stock companies rose up from 11,114 (paid up capital Rs. 290 crores) in 1939 to 14,859 (paid up capital Rs. 390 crores) in 1945. Fourthly, thanks to the war-time boom, many industries like cotton textile, paper, jute, cement and sugar generated fabulous profits, helped by inflationary conditions. Fifthly, on account of the inflationary conditions helped by large scale currency expansion, prices went on rising continuously leading to the imposition of price and distribution controls by the government in a number of items. These controls were destined to become permanent features of the Indian scene. Lastly, along with corporate expansion and rise in profits, many unhealthy and undesirable trends in Company formation and management crept in. Interlocking of funds and diversion of profits, defrauding of share-holders and other malpractices took place on a large scale. Also, there was wide-spread hoarding, black marketing and price manipulations. It was during these years that Indian business came to acquire the prevailing unsavoury image in public eyes from which it has not recovered ever since. From time to time the public including shareholders urged for greater government control over the formation and management of companies in public interest. The general situation was further aggravated by the widely held belief which is not wholly true that throughout this period of mounting profits the working class was denied its rightful share and thus the capitalist were gaining at the cost of the workers. This pervasive anti-business mood was to form the back-drop for the post-war and post-independence era of government control over business.*

## Independence, Partition and After

The emergence of India as an independent nation on August 15, 1947 coupled with the partition of the country was the beginning of a new glorious era in the history of our country. On the one hand the independent Government embarked on a vigorous policy of industrialization and encouragement of industry. On the other hand there was a temporary dislocation on account of the breaking of the economic and political unity of the country as a result of partition and the wide-spread communal disturbances in parts of the subcontinent that accompanied it. India got 91

*For details see N.K. Sengupta, *Corporate Management in India,* Vikas (New Delhi).

per cent of the total number of industrial units, 93 per cent of the total number of workers employed and about 97 per cent of the total value of mineral production. However, she also lost a very significant market in general and almost the entire supply of raw materials in two of her major industries, jute and cotton. About 81 per cent of total production of raw jute went out of India, whereas all the mills stayed in India. Similarly, although of the 394 cotton mills in undivided India, only 14 went to Pakistan, nearly all the supply of long and medium staple cotton which used to come from West Punjab and Sind was now lost to India.

Governmental efforts in the earlier years had necessarily to be concentrated on extending the area of jute cultivation in Eastern India which very often meant loss of food crops, and on importing long and medium staple cotton abroad which imposed severe strain on the country's foreign exchange resources. The dislocation of railway and roadways traffic and of inland river navigation in Eastern India also produced some disturbing effects on the smooth growth of industrial activity. Industries like hosiery, woolen, glass and metal works suffered from the migration of skilled workers, mostly Muslims, to Pakistan, although this was perhaps more than made up by the inflow of fresh managerial and entrepreneurial skill from those who migrated from Pakistan to India.

Governmental efforts were directed to improving the climate of industrial relations, e.g., the well-known tri-partite industrial conference (1947) which among other things called for a three year truce between capital and labour and granting comprehensive measures for determination of wages and conditions of labour, granting of tax concessions to industry in the budget of 1948-49, the continuance of cheap money policy, the setting-up of the industrial Corporation in 1948, and various welfare measures like the Factories Act, 1949. On April 7, 1948 the Parliament adopted an Industrial Policy Resolution laying down the broad objectives of Government Policy in the field of industrial development and demarcating the respective spheres for public and private sectors. This Resolution stressed the need for a policy of 'mixed economy' and thus struck a middle course between those who stood for nationalization of private business, and those who advocated free enterprise, the Government also took steps to clarify its policy towards foreign capital in a policy statement made by the Prime Minister on April 6, 1949. In this the Government categorically declared its intention not to discriminate between foreign capital and Indian capital, welcome foreign investment in priority areas and proposed no to impose on foreign companies any restrictions which were not applicable to similar Indian enterprises. All these appeared to have had a market effect, and from 1949 onwards industrial production recovered from the slump since 1945. This rising trend was maintained during 1949 and 1950 except in jute and cotton. This was also facilitated by Government assistance to industrial units for replacement, modernization and import of capital goods wherever required, liberalization in the depreciation allowance and exemption of duties in the case of industries like sugar. From 1950 when the Constitution came into effect and the Planning Commission was set up, we entered into a new era of planned economic development in which the Government had necessarily to play a dominant role in the field of industrial development, not only from the point of view of building a dominant public sector but also for encouraging and regulating private sector industry in the same breath in accordance with the priorities laid down in the Constitution and the Plans. The Industrial Policy Resolution of 1956 massively enlarged the areas of industrial activities reserved for the public sector and correspondingly reduced the role of the private sector. But the broad principle of mixed economy remained.

Since 1950-51, India has passed through twelve Five Year Plans and several Annual Plans and is now through the 13th Five Year Plan. The role of the private sector industry was fairly significant in the plan frame upto the 3rd Five Year Plan, but became somewhat eclipsed during the sixties and the seventies as a result of the increasing dominance of populist and socialist postures. The Sixth Plan was marked by the return of the private sector into the plan frame on a low key. This trend continued in the 7th Plan and the 8th plan. The 8th Plan registered an unprecedented high growth rate of 6.5 per cent of the GDP, and much of it was accounted for by the private sector investment. Total investment grew at the rate if 12.5 per cent annum; public investment at 4 per cent. The financial and the balance of payment crises that the nation faced from the onset of the 1990s compelled the acceptance of deregulation, a reduced role for public sector, making the public sector efficient and surplus-generating, and much greater reliance in general on the private sector for industrial and infrastructure development. The point to emphasize in that the plan priorities play an important role in business including the public sector deciding on which areas to grow and which areas to cut down.

Meanwhile several international developments also affected the issue of Government Business inter-face in India. First, the collapse of the Soviet Union and with that all the communist countries in the Eastern Europe led to a setback in leftist ideas of Government ownership and control on business and to the predominance of market oriented capitalism. This had its impact on our country as well. India in line with other countries such as Britain, France and Russia passed through a phase of privatization and withdrawal of Government's micro-economic controls. But from 2008 onwards we had the other extreme in the free market world. The Wall Street collapse of the banking system leading to global crisis which affected the Western Europe and the East Asia. This crisis in the capitalist system almost compensated for the fall of the Soviet Union and other communist countries. An interesting development was that China, although not formally abandoning communism, abandoned the Marxist system of economy for all practical purposes and turned to market capitalism, in that process showing unmatched record of growth. India while influenced somewhat by Margret Thatcher's privatization programmes in Britain went only a little in the direction, but on the whole adopted the policy of freeing enterprises from Government control from 1991 onwards. In the process India's economy advanced significantly and set new visions of growth during the 1990s and first decade of the 21st century.

Thus India is in steps with the prevailing dominant trend in Government business interface in the world scenario.

Aspects of Government's Role

(i) Government as regulator of business;
(ii) Government as promoter of business;
(iii) Government as entrepreneur;
(iv) Government as planner;
(v) Government as consumer.

Under the first head we can study the entire gamut of regulatory legislation and policies. On the one hand there is a very large indirect area of Government control over the functioning of private sector business through budgetary, fiscal or monetary policy. These relate to the broad macro-economic management of the economy, a role that Government has necessarily to assume even in market economy conditions. But as against this there is also a fast expanding area of direct administrative or physical controls, legislative and non-legislative, through which the Central government in India seeks to ensure that private investment and production in industry and the use of scarce resources including foreign exchange conform to Government's basic social and economic objectives and also the priorities indicated in our Give year Plans. While in the earlier years of our planning the indirect controls were definitely playing a more important role than direct administrative controls, in later years the latter seem to have acquired similar if not greater importance. In today's economic landscape they are as important as indirect controls, They become necessary tools in a system that sought to steer a middle course between two conflicting demands, both fairly vocal in our society, one seeking a policy of total nationalization of the means of production and distribution and the other advocating by and large a policy of free enterprise with limited regulations and a limited public sector. The excessive use of administrative controls leads to the play of whims and prejudices which often lead to corruption. There was a belief that in the early days of licensing the house of the Birlas managed to get industrial licenses in nearly every industry in which the Tata house companies were established. There were recurrent, complaints that foreign companies applying for industrial license for project to be located in a state were advised to relocate it in another state and the application was kept pending indefinitely. There were whispers about the peddling of money or political power for obtaining licenses. This phase ended only after the sea changes from 1991 onwards which dismantled, the license permit Raj. A regime of administrative controls avoids total nationalization of all resources, but at the same time allows the operation of a very substantial sector of the economy in private hands subject to certain social and national priorities and objectives, and not according to the dictates of the market. There were innumerable administrative controls over the working of private business. But we can broadly identify the following major areas which affected business before the 1990's.

(i) Industrial policy and licensing;
(ii) Anti-Monopolies Law and Law on Competition;
(iii) Company Law;
(iv) Capital issue control (Primary Market);
(v) Control over Stock Exchanges (Secondary Market);
(vi) Import control including control over capital goods imports;
(vii) Foreign exchange control;
(viii) Export regulations
(ix) Regulation of foreign investment and foreign collaboration;
(x) Commodity control including informal control over the price and the distribution of commodities.
(xi) Environmental and anti-Pollution control.

But we need to highlight that since the starting of the economic reforms in July 1991, some of them have disapproved. There is a general movement towards deregulation and progressively diluting or even removing these control thereby allowing industry freedom and flexibility. Many of the old administrative controls have been removed, although some of the old procedural hang-overs still persist. There are many crucial aspects of deregulation which still remain unattempted, because they are politically difficult. One such area is insurance where despite a lot of international pressure for deregulation and privatization and despite the clear recommendations of a government-appointed committee (the R.N. Malhotra Committee) for partial privatization of the State-owned insurance companies and for permitting private sector companies including foreign enterprises government under trade union pressure could not take any step except announcing a regulatory authority for insurance industry, But after a lot of dithering the government at long last permitted private sector insurance companies with a ceiling of 26 per cent foreign share-holding. An Insurance Regulatory Authority was also established. There is still considerable political opposition. But it heralded new era. The promotional role of the Government in relation to industries becomes more pronounced. It can be see in providing finance for industry, in granting various fiscal incentives and in creating infrastructure facilities for industrial growth and investment. The State Governments also get directly and intimately involved in the promotional process. A study of the Government's entrepreneurial role takes into account the impressive growth of the public sector in India from a small beginning to its present dominant position towering over the industrial landscape, In its role as planner the Central Government indicates the various priorities in the Five-Year Plans and also the sectoral allocation or resources.

But this analysis of Government's role into several aspects is purely for the facility of understanding. These are not really separate compartments, but integratedly connected with one another. Thus in pursuing its regulatory role Government has often found it necessary to take over management or even ownership of private sector undertakings or even of an entire industry in larger national interest. In these instances Government's regulatory role shades off imperceptibly into an entrepreneurial role. Sometimes in a reverse order Government having set up units of production or business in particular field may in national interest or in the interest of production or coordination have taken over control of the existing private units in that field. The regulatory and promotional roles are also very often complementary. To take one example, public sector financial institutions and nationalized banks are both promotional and regulatory agencies. On the one hand, they promote industry by providing finance. On the other hand, for about three dealers, after the almost total nationalization of industrial finance, they commanded the crucial power of sanctioning or denying long-term credit or short-term loans. By withholding finance from non-priority industry or inefficient units they can almost serve the role of a regulatory agency of the Government. Government's promotional role often turns imperceptibly into Government's purchase policy. Government is the largest purchaser of goods in the economy, and many industries such as jute, textile, engineering, automobile and railway wagon-building are heavily dependent on Government purchases. Budgetary cut-backs on purchase lead to severe recession. The role of DGS&D, the principal purchasing agency, is crucial for many industries. An area where the regulatory, promotional purchase and the entrepreneurial rules of the Government have converged together in recent times is the revival of sick industrial units. Central and State Governments together with financial institutions and nationalized banks often get involved in joint operations aimed at rescing units from industrial sickness which has become a pervasive trend today and nursing them back to health and viability. Finally, Government's pervasive role as planner of the economy embraces all the other roles. Planning for future economic development inevitably means regulatory, promotional, consumer and entrepreneurial action. Despite the declining role of centralized planning in recent years and the advent of indicative planning, the role for planning will remain important on account of the State's undiminished role in macro-economic management, in the development of the infrastructure in laying down the rules of the game for the private sector and finally, in ameliorating the living conditions of the poor. The recent currency turmoil and steep deceleration in the Wall Street in USA, in Europe and the Asia Pacific region, almost as dramatic as the economic growth of some of these countries in recent decades, has once again underscored the role of effective government support and intervention.

## CHAPTER 2

# Constitutional Framework of Government Control of Business in India

In any discussion on the interfere between private business and Government, the provisions in the Constitutions of India which support or restrict Government activities in economic life occupy a prominent place. In the U.S. Constitution there is an in-built prejudice in favour of *laissez faire* and the Federal Government had to extend its regulation to private business on many occasions by liberal interpretation of the 'Commerce Clause' and the 'Taxing Clause' backed by the decisions of the Supreme Court. In contrast the Indian Constitution is based on the concept of the 'Welfare State' as distinguished from a 'police State'. The Preamble itself declares that the aim of the State among other things is to secure to all citizens social and economic justice. With this end in view the Constitution contains numerous provisions which assert the right of the State not only to intervene in private business, but also to commence and conduct business under its ownership as countervailing force. The Directive Principles of State Policy relating to social and economic matters (Article 38, 39, 41-43 and 43A)[1] discarded the old doctrine of *laissez-faire* and established the right of Government to regulate and control private business in a drastic manner.

Contrary to a popular impression, the directive principles are not to be taken lightly merely because these are not justifiable. But they represent the broad sign posts which State Policy must follow. Also, it is not correct to say that they have no binding force. They are in the nature of moral precepts for the State authorities. The Government may not have to answer for any breach of a directive in a court of law, but it will certainly be accountable before the public at large for their observance. As pointed out by Mathew, J. in the Kesavananda Bharati case, although these provisions are expressly made unenforceable, that does not affect their fundamental character. They are as important as the fundamental character. They still very much form part of the constitutional law of the land. They are as important as the fundamental rights of the individual. They are fundamental in the governance of the country (Kesavananda Bharati vs. State of Kerala, (1973) 4 SCC 225-877). The directive principle impose an obligation on the state to take positive action for creating socio-economic conditions in which there can be an egalitarian social order with social and economic justice to all. As pointed by Mathew, J. in the judgement whether at the particular moment in the history of the nation. A particular fundamental right should have priority over the moral claims embodied in part IV (directive principle) or must yield to them is a matter which must be decided by each generation in the light of its experience and values.

Of special significance are Articles 38, and 39. The former declares that the State shall strive to promote the welfare of the people by securing and protecting as effectively as it may a social order in which justice, social, economic and political, shall inform all the institutions of national life. Article 38 (2) inserted by the 44th amendment Act, 1978 further enjoins that the State shall in particular strive to minimize the inequalities in income and endeavour to eliminate inequalities in status, facilities and opportunities not only amongst individuals, but also amongst groups of people residing in different areas or engaged in different vocations.

Article 39 directs that State shall in particular direct its policy towards securing:

(a) that the citizens, men and women equally, have the right to an adequate means of livelihood;

(b) that ownership and control of the natural resources of the community are so distributed as best to subserve the common good; that the operation of the economic system does not result in the concentration of wealth and means of production to the common detriment;

(c) that the operation of the economic system does not result in the concentration of wealth and means of production to the common detriment;

(d) that there is equal pay for equal work for both men and women;

(e) that the health and strength of workers, men and women, and the tender age of children are not abused and that citizens are not forced by economic necessity to enter avocations unsuited to their age or strength;

(f) that children are given opportunities and facilities to develop in a healthy manner and in conditions of freedom and dignity and that childhood and youth are protected against exploitation and against moral and material abandonment.

The subsections (b) and (c) are particularly relevant in so far as they have been declared to be the driving force behind a number of specific laws or policy measures affecting business. In pursuance of these provisions our Government has, on the one hand, introduced remedial legislation and reform on a large scale. On the other hand, it has effected nationalization of existing private business concerns, or vested their business and assets in statutory public corporations, e.g., life insurance, road transport, civil aviation, commercial banking, or set up a large number of public sector projects. In fact the adoption by Parliament of the socialist pattern of society as the objective of our social and economic policy in December 1954 followed directly from these directive principles of our Constitution. Of considerable importance for business, also, is the recently inserted article 43 A which states: "The State shall take steps, by suitable legislation or any other way, to secure the participation of workers in the management of undertakings' establishments or other organizations engaged in any industry."

The two most important limitation on the powers of the Central Government in the matter of regulation of business comes from (i) the division of powers between the States and the Central Government and (ii) the Fundamental Rights (Chapter III) of the Constitution.

## CENTRE-STATE DIVISION OF LEGISLATIVE POWERS

List I in schedule VII contains the subjects which are within the exclusive legislative powers of Parliament, and to that extent within the executive powers of the Central Government. In it the following entries relate to economic matters:

7. Industries declared by parliament by law to be necessary for the purpose of defence or for the prosecution of war.

41. Trade and commerce with foreign countries; import and export across customs frontiers; definition of customs frontiers.

42. Inter-State trade and commerce.

43. Incorporation, regulation and winding up of trading corporations, including banking, insurance and financial corporations but not including co-operative societies.

45. Banking.

47. Insurance;

48. Stock exchanges and future markets.

51. Establishment of standards old quality for goods to be exported out of India or transported from one State to another.

52. Industries, the control of which by the Union is declared by Parliament by law to be expedient in the public interest.

53. Regulation and development of oilfields and mineral oil resources; petroleum and petroleum products; other liquids and substances declared by Parliament by law to be dangerously inflammable.

54. Regulation of mines and mineral development to the extent to which such regulation and development under the control of the Union is declared by Parliament by law to be expedient in the public interest.

List II contains the following entries which are within the exclusive sphere of the State:

23. Regulation of mines and mineral development subject to the provisions of List I with respect to regulation and development under the control of the Union.

24. Industries subject to the provisions of entries 7 and 52 of List I.

25. Gas and gas-works.

26. Trade and commerce within the State subject to the provisions of entry 33 of List III.

27. Production, supply and distribution of goods subject to the provisions of entry 33 of List III.

32. Incorporation, regulation and winding up of corporations, other than those specified in List I, and universities, unincorporated trading, literary, scientific, religious and other societies and associations; co-operative societies.

List III, which contains the concurrent subjects, also has a number of entries impinging upon the freedom of private enterprise, e.g.

20. Economic and social planning.

21. Commercial and industrial monopolies, combines and trusts.

32. Shipping and navigation on inland waterways as regards mechanically propelled vessels, and the rule of the road on such waterways, and the carriage of passengers and goods on inland waterways subject to the provisions of List I with respect to national waterways.

Trade and commerce in, and the production, supply and distribution of:

(a) the products of any industry where the control of such industry by the Union is declared by Parliament by law to be expedient in the public interest, and imported goods of the same kind as such products;
(b) foodstuffs, including edible oilseeds and oils;
(c) cattle fodder including oilcakes and other concentrates;
(d) raw Cotton, whether ginned or unginned, and cotton seed; and
(e) raw jute.

34. Price control.

35. Mechanically propelled vehicles including the principle on which taxes on such vehicles are to be levied.

38. Electricity.

List II enumerates the State subjects and List III the concurrent subjects. It must be admitted that a number of entries interspersed in the three lists concerning economic matters seem to overlap and this has led to many significant Constitutional controversies. One interesting controversy was Tihramji vs. State of U.P. in which entry 52, in List I, entries 24 and 27 in List II and entry 33 in List III got involved in connection with the regulation of sugar industry. The judgement of the Supreme Court to some extent diluted the power of the Central Government to regulate all aspects and stages of an industry like sugar in so far as raw materials like sugarcane were excluded from its purview. The position today is that Parliament can regulate only the process of manufacture and the products of industry, but it cannot regulate the supply of raw materials to the controlled industry except to the extent the raw materials fall under entry in List III.

But on the whole in the matter of economic and industrial regulation, under the Constitution the Centre has very wide powers, and its supremacy vis-à-vis the State has been established. Under entry 52 of List I it can control industry. Under entry 33 in List III it can control the products of controlled industry, imported goods, and important raw materials like cotton and jute. Under entry 42 in List I it can regulate inter-state commerce, and under entry 34 in List III it can control price. It is also significant that despite Tihramji case the Centre passed an order in 1955 under which power has been taken to control movement of sugarcane.

## FUNDAMENTAL RIGHTS

This chapter obviously constitutes the major Constitutional limitation on Government's power to regulate the economy of our country and the activities of the private sector. The main limitations are found in the following Articles:

1. Article 14 guaranteeing equality before the law and equal protection of the laws.

2. Article 19 which contains the so-called 'seven freedoms' under our Constitution runs as follows:

1. All citizens shall have the right:

(a) to freedom of speech and expression;

(b) to assemble peacefully and without arms;

(c) to form associations or unions;
(d) to move freely throughout the territory of India;
(e) to reside and settle in any part of the territory of India;
*(f) to acquire, hold and dispose of property, and
(g) to practice any profession, or to carry on any occupation, trade or business.

2. Nothing in sub-clause (a) of clause (1) shall affect the operation of any existing law or prevent the State from making any law in so far as such law imposes reasonable restrictions on the exercise of the right conferred by the said sub-clause in the interests of the sovereignty and integrity of India, the security of the State, friendly relations with foreign States, public order, decency or morality, or in relation to contempt of court, defamation or incitement to an offence.

3. Nothing in sub-clause (b) of the said clause shall affect the operation of any existing law in so far as it imposes, or prevent the state for making any law imposing, in the interests of the sovereignty and integrity of India or public order, reasonable restrictions on the exercise of the right conferred by the said sub-clause.

4. Nothing in sub-clause (c) of the said clause shall affect the operation of any existing law in so far as it imposes or prevents the state from making any law imposing, in the interests of the sovereignty or integrity of India or public order of morality, reasonable restrictions on the exercise of the right conferred by the sub-clause.

5. Nothing in sub-clause (d) and (e) of the said clause shall affect the operation of any existing law in so far as it imposes, or prevent the State from making any law imposing, reasonable restrictions on the exercise of any of the rights conferred by the said sub-clauses either in the interests of the general public or for the protection of the interests of any Schedule Tribe.

6. Nothing in sub-clause (g) of the said clause shall affect the operation of any existing law in so far as it imposes, or prevents the State from making any law imposing, in the interests of the general public, reasonable restrictions on the exercise of the rights conferred by the said sub-clause, and in particular, nothing in the said sub-clause, shall affect the operation of any existing law in so far as it relates to or prevents the State from making any law relating to:

(i) the professional or technical qualifications necessary for practicing any profession or carrying on any occupation, trade or business, or

**Debated by the 44th Amendment Act, 1978.*

(ii) the carrying on by the State, or by a corporation owned or controlled by the State, of any trade, business, industry or service, whether to the exclusion, complete or partial, of citizens or otherwise."

Of the seven freedoms, those in Article 19 (I) (f) and (g), the former conferring on the citizens of the right to acquire, hold and dispose of property and the latter containing the right to practice any profession, or to carry on any occupation, trade or business, are of direct relevance to business. Sub-clause (5) abridges sub-clause (1) (f) by stating that this right is subject to any law made by the state imposing reasonable restrictions in the interests of the general public. Similarly sub-clause (6) subjects the right conferred by sub-clause (1) (g) to the right to any law made by State imposing reasonable restrictions in the interests of the general public, and also to the right of the State to provide by law for carrying on by it or by a corporation owned or controlled by it of any trade, business, industry or service whether to the exclusion, complete or partial, of citizens or otherwise. It should therefore be noted that Article 19 itself limits uncontrolled exercise of these rights by empowering the State to impose by law reasonable restrictions in the larger interests of the public. Thus the Constitution strives *to strike a balance between individual liberty and social control.*[2] It does not leave TO THE Court, as the American Constitution does, to decide on the extent of permissible State intervention.

Article 31 as it originally stood contained the right of property and the right to enjoy and dispose of property subject only to reasonable restrictions, but also providing for the right of the State to compulsorily acquire or requisition property for a public purpose by law, and the right of compensation to the owner in such cases of acquisition or requisitioning of property, a right common to all persons including those in private business. Article 31 was omitted by the 44th Amendment Act, 1978. 31 A, 31 B and 31 C are as follows:

Of them the most significant provisions are Article 19 (1) (f) and Article 19 (6) (ii). The former can be said to constitute the safeguard of "due process of law" for property and business rights of the American pattern. By virtue of it the Supreme Court can decide whether the restrictions imposed by the State are reasonable or not. Thus although our Constitution acknowledges that there cannot be any such thing as absolute or uncontrolled liberty and that the State can under 19 (1) and (6) restrict the exercise of freedom of property, trade, profession and business guaranteed under Article 19 (f) and (g), these restrictions must be reasonable ones, and cannot be imposed by the executive without legislative authority. The power of judicial review is derived from the word: reasonable" which qualifies the world "restrictions" in each of these clauses. In determining reasonableness for Courts can take into account not only public interest, but also whether the restrictions sought to be imposed by the legislature has a reasonable relation to the authorized purpose, or is an arbitrary abridgement of the freedom guaranteed by the Article. Thus we have judicial supervision of the constitutionality of legislative and executive action.

Prior to the Supreme Court's award on bank nationalization in 1969 one view held among jurists in the light of two decades of the Court's decision was that the Court had virtually abandoned its role in relation to Article 19 (1) (f) and (g) and had followed a policy of deferences to the legislative verdict in determining the reasonableness of a restriction, and that as a result "private economic interests do not enjoy much of a substantive protection under the Constitution."[3] But this view seems to be based on a somewhat unrealistic comparison between the attitude of the U.S. Supreme Court towards this question and that of our Supreme Court. It ignores the fact that whereas the attitude of the former was all along conditioned by the prevailing laissez faire economic philosophy, in India the long tradition of close government control of business specially during the war years, and the universally accepted need after independence for government supervision of the economy in the interest of planning and development were bound to cast a profound influence on the attitude of the courts. As has been well observed, *It was the fundamental rights which were the newcomers on the constitutional scene, and not governmental restrictions on the liberties and rights of citizens.*[4] Secondly, soon after the Constitution came into being it was realized that Article 19 as it stood would obstruct the State in pursuing some of the Directive Principles (Saghir Ahmed vs. U.P. Roadways, 1951) and the result was the Constitution (First Amendment) Act, 1951. It introduced in Article 19 (1) sub-clause 6 (ii) which authorized "the carrying on by the State, or by a corporation owned or controlled by the State of any trade, business, industry or service, whether to the exclusion complete or partial, of citizens or by a corporation owned or controlled by the State of any trade, business, industry or service, whether to the exclusion complete or partial, of citizens or otherwise." This further lessened the scope of judicial review. Taking recourse to this provision Government has nationalized many institutions which earlier operated in the public sector. Government also created monopoly of public institutions in a number of fields like insurance or other commercial organization operating side by side with privately owned organization. As a result of this amendment it is constitutionally possible for the Parliament to introduce Communism in India at a stroke by nationalizing trade and industry and thus abolishing the private sector altogether.

In such a context some degree of judicial deference towards legislative acts was perhaps inevitable. Thus in Balsara vs. State of Bombay 1951 the Court held that if a law seek to carry out an object in pursuance of the Directive Principles it cannot be called unconstitutional even if it offends a fundamental right, for what the State is required by the Constitution itself to do cannot be said to be unreasonable, e.g. Article 43 (minimum wages), Article 47 (restriction on the sale of liquor etc). In the case of West Bengal vs. Subodh Gopal, the Supreme Court held that under our Constitution the legislature possessed a larger measure of police power that what had earlier been supposed. Nevertheless the courts have intervened in innumerable cases and invalidated State regulatory measures on the ground that these violated the constitutional guarantees of fundamental rights. But once the legislature has proceeded to plug the loophole and enact a new law the attitude of our Courts has not generally been one of confrontation, but of defence to the wisdom of the legislature.

The courts also for a long time interpreted Article 31 in a manner which invalidated State actions, and Article 31 had to be amended several times (the First, the Fourth, the Seventeenth and the Twenty-fifth amendments) with a view to carrying out the objective envisaged in Article 39 of effective control of the material resources and the means of production and for transfer of ownership to the State. Thus the Fourth Amendment (1955) recast the entire 31-A by providing that no law providing among other things for:

1. The taking over of the management of any property by the State for a limited period in the public interest or for proper management,
2. The amalgamation of two or more corporations in the public interest or for proper management,
3. The extinguishment or modification of any right of managing agents, managing directors, directors etc. or of any voting rights of shareholders, or
4. The extinguishment or modification of any rights arising out of any agreement, lease or licence in respect of any mineral or mineral oil shall be void on the ground that it is inconsistent with any rights conferred by article 14, 19 or 31.

It is also laid down that when a law provided for the acquisition of a person's property for a public purpose and also provided some compensation, the adequacy of the compensation shall not be questioned in a Court. As the Supreme Court, in spite of this amendment, continued to hold that the expression 'compensation' meant full monetary equivalent of the property or the market value,[5] the 25th Amendment (1971) substituted the word 'amount'. But again, the Supreme Court by a majority judgement in the famous Kesavananda Bharathi case in 1973[6] held that the amount which has to be fixed by the legislature cannot be arbitrary or illusory, but must be determined by a principle which is relevant to the acquisition of property. Thus it revived an area for judicial intervention. The 25th Amendment Act, 1971 also introduced a new article, 31-C which provides that any law which seeks to implement the directive principles in Article 39 (b) or (c ) shall not be void on ground of being inconsistent with Article 14, 19 or 31, and no law which declares that it is for giving effect to these principles shall be challenged in any Court on the ground that it does not give effect to this policy. The immediate background to this was the Supreme Court's judgement striking down the banks' nationalization, and Parliament's desire to settle the issue by appropriate amendment of the Constitution. But the Supreme Court's decision in the Kesavananda case holding judicial review as an essential feature of our Constitution has somewhat toned down the effectiveness of Article 31-C. However, the 42nd Amendment (1976) proceeded to assert Parliament's sovereign right to amend the Constitution and to place all amendments beyond the scope of judicial review. Further, the insertion of the adjective 'socialism' by the 42nd Amendment in the Preamble to describe the Indian Republic appears to underline the Constitution's distinct preference for a socialist type of economy away from *laissez faire* and unrestricted private ownership. This, together with Article 31-C as amended by the same Amending Act made it unambiguously clear that the Directive, Principles would prevail *en bloc* over the Fundamental Rights contained in Article 14, 19 and 31. That the courts could not ignore this significant change in the Preamble is clear from the Supreme Court's verdict in the Excel Wear Case (A Excel Wear vs. Union of India A. 1979 SC 25) that though the Indian Constitution envisaged private ownership of property and business, the insertion of the world 'socialist' would enable the courts "to learn more and more in favour of nationalization and State ownership of an industry." The same trend was further accentuated by the 44th Amendment Act, 1978, although undertaken by the Janata Party Government, which repeated Article 19 (1) (f) and 31 (2) from the Constitution. Taking the recent constitutional changes together it is possible to take a view that from 1979 onwards the thrust in our constitution is not in favour of a mixed economy, but State ownership of production and distribution. No court can now entertain a complaint from a displaced private owner on the ground that a confiscatory legislation or nationalization without compensation is unconstitutional because it takes away his fundamental right to property. However, it should also be emphasized that the Supreme Court can grant relief if it ventures to assert its doctrine of no amendment of the constitution's basic structure notwithstanding clause (4) and (5) of Article 368 (Basu, DD Constitutional Law of India, 2nd edn. Page 3, 1980). However it is significant to record that during the debate of the 44th Amendment Bill Prime Minister Indira Gandhi announced that the object behind inserting the world 'socialist' was not to achieve collectivism or State socialism but only equal opportunity of socio-economic reform.

However, Parliament's power to amend is still subject to the limitations laid down by the Supreme Court in the Minerva Mills Case (1980), that the basic structure of the Constitution cannot be changed by Parliament.

It is of interest to note that in recent years a large number of socioeconomic legislations have been included in the Ninth Schedule (188 at the end of 1983) which by virtue of Article 31-B is completely outside the scope of judicial review. Among these are the Industrial (Development and Regulation) Act, 1951 and the M.R. T.P. Act, 1969.

One interesting point to remember is that the freedom under Article 19 (1) is available only to citizens. Another is that it is available only to natural persons who are citizens, not to corporations.

Of some relevance to us, also, is part XIII of the Constitution containing Articles 301-307. Article 301 declares that trade, commerce and intercourse throughout the territory of India shall be free. This freedom is however different from the freedom guaranteed under Article 19. The former can be invoked by citizens and foreigners, while the latter is available only to citizens. Secondly, the right under Article 301 is only a constitutional; right which is justifiable while the right under Article 19 is a fundamental right which is justifiable. Article 302 enables Parliament to impose restrictions on this freedom in the public interest. Unlike in Article 19 the word 'restrictions' is not qualified by the word 'reasonable'. This seems to make reasonableness not-justified by the word 'reasonable'. This seems to make reasonableness not-justifiable and thus gives Parliament a much larger authority. In contrast the restrictions to be imposed by the State Legislation under Article 304 (b) on the freedom of trade are required to be 'reasonable'. The object of the 'freedom' guaranteed by Article 301 as supported by the case law, is to ensure that the economic unity of India is not broken up by internal barrier and that the flow of trade runs smooth throughout the territory unhampered by restrictions at various points. It has however been settled that tax laws, or purely regulatory measures, like licensing of vehicles, marketing, and health regulations cannot be challenged as offending article 301 unless they can be shown as colourable measures to restrict the flow of trade, commerce and intercourse.

In conclusion we should note that the Indian Constitution envisages a 'mixed' economy in which nationalized undertaking co-exist with private enterprise, and the constitutional guarantees for freedom and equality of private enterprise are tempered by the recognition of the need for drastic regulation by Government in many respects. The freedom enjoyed by private enterprise is not absolute, but subject to serious limitations under Articles 19, 31,302, 303 and 304. Expressions, such as "In the interest of the general public" in Article 19 (5), give the State very wide authority to impose by the law reasonable restrictions on the ground of the general social and economic policies of the State. It is important to note that even when the government is wanting to make major policy changes in several directions such as permitting the private sector including foreign companies to enter into the insurance sector, or partially privatizing the monopoly public sector insurance companies, the existing law for full government monopoly in insurance in pursuance of the constitution's provisions is being held as a serious obstacle.

The Supreme Court has repeatedly held (e.g. Dwarka Prasad vs. State of U. P., 1954) that a restriction is reasonable only when there is a proper balance between the rights of the individual and those of the society, between his fundamental right to freedom and the overriding need for social control in public interest. Indeed there is a balance in jour constitution between private enterprise and Government control with the balance titled in favour of the latter. Incidentally the Courts in India have always operated free from Government control and activism by the Supreme Court and High Courts always played an important role in the inter-face between the Government and Business. The recent judgment of the Supreme Court on the Vodafone case where the Court turned down a big assessment by the Income Tax Department on a foreign company is an illustration in point. This kind of activism improves the psychology of foreign investors and attracts foreign investment. Similarly, the Supreme Court turning down the Government case in the so called 3G issue has also proved that the judiciary has in cases given verdict against Government's excessive zeal thereby bringing about a certain degree of moderation in the inter-facing between

Government and Business. But the scraping of licenses issued to a number of foreign companies such as Telenor did make foreign investors apprehensive. The Supreme Court's recent judgment in the Vodafone case turning down the Income Tax Department tax claim on a transaction between two non-resident companies in respect of Indian properties, was no doubt welcomed by foreign investors, But talks of a new law on this with retrospective effect have disturbed them. Besides some foreign companies whose telecom licences were cancelled by the Supreme Court have sought recourse to international arbitration.

Before we leave this subject, it is important to remember that much of the power that the Central Government in India exercises in the economic field is not derived from the Constitution of India, but from the system of planning that has been in vogue since 1951. The Planning Commission that was created in 1950 by a government resolution as an executive organ of the Central Government is charged with the responsibility of determining the size of the Five Year Plans and the Annual plans of the States including the pattern of financing and allocating Central Plan assistance to the States. To the extent that many of the states become heavily dependent on Central funding of their Plans they also become subservient to the Planning Commission and thus lose part of their sovereign position under the Constitution. As the Planning Commission also determines the Plan size of the Central Ministries and approves all major Plan projects of these Ministries it comes to assume a commanding position in India's economic system.

## REFERENCES

1. Inserted by the Constitution (Fdrty0Second) Amendment Act, 1976.
2. Gopalan Vs. State of Madras (1950) S. C. R 88 (253-54).
3. Alice Jacob, "Public Control of Private Enterprise: Judicial Process and Policy Perspectives", 1967, Journal of Indian Law Institute, p. 171.
4. R. B. Tewari, "Private Enterprise and Govt. Regulations" in Indian Law Institute-Government Regulation of Private Enterprise, p. 53.
5. Cooper Vs. Union of India, A.I.R 1973 S.C. 1641.
6. Kesavananda Vs. State of Kerala, A. I. R. 1973 S.C. 1641.
   This judgment is more famous because it upheld Parliament's power to amend even fundamental rights (without destroying the essential features or basic structure of the Constitution) and thus over-ruled Golaknath's case which had held otherwise.

CHAPTER 3

# Industrial Policy and Industrial Licensing: A Bugbear before 1991—But a damp squib now

From 1951 on to the massive economic reforms of 1991 -92, industrial licensing constituted the key element in the Indian Government's industrial policy. This meant a tight investment licensing system administered primarily through the Industries (Development and Regulation) Act, 1951 and supplemented by a host of other regulatory laws and administrative practices. Most of these controls professedly arose from the system of planning in India and from the provisions in the Constitution preaching socialist pattern of society, equality of wealth and opportunities and egalitarianism in general.

Until 1991 the inner core of policy and legal instruments consisted of (i) the Industrial Policy Resolution 1956, the basic policy document, (ii) the Industries (Development and Regulation) Act, 1951, the central legal instrument, and (iii) the Government's Industrial Licensing Policy within the overall frame of the Industrial policy Resolution. Together these controls constituted the classic interface between government and publishers.

Apart from this inner core of three direct controls, there was also an outer circle of several indirect but important controls, the most important among them being (i) the M.R.T.P. Act. (ii) Capital Goods Import Control, and (iii) Government's policy with regard to foreign investment and foreign collaboration. All Companies which were covered by the provisions of the M.R.T.P. Act dealing with concentration of economic power were required to obtain Central Government's special approval under that Act to pay new project over and above the industrial licence. If any project involved the import of capital equipment or machinery, a Capital Goods clearance for which there is a separate procedure becomes necessary. For getting foreign equity investment or technical collaboration a Company needed yet another separate approval of its project from an official body, viz. the Foreign Investment Board. Yet another clearance called the FERA clearance (approval under section 29 of the Foreign Exchange Regulation Act to the continuance of existing business by foreign controlled companies) affected a substantial segment of Indian industry for several years from 1974 onwards. These policies and procedures had an important bearing on the formulation and implementation of new projects in our country's Industrial system. In this chapter we shall examine the three direct instruments of control. Viz. Industrial Policy Resolution, the Industries (D&R) Act and the Industrial Licensing system, and which still remain the major policy instruments despite the number of policy announcement made subsequently.

Government of India's first Industrial Policy Resolution (1948) called for a dynamic national policy directed "to a continuous increase in production by all possible means, side by side with the measures to secure its equitable distribution." For implementing that policy, the Resolution stressed the need for the state to play "a progressively active role in the development of industries." The resolution made it clear that 'for some time to come, the State could contribute more quickly to the increase of national wealth by expanding its present activities where it is already operating and by concentrating on new units of production in other fields, rather than on acquiring and running existing units.' It was indicated that "meanwhile, private enterprise properly directed and regulated, has a valuable role to play." The public and private sectors were thus given complimentary roles in promoting industrial development. The manufacture of arms and ammunition, the production and control of atomic energy, and the ownership and management of railways were to be the exclusive monopoly of the Central Government. The responsibility for setting up new undertaking was reserved to the State in the following six basic industries, except where, in the national interest, the State itself found it necessary to secure the co-operation of private enterprise:

(i) Coal.
(ii) Iron and Steel.
(iii) Aircraft manufacture.
(iv) Ship-building.
(v) Mineral oils.
(vi) Manufacture of telephone, telegraph and wireless apparatus (excluding radio receiving sets).

## INDUSTRIAL POLICY RESOLUTION, 1956

The need for further amplification of this policy and for extending the scope and coverage of the public sector arose due to subsequent developments in the political and economic spheres. The Directive Principles of State Policy enshrined in the Constitution adopted in January 1950 indicated the socioeconomic goals towards which the efforts of the State were to be oriented. In the light of these principles, planning for economic development assumed special importance. A National Planning Commission was accordingly set up in March 1950 and the nation's First Five-Year Plan was finalized by the end of 1952. While the First Five Year Plan was under implementation the pursuit of a socialist pattern of society was accepted by Parliament in 1954 as the principal objective of social and economic policy. With the completion of the First Five-Year Plan, it became clear that there was urgent need for accelerating the pace of economic development through the expansion, among other things of heavy industries. Taking these changes and needs into account, Government reformulated their industrial policy in April, 1956.

The Resolution of 1956 declared:

The adoption of the socialist pattern of society as a national objective, as well as the need for planned and rapid development, requires that all industries of basic and strategic importance, or in the nature of public utility service, should be in the public sector. Other industries which are essential and require investment on a scale which only the State in the present circumstances could provide, have also to be in the public sector. The State has, therefore, to assume direct responsibility for the future development of industries over a wider area."

This revised Industrial Policy Resolution classified industries into three categories having regard to the part which the State would pay in each of them. In the first category were placed the industries the future development of which was to be exclusive responsibility of the State (Schedule-A). The second category consisted of industries which would be progressively State-owned and in which the State would therefore generally take the initiative in establishing new undertakings but in which private enterprise would also be expected to supplement the effort of the State (Schedule-B). The third category included all the remaining industries where future development would generally be left to the initiative and enterprise in the private sector. The following industries were placed in the first and second categories respectively.

**Schedule 'A'**

1. Arms and ammunition and allied items of defence equipment.
2. Atomic energy.

3. Iron and steel.
4. Heavy castings and forgins of iron and steel.
5. Heavy plan and machinery required for iron and steel production, for mining, for machine tool manufacture and for such other basic industries as may be specified by the Central Government.
6. Heavy Electrical plant including large hydraulic and steam turbines.
7. Coal and lignite.
8. Mineral oils
9. Mining and iron ore, managanese ore, chrome ore, gypsum, sulphur, gold and diamond.
10. Mining and processing of copper, lead, zinc, tin molybdenum and wolfram.
11. Minerals specified in the schedule to the Atomic Energy (Control of Production and User) Order, 1953.
12. Aircraft.
13. Railway transport.
14. Air transport.
15. Ship building.
16. Telephone and telephone cable, telegraph and wireless apparatus (excluding radio receiving sets).
17. Generation and distribution of Electricity.

**Schedule 'B'**

(i) All other minerals except "minor minerals" as defined in Section 3 of the Minerals Concession Rules, 1949.
(ii) Aluminium and other non-ferrous metals not included in Schedule 'A'.
(iii) Machine Tools.
(iv) Ferro-alloys and tool steels.
(v) Basic and intermediate products required by chemical industries such as the manufacture of drugs, dyestuffs and plastics.
(vi) Antibiotics and other essential drugs.
(vii) Fertilizers.
(viii) Synthetic rubber.
(ix) Carbonisation of coal.
(x) Chemical pulp.
(xi) Road Transport.
(xii) Sea Transport.

The Resolution made it clear that "the division of industries into separate categories does not imply that they are being placed in watertight compartments. Inevitably, there will not only be an area of overlapping but also a great deal of dovetailing between industries in the private and the public sectors. It will be open to the State to start any industry not included in Schedule 'A' and Schedule 'B' when the needs of planning so require or there are other important reasons for it." It further declares that the expansion of the existing private units in Schedule 'A' is not ruled out. There is also the possibility of the State securing the cooperation of private enterprise in establishing new units when the national interest so requires. In such cases 'the State will ensure either through majority participation in the capital of otherwise that it has the requisite powers to guide the policy and control the operations of the undertaking.' The growth of private enterprise in Schedule 'B' industries "with State participation" was also envisaged. Thus the genesis of 'joint sector' or even of what Shri T. A. Pai has called 'national sector' can be said to lie in the 1956 Industrial Policy Resolution.

Stressing further the complementary role of both the sectors, the Resolution declared "further, heavy industries in the public sector may obtain some of their requirements lf light components from the private sector, while the private sector, in turn, would rely for many of its needs on the public sector. The same principle would apply with even greater force to the relationship between large scale industries."

Other principles emphasized in the Resolution were:

(i) Reduction of disparities in income and wealth and to prevent monopolies and the concentration of economic power in different fields in the hand of a small number of individuals;

(ii) Fair and non-discriminatory treatment to public and private sector units where they co-exist;

(iii) Encouragement to cottage and village and small scale industries and modernizing them so as to improve their competitive efficiency;

(iv) Progressive reduction of disparities in levels of development between different regions;

(v) The maintenance of industrial peace;

(vi) Improvement of living and working conditions of workers and raising the standard of their efficiency;

(vii) Developing the country's resource of technical and managerial personnel;

(viii) Participation of workers, technicians and professional in management;

(ix) Responsibility of public enterprises to augment the revenue of the State and provide resources for further development in fresh fields.

To sum up, the Industrial Policy Resolution of 1956 gives the broad policy framework of industrial development in India. In spite of considerable changes in emphasis among various sectors which took place from time to time, this Resolution remained the Magna Carta for Indian Industry till its replacement by the July 1991 Industrial Policy which in many respects sought to return to the spirit of 1956.

## INDUSTRIES (DEVELOPMENT AND REGULATION) ACT, 1951

Unlike most of the administrative controls over business in our country, industrial licensing did not originate during the Second World War, but only in 1951 when the First Five –Year Plan began. Its legal frame is provided by the industries (Development and Regulation) Act, 1957 which, as the name implies, is concerned with the regulation and development of industry in accordance with the principles indicated by the Industrial Policy Resolution (1948, 1956) and also the priorities indicated by each Five-Year Plan.

This Act has been described as "the single most important piece of economic development legislation" in our legal structure. Along with the Companies Act, 1956, and the Monopolies and Restrictive Trade Practices Act, 1969, it confirmed on Government powers of almost total regulation and control over the working of the private industry and corporate sector in a manner almost unique in the world. The Act also become a subject of severe controversies, as various policies and assumptions implied in it have been questioned by sections of businessmen, politicians both of the rightist and the leftist varieties, and also by economists of various schools.

### Objectives

The objectives behind regulation and licensing of industries can be summed up as follows:

(i) Regulation of private industrial development in accordance with the planned priorities.

(ii) Channelization of investment into priority industries.

(iii) Avoidance of the concentration of ownership and control over large segments in industrial fields by large industrial houses.

(iv) Prevention of locational concentration so as to encourage dispersal of industries to under-developed regions and ensure balanced growth.

(v) Promotion of small scale and cottage industries and reducing undue competition between them and large scale industries.

(vi) Optimum utilization of the scarce foreign exchange resources.

(vii) Enabling government to take over management of undertakings which are being conducted in a manner detrimental to the industry or public interest.

### Mian Provisions

The important provisions of the Act may be summed up in the following manner:

1. All existing industrial undertaking in the scheduled industries, i.e. industries which are listed in the First Schedule of this Act should be registered with the Government within the prescribed period and issued with certificates of registration (Section 10);
2. No new industrial undertaking of a major size can be started in the scheduled industry (Section 11), no new article can be manufactured (Section11-A) and no substantial expansion of an existing undertaking can be effected (Section 13) without a licence to be issued by the Central Government.
3. No change of location of an industrial unit can take place without the express permission of Central Government.
4. Central Government has also power to revoke registration of licence in case of any misrepresentation, etc. by the party concerned, or failure on the part of licences to take effective steps (Section 12).
5. Under Section 15 of the Government has powers to order investigation into the working of industrial undertakings. Under Section 16 if this investigation reveals that the undertaking to the particular industry or to the country's economic development, the Government has powers to issue directions to the management, in respect of prices, production, quality, the management of the undertaking and other areas of its performance. In the event of the undertaking not carrying out these directions, Government can take over its management for a specific period and appoint an authorized controller to manage the company (Section 18). It is important to note that this' power to take over management and control of an undertaking embodied in sub-section A to F of Section 18 has been made non-justifiable.
6. Section 18-G gives the Central Government comprehensive powers to control and regulate the supply, distribution and prices of any of the articles produced by an industry listed in Schedule-A, and no order made for this purpose can be called in question in a court of law.
7. For the purpose of advising the Central Government on matters concerning the development and regulation of scheduled industries

Section 5 of the Act authorizes the establishment of a Central Advisory Council for Industry with necessary sub-committees and standing committees. This Council consists of representatives from the Central Government and from owners or employers, consumers, labour and certain other sections including primary producers, Central Government is required to consult this Council with regard to the making of any rules and improvement under the Act and may consult it 'with regard to any other matter connected with the administration of this Act.'

8. Developmental Councils are to be constituted in respect of each scheduled industry or groups of industries (Section 6). The functions that may be assigned to these Councils are enumerated in the Second Schedule. The more important of them are: recommending production targets and co-ordinating production programmes; suggesting norms of efficiency in order to eliminate waste, maximize production, and reduce cost; standardizing products; assisting in the distribution of controlled materials; facilitating the training of technical and skilled personnel; promoting scientific and industrial research; investigating the possibility of decentralizing stages and processes of production; improving business management practices; advising Government on matters pertaining to the industry or group of industries.

The Development Councils along with the Central Advisory Council for Industries represent the more positive side of the act. The idea of such Councils was borrowed from the Development Councils of UK and also shows the influence of the French technique of indicative planning through the modernization councils. They were set up in about 20 industries and have been utilized for the formulation of the targets and programmes for the Five-Year Plans. Through them the planning of industrialization is sought to be made the joint effort of the Government and the private sector. They have also brought out better undertaking between Government and industry. Their expenses are met out of a levy on the assets or goods manufactured in a particular scheduled industry. Contrary to some doubts in the beginning, these Councils have on the whole worked as homogeneous bodies and also brought about suitable dialogue between Government and the private sector. The strains that developed in the relationship between Government and business doing 1970s and 1980s could perhaps be eliminated to a large extent if these Councils were again reactivated and utilized in the spirit envisaged by the Act. Unfortunately they have become in recent years largely non-technical bodies which merely set some vague targets but lack the effectiveness to implement them.

A common criticism from private sector industry was that industrial licensing has been used more as an ideological instrument of socialism than as a happy medium of a mixed economy. It is difficult to endorse this contention except with reference to the period 1967-73 i.e. from R. K. Hazari's study on industrial licensing to the industrial licensing policy of 1973. On the other hand, between 1951, a great deal of pragmatism and emphasis on industrial growth seem to have characterized the working of the policy, and licences were often than not granted for asking.

Inevitably, the liberal application of the policy led to abuses on a sizeable scale by the private sector, in particular, some of the industrial houses. The distrust of the private sector, the general hostility to large industrial houses, and ht resultant restrictive policy and hardening of procedure which marked the period from 1967 to 1974 were largely a reaction to these abuses. A certain ideological view, and need for populism intensified this process.

## THE NEW INDUSTRIAL POLICY OF JULY 1991

Despite the impressive growth performance of the 1980s, serious budgetary and fiscal deficits of the Government and severe pressure on the country's balance of payments position led to a critical economic and financial situation by 1991, further aggravated by the political uncertainty. By the time there was a new deregulatory and liberal economic regime and drastically reducing the government's licensing and regulatory functions. This was the rationale behind the sweeping changes in industrial and trade policies brought about by the Narasimha Rao government in 1991 and 1992. A series of measures were introduced then by the government to bring about industrial deregulation and to substantially liberalise the provisions relating to domestic and FDIs. This reforms process has been continued and sustained. Since then the industrial policy reforms have reduced the industrial licensing requirements. Removed restrictions on investment and expansion, and facilitated easy access to foreign technology and foreign direct investment.

The following were the major reforms in the new industrial policy:

(i) All industrial undertakings are exempt from obtaining an industrial license except for
 (a) 3 industries reserved for the public sector
 (b) 5 industries retained under compulsory licensing. They are

1. Distillation and brewing of alcoholic drinks.
2. Liquors and cigarettes of tobacco and manufactured tobacco substitutes.
3. Electronic Aerospace and defence equipments of all types.
4. Industrial explosives indulging detonating fuels, safety fuels, gunpowder, nitrocellulose and matches.
5. Hazard in chemicals.
   (a) Hydrocyanic acid and its derivatives.
   (b) Phosgene and its derivatives
   (c) Isocyanides and di isocyanides
   (d) Hydrocarbon

All those waiting to do manufacturing of these items are required to apply for industrial license to this Secretariat for Industrial Assistance (SIA) located in the Ministry of Commerce and Industry in New Delhi in the prescribed from. There is an inter-Ministerial licensing committee to consider licensing application and recommend approval or rejection. No licence is permissible in items of manufacture reserved for the small scale sector or if the proposal is subject to locational restriction.

(i) The areas reserved for the public sector have been reduced from earlier 29 (17 in Schedule A+12 in Schedule B of 1956 Policy) to 3. These are areas where security and strategy concerns predominate (Annexure l).

(ii) 112 high priority industries, identified under the National Industrial Classification, 1987, Qualify for automatic approval up to 50/51/74/100 per cent FDI, depending on the nature of activity. (Annexure IV).

(iii) Industrial undertakings are free to select the location of a project. The only restriction in force is that the proposed project should not be located within 25 kms from the periphery of the standard urban area limit of a city having a population of more than 1 million according to 1991 census (Annexure V). Exception are the non-polluting industries, the industries located in an industrial area designated by the concerned state government before July 25, 1991.

(iv) Entrepreneurs are required to obtain Statutory Clearances relating to Pollution Control and environment fir setting up an industrial project.

(v) The exemption from licensing will apply to all substantial expansions of existing units provided the item is not listed in annex I/II and is not reserved for the small scale sector.

(vi) Foreign investments up to 100 per cent will be allowed to trading companies primarily engaged in:
  (a) Exports;
  (b) Bulk imports with export exbonded warehouse sales;
  (c) Cash and carry wholesale trading; and
  (d) Other import of goods and services provided at least 75 per cent is for procurement and sale of goods and services among the companies of the same group and for third party use or onward transfer/distribution/sales.

(vii) Foreign technology agreements up to payments not exceeding USS2 million and royalties up to 5 per cent on domestic sales and 8 per cent on export sales, subject to a total payment of 8 per cent on sales over a period of 10 years, will not get automatic clearance.

(viii) Chapter III of the MRTP co was removed except for one section viz. Section 27 which deals with the splitting of monopolies. The Act regulated the economic activities of enterprises that were classified either as large houses or as dominant undertakings. (based on market share). This is expected to release Indian industry from regulations that earlier controlled substantial expansions. There would now be no need for prior approval from the government for new undertakings, expansions, mergers, amalgamations, takeovers, appointment of directors, etc.

(ix) No licenses or approvals needed from the Government of India for the small scale industry sector only with the exceptions of articles listed in Annexure I and Annexure II.

(x) Reservation of products for exclusive manufacture (812 products at present) in the small scale.

(xi) Investment ceiling on plant and machinery for SSI units which was raised from Rs, 60 lakhs to Rs. 3 crore in 1997 has been reduced to Rs, 1 crore in 1999. The investment limit for tiny units, however, continues to be at the level of Rs. 25 lakh.

(xii) Export obligation of non-SSI units producing reserved items has been reduced from 75 per cent to 50 per cent.

(xiii) Infrastructural support to Entrepreneurship Development Institutes (EDLs) to augment their training capabilities

(xiv) Quality certification scheme launched to improve SSI product quality. Financial support to acquire ISO 9000.

(xv) Priority sector lendings of SSIs.

(xvi) In order to ensure that credit is made available to all segments of the SSI sector. RBI has issued instructions that out of the funds normally available for the SSI sector. 40 per cent be given to units with investment in plant and machinery upto Rs. 5 lakhs, 20 percent to units with investment between Rs. 5 lakhs and Rs, 25 lakhs and remaining 40 per cent for other unit. Banks have been asked to operationalise more specialized SSI branches. The single window scheme of SIDBI is also being extended to all districts.

(xvii) Announcement of a new Credit Insurance Scheme in the Budget (1999-2000) for providing adequate security to the banks to improve flow of investment credit to SSI units, particularly export oriented and tiny units.

(xviii) To coordinate the latest development with regard to the World Trade Organisation (WTO), agreements and organizing WTO Sensitisation Seminars, Workshops.

Clearly, there is an intention to shift the main responsibility for investment decision from the Ministers and bureaucrats on whom it was vested for the last forty years back to where it should logically belong, viz., the entrepreneurs and the industrial managers. A determined pursuit of these policies should free India from the policy aberrations and ills which have afflicted her during these decades.

The process of economic reforms has in fact been proved irreversible. All governments to the date, coming after Narasimha Rao seem to have followed liberalization and economic reforms with a view to bringing about rapid and substantial economic growth and move towards globalization of the economy. The result has been on astonishing break-through.

While during the seventies and the eighties, the average annual GDP growth seldom exceeded 2 or 3 per cent, it rose at 6 per cent during the nineties 8 or 9 per cent during the first decade of the present century. The new industrial policy should also be viewed with several other measures by the government. Provisions related to foreign investment, industrial licensing, foreign exchange control etc. have been relaxed substantially. The capital market has been opened up top foreign investment and restrictions on imports have been substantially removed. The industrial policy reforms have reduced the industrial licensing requirements to a select number of hazardous and environmentally sensitive industries, removed restrictions on investments and expansion by MRTP Houses, reserved only 6 industries for public sector and facilitated easy access foreign technology.

For our present purposes we need not go through the details of the extremely negative and conservative licensing policy of the Government during the Seventies and Eighties. With the spectacular deterioration of the

Government's financial position in 1989-90 necessitating an approach is the international Monetary Fund for a bail out, there was inevitably a move towards dismantling of the costly Licensing Permit Raj. Licensing policy was relaxed as never before and import restrictions and foreign exchange restrictions were removed. The responsibility of entrepreneurial decisions was transferred to the entrepreneur and managers after nearly three decades from the officials and ministers.

This coincided with another key change Indian Economy had been insulated from the world during these three decades through a variety of measures such as import control foreign exchange control and regulation of foreign investment and foreign technological collaborations, and also control on exports. Now India became a part of global economy. An Indian company was no longer under a compulsion to obtain now materials and intermediate goods locally and could now buy them from anywhere in the world, Similarly it could sell its products in any other country wherever it could obtain the best price.

## RESERVATION FOR SMALL SCALE INDUSTRY

A small scale unit is defined as an undertaking of the capital investment in plant and machinery does not exceed M Scores i.e. M 50 million. Government has reserved certain items for exclusive manufacture in the small scale sector. This list at one time covering over 700 items which stands reduced. These units can get themselves registered with the Director of Industries (District Industries Centre of the State). These units are also free from locational restrictions.

### Locational Restrictions

No industrial license is to be given (1) if the proposed location is within 25 km of the limits of 23 cities having population of 10 lakhs as per the 1991 census. But the locational restriction does not apply.

1. If the unit is to be located in an industrial area
2. In the case of electronics, computer software, printing and any other industry notified as "non-polluting industry."

## ENVIRONMENT CLEARANCE

While the scheme for industrial licensing has been virtually eliminated in recent years, environmental clearance has become prominent. All entrepreneurs are required to take statutory clearance relating to pollution control and environment is required of projects in 31categories of industries as justified by the Ministry of Environment & Forests (27. 1. 94 Justification) under the Environment (Protection) Act, 1986 e. g. petrochemical complex, petroleum refineries canal, thermal power plants and fertilizers.

However, if the projects is less than 10 crores i.e. 1 billion, environmental clearance is not necessary unless it is in the areas of pesticides, bulk drugs, asbestos, paint conflexes, mining, distilleries, dyes, foundries, electroplating industries, travel roads in Himalayan areas and towards projects of certain parameters.

Separate guidelines have been viewed by the Environment Ministry in respect of certain ecologically fragile areas like Aravalli range, Doon Valley and Coastal areas unfortunately environmental clearance has now emerged as the new bugbear in place of licensing. Environmental authorities have held up clearance to many coal mines or coal-related steel mill projects for years and this has created a new controversy.

Unfortunately for our country Governments' control has generally taken the form of direct discretionary case by case control rather than indirect non-discretionary controls such as budgetary, fiscal or monetary controls. This is partly a hangover from the colonial days and partly a result of the planning system we adopted after independence. This invariably reduces government control into the emergence of powerful Govt. bodies which receive a specific application in respect of every action and gives a specific decision. This complicates the problem of interfacing. Not only do we insist on multiple approval of the same business action from different Govt. authorities, but within each authority there is a vertical line of hierarchy through which each case has to pass through. Too many things are required to go through Central or State Secretariats. And the Secretariat insists on detailed examination of every case horizontally and vertically oblivious of the time element and the urgency of particular cases. Our administrative control system applied by the Secretariat culture is simply not capable of high speed decisions which are the need of present times. The results more often than not are inordinate delays, lack of clarity, loss of priority, emphasis on things not relevant and inevitably, as a result of all this corruption.

# CHAPTER 4
# Company Law

Company Law according to its traditional view is concerned with the organisation and functioning of joint stock companies, the incorporation of these companies, their constitution and the inter-relationships amongst members, their management and eventually with the manner of dissolution. Today it has become the principal law of organisation and management for corporate business. Sir Francis Palmer, the famous commentator on English Company Law, said in his book towards the end of the last century, "that now-a-days looking to the vast number of persons as directors, shareholders, officials, customers, creditors or otherwise in companies. there are but few businessmen who can escape the task of acquiring some knowledge of Company Law." This has become much more true today. As against the traditional view there is also a modern view which seeks to enlarge the scope of company law and make it a major instrument of the national, social and economic policies in relation to business.

In recent years there has been a vigorous debate in the West on the precise role of company law and its adequacy in the context of the present day economy. There are those called "preservationists" and those who are called "reformers". In a way both the schools are vigorously engaged in re-examining the very basis of company law. Both are concerned with the need for sweeping changes in company law. The former put the emphasis on tidying up the law as it now stands in respect of such things as the powers and position of the shareholders or of the Directors and the Chief Executive, but their essential thrust is on improving and streamlining the present structure, not on changing its scope and objects. But the reformers go much further. They question the relationship of the company with its environments and the modes by which this relationship is expressed and call for a fundamental review of both its internal mechanism and external role. Some of the reforms advocated by the Jenkins Committee in England and already implemented, and the controversy over the Bullock report which has suggested putting worker-directors in board-rooms, and the recent Cadbury report on the structure of company broads including a part-time Chairman and a full-time Chief Executive are indeed of far-reaching significance, and indicate that even in England, the home of company law, the traditional concept is fast disappearing. Indeed there is increasing realisation in most of the western countries that much of the legislation for joint-stock enterprise now in force is not in tune with contemporary conditions and ideas, and that private enterprise working in the corporate form should in some way, leaving its autonomy unaffected, be made answerable to the society for its decision and actions.

In this respect, India has been far ahead of most of the western countries in the last two decades. Until 1956 our company law from its modest beginning in a law of 1850 (on the model of the English Companies Act 1844), which merely provided for registration of joint-stock companies, generally followed the course of British Company Law. Changes were introduced in 1860, 1866 and 1892 and again in the Companies Act 1913 closely reflecting changes in the British law from time to time such as the introduction of limited liability. There were some half-hearted attempts in 1913 to introduce special provisions to take care of special Indian features such as the system of managing agency, but without any success.

It was the strains and stresses in the Indian economy created by the Second World War which focused public attention on the need for revitalising the Companies Act, 1913. There had been very serious complaints of malpractices and manipulations in company formation and management during the war. It was, therefore, felt that the existing Act contained some very serious lacunae and was unable to control the, activities of dishonest businessmen and financiers. The advent of Independence and the adoption of the Constitution in 1950 with its Directive Principles of State Policy further highlighted the need for the revision of the Companies Act. The idea grew that the Companies Act should no longer be regarded in its orthodox sense as just a mechanism for the regulation of joint-stock enterprise and to take care only of the shareholders and the creditors and that it has a much greater role to playas a principal instrument of Government's social and economic policy. The acceptance of Socialist Pattern of Society as our national goal in 1954 further strengthened this approach. The result was the Companies Act, 1956 which, along with its amendments, is the substantive law in our country today. It is based substantially on a report submitted by the Bhaba Committee (1950) which appeared to have accepted the modern view that seeks to entrust company law with a much larger responsibility in contrast with the traditional view of the company law. Inevitably, therefore, it contained a large number of new, and—to Western eyes—startling provisions for public control over the functioning of joint-stock companies.

The following were declared as the basic objectives of the Companies Act, 1956 by Shri C.D. Deshmukh, the then Finance Minister while moving the bill in the Parliament:

(i) Minimum standard of business integrity and conduct in promotion and management of companies;

(ii) Full and fair disclosure of all reasonable information relating to the affairs of the company;

(iii) Effective participation and control by shareholders and the protection of their legitimate interests;

(iv) Enforcement of proper performance of their duties by company management;

(v) Powers of intervention and investigation into the affairs of companies where they are managed in a manner prejudicial to the interest of the shareholders or to the public interest.

## 'COMPANY' DEFINED

The word 'company' is a loosely used expression with different meanings in different contexts. In common parlance, the word is applied to almost any form of business including individual businessmen. It is also difficult to define it in precise legal terms. In legal theory, a company can be defined as 'an association of a number of persons for a common object, that object normally being the economic gain of its members' (Gower, Modern Company Law). But even this definition does not conform to the economic realities of today. It is difficult, in the present day context, to restrict the expression 'company' to trading concerns alone. In fact, many non-profit-making bodies are also registered under the Companies Act and are subject to the same rules as trading companies. Similarly, it will be unreal to describe a holder of shares in a modern joint-stock company as associating with the other members in running the business. It would not even be correct to describe a modern shareholder as a co-owner of the business. In reality, he is simply a supplier of capital rather than an owner of the business. Thus none of the accepted definition of a joint-stock company seems to express the correct legal and practical position of a company. A modern company has three outstanding characteristics:

(i) Corporate personality;

(ii) Limited Liability; and

(iii) Transferability of shares.

We should identify a company only with reference to these characteristics. The definition of a company as given in Section 3 of the Companies Act is that a 'company' means a company formed and registered under this Act or an existing company formed and registered under any of the previous company laws in India.

## Partnerships and Companies

It is useful to note in brief the distinctions between a joint-stock company and a partnership both of which are very common forms of business enterprise. In India, partnerships, to which the word 'company' is sometimes colloquially applied, are governed by the Indian Partnership Act.

Many of the present day companies originated out of partnership firms. With the growth of industries and business, and as more and more money was needed and the liability of the members increased, partnerships were replaced by companies to which many people can contribute money while sharing liability in a very limited way only. Thus, joint-stock company has today become the commonest form of business organisation. The fundamental differences between a partnership and a company, both of them associations of more than one person for the purpose of doing business for profit may be enumerated as follows:

(i) Unlike a company, a partnership has no separate legal personality. It means the persons constituting the partnership. It is thus available only for a very small number of persons having trust and confidence in one another to come together. But a company, which is a distinct legal person subject to legal duties and entitled to legal rights, is available for a large number of people. Most of the other differences follow from this corporate personality of a company.

(ii) The liability of a shareholder in a company is usually limited to the extent of the money contributed by him (unless it is an unlimited liability company). But the liability of a partner in a firm is unlimited.

(iii) Partners in a firm can make any agreement between themselves regarding conduct or management of the firm. But shareholders cannot make certain arrangements between themselves, as for example, a company cannot buy shares of the company.

(iv) In a partnership, unless there is an agreement, each partner can participate in management. But in a company, management is usually carried on by the directors only, and a shareholder has ordinarily no right to participate in management.

(v) The death of a partner dissolves partnership. But a company has perpetual succession.

(vi) A partnership cannot have more than 20 members (10 in the case of a banking firm). There is no such maximum limit in the case of a public company although a private company cannot have more than 50 members.

(vii) A partnership cannot transfer his shares without the consent of co-partners. But in the case of a public company, there is no such restriction on transfer of shares.

## Types of Companies

There are three basic types of companies in our law:

(i) Companies limited by share—popularly known as limited companies. This is the normal form of a joint-stock company in our country. Such a company obtains finances by the issue of shares to a large number of people. The liability of these shareholders is limited to the share money actually paid or to be paid by them.

(ii) Companies limited by guarantees. In a guarantee company the liability of the members is limited by the memorandum to such amount as the members may undertake to contribute to the assets of the company in the event of its being wound up. In such a company the members are really guarantors of the company's debts upto the guaranteed amount. They have no obligation to subscribe while the company is a going concern, but have obligation only when it is wound up to pay the guaranteed amount to meet the liabilities of the company. Law assumes that the working capital of a guarantee company will come from other sources, e.g. endowments, grants, fees, etc. A guarantee company is particularly suitable for a non-profit-making association.

(iii) Companies with unlimited liability. An unlimited company is defined by the English Companies Act as a 'company not having any limits on the liability of its members.' However, in Indian company law, an unlimited company is largely a matter of theoretical interest. In practice, there is no known unlimited company in existence today.

Each of these three types may again be formed as either public company or private company. As the principle of limited liability holds almost universal sway, the commonest types of companies today are the public limited and private limited companies, the word 'limited' connoting their limited liability.

We may note another class of companies, either limited by shares, or by guarantees under the category of associations not for profit. These are usually registered under Section 25 of the Indian Companies Act. These are generally for promotion of art, science, religion etc., and are commonly known as guarantee companies. But they are not to be confused with societies, clubs and professional associations governed by the Societies Registration Act of 1860 which also allows them to hold property, buy and sell, borrow or lend in furtherance of the object.

*Public and Private Companies:* The general presumption in the Act is that a company is a public company unless it clear from its constitution that it is a private company. In other words, in our Act, there is a statutory presumption which is rebutable that the company is not a private one. Section 3 (iii) defines a private company as a company which by its articles:

(i) restricts the right to transfer its shares,
(ii) limits the number of its members to fifty (excluding those who are or were employees at the time of the acquisition of shares); two or more persons jointly holding shares being counted as a single member; and
(iii) prohibits any invitation to the public to subscribe for any shares of the company.

A public company is defined in Section 3 as one which is not a private company. The minimum number of members in a public company is 7 (Section 12) and the minimum number of Directors 3 (Section 252). In contrast the minimum number of both members in a private company and directors is two. The maximum number of directors in a public or private company is not laid down in the Act. But the articles of the company usually provide for it. Section 45 lays down that if the membership of a private or public company falls below two or seven respectively and if the company carries on its business for more than six months, it forfeits its limited liability and the members become personally liable for any action after six months.

It should be borne in mind that most of the rigorous provisions of the Act apply only to public companies for the simple reason that they do business with the money offered by innumerable investors whose interests require to be safe-guarded.

In passing, it should be noted that only the shares and debentures of public limited companies and not those of private limited companies can be quoted on stock exchanges.

The Companies Act also lays down a relatively simple procedure for conversion of a private company into a public company. According to Section 44, the articles of association have to be altered deleting the basic restrictive clauses applicable to a private company. The number of members is required to be raised to 7 and that of directors to 3. The company also has to file with the Registrar a statement in lieu of a prospectus. A public company can be converted into a private one by inserting in its articles the three restrictive provision with the approval of the Central Government [Article 31 (1)].

There is also a category of 'deemed' public companies. Section 43A lays down that if 25 per cent or more of the paid up capital of a private company is held at any time by one or more bodies corporate, it would be deemed to have become a public company and will be subject to all the provisions of the law applicable to public companies except that:

(i) the three restrictive clauses of a private company need not be deleted, and
(ii) its membership may be less than seven.

Also such a company need not comply with the following restrictions:

(i) It is not necessary to have the presence of five members in a general meeting in order to have quorum.
(ii) The profit and loss account filed with the Registrar need not be open to inspection by the public provided the Government approves. (Section 220).
(iii) Filing of statement in lieu of the prospectus under Section 44 is not necessary unless the company raises subscription from the public by complying with the provisions of Section 70.

The object of this amendment is to ensure that private companies, which employ sizeable amount of public money or operate on a large-scale are made subject to more or less the same restrictions and limitations. A 'deemed' public company also forfeits the word 'private' in its name. A private company will not be so 'deemed' as a public company where:

(i) its entire paid up capital is held by a single Indian private company or one or more foreign companies; or
(ii) the shares are held by one or more foreign bodies corporate which or each of which, if incorporated in India, would be regarded as a private company; or
(iii) any shares in it are held by one or more private companies in which no other company holds shares and the total membership of all these companies including the private company in question does not exceed fifty.

Shares of the following description need not be taken into account in calculating the subscribed 25 per cent if these shares are held by a banking company (i) as a trustee or on behalf of a trustee and the shares have not been set apart for the benefit of any body corporate or (ii) as executor of a shareholder who has not bequeathed them to any body corporate or they have not been bequeathed on behalf of an executor or administrator of the deceased.

A deemed public company can become a private company again with the Central Government's approval when it ceases to fall within the purview of Section 43 A. The amending Act, 1974 has introduced in Section 43 A, certain new provisions under which a private company whose average annual turn-over during the three previous years is not less than Rs 1 crore, or a private company which holds not less than twenty-five per cent of the shares in a public company shall become a public company under Section 43A.

*Holding and Subsidiary Companies:* According to Section 4(a) which defines 'holding' and 'subsidiary' companies, a company is a holding company and another company its subsidiary, if—

(i) the former controls the composition of the Board of Directors of the latter or
(ii) the former controls more than half of the voting power of the latter or
(iii) the latter is a subsidiary of a subsidiary of the former.

A foreign company is considered to be a holding company or a subsidiary under Indian law if it is so considered under the law of its country of incorporation, even though it may not satisfy the definition of a holding or subsidiary company under Indian law. According to Section 42 a subsidiary company cannot be a member of its holding company except where—

(i) it is concerned as the legal representative of a deceased member of the holding company or
(ii) where it is concerned as a trustee or
(iii) where the shareholder is a security for the purpose of a transaction entered into by it in the ordinary course of business which includes lending of money.

*Government Company:* This is also a new concept introduced by the Companies Act of 1956. According to Section 617, a company, in which not less than 51 per cent of the paid up capital is held by the Central Government, a State Government or Governments or partly by Central Government and partly by one or more State Governments, is called a Government company. A Government company can be either public or private, although they need not write the word 'private' after their names. Section 619 lays down certain special provisions in respect of Government companies, as for example:

(i) A Government company is subject to a regular system of special audit under the direction of the Comptroller and Auditor General in addition to the normal statutory audit (Section 619); and

(ii) A Government company operates under the overall control of the Parliament or the State Legislature as the case may be and an annual report on the working and affairs of every company along with the audit report made by the Comptroller and Auditor General has to be laid down on the floor of the concerned legislature (Section 619A). Under Section 619B newly inserted by the 1974 amending Act the provisions of Section 619 are to apply to any company in which not less than fifty one per cent of the paid up share capital is held by the Central or State Government or Government companies and public financial institutions in combination as if it were a Government company. Section 620 authorizes the Central Government to exempt by notification in the Official Gazette any Government company from compliance with any of the provisions of the Companies Act.

*Foreign Company:* Indian Company Law contains certain special provisions for the foreign companies (Sections 591-603). A foreign company is defined in Section 591 as one which incorporated outside India and which has established a place of business in India. The 1974 amendments have introduced a new sub-section to this section which enjoins that when Indian citizens or corporate bodies hold fifty per cent or more of the share capital in such a company, the company shall comply with the provision prescribed in the Act with regard to its business in India as if it were a company incorporated in India. The Registrar of Companies, New Delhi is the Registrar for foreign companies. Such companies are required to submit all the documents prescribed to be delivered under the law to him, and also copies of these documents to the Registrar in the State which has their principal place of business. The provisions of the Indian Companies Act relating to many matters e.g., the issue of prospectus, the provisions relating to changes, are applicable to the foreign companies, The Registrar has the power to call for information from these companies [Section 234 (8)]. It is incumbent upon foreign companies to exhibit in English the name, the country of incorporation and the nature of the liability of members in the prospectus, on the outside of every place of business and in all business letters, notices and official publications, etc, A company, which ceases to do business in India, can be wound up through a court as an unregistered body although it may still exist according to the law of the country of incorporation.

## Main Features of the Act

The Companies Act contains a large number of measures by which the control of the shareholders embodied in Ordinary Resolution and in some cases a Special Resolution, in General Meetings, is made a necessary condition for taking and implementing decisions over a large area of Company Management. In this way, the Act tries to restore to the Indian shareholder some of the authority which they have under the Law, but which they have not been able to exercise effectively. Similarly, the Act also tried to restore the authority of the Board of Directors which had been lying under a shadow, so to say, as a result of the rise of the managing agency as the dominant form of corporate management in our country, In order to reduce this stranglehold of big business houses on industry through the instrument of managing agents, this Act contained drastic regulatory provisions with a view to making the managing agents accountable to both the Board of Directors and the shareholders of the Company. In fact the Act sounded the death-knell of this historical institution. It was allowed under stringent restrictions and on a sort of grace period until it was finally abolished with effect from 3rd April, 1970 by an amendment of the Act.

This Act also contains startling provisions for Central Government's control over the appointment and remuneration of Managing Directors, whole-time directors and managers as defined under the Act. No managing director, etc. can be appointed or reappointed in a public limited company or in a private limited company which is the subsidiary of a public limited company or a 'deemed' public company without the Central Government's approval (Section 269). Similarly, their remuneration for which the Act itself lays down some statutory limits (not more than 5 per cent of the net profit for an industrial Managing Director etc. and not more than 11 per cent for all of them taken together) requires to be approved by the Central Government by virtue of the administrative ceilings which the Central Government have been enforcing since 1959 over and above these statutory ceilings as conditions for approval. There has been considerable relaxation in recent times in the wake of the liberalisation process from 1991 onwards and companies in general are not required to apply for government's specific approval so long as they fix the remuneration within the guidelines.

Thirdly, Indian Company Law has placed certain restrictions on loans made or guarantees given by one company to another. These restrictions are more stringent in the case of transactions involving companies under the same management (Section 370). The Act also prescribed (Section 372) certain limitations on a company investing in the share of another company depending on the proportion of such investment to the subscribed capital of the investing company on the one hand and on the other that of the corporate body in which the investment is made. Prior approval of the company, in general meeting and of the Central Government, is necessary if:

(i) the investment is in excess of 10 per cent of the subscribed capital of the corporate body in which the investment is made;

(ii) the aggregate of all such investments made in all corporate bodies in the same group is in excess of the 20 per cent of the share capital of the investing company; or

(iii) the aggregate of such investment made in all the corporate bodies is in excess of the 30 per cent of the investing company.

This limit of 30 per cent is, however, not applicable to an investing company under certain conditions. They have also been applied to the investments made by a holding company on its subsidiary;

(i) Banking or Insurance Companies;

(ii) a company established with the object of financing industrial enterprises; or

(iii) a private company which is not a subsidiary of a public limited company.

Fourthly, the Act also contains a number of provisions for maintenance of proper books of accounts by companies, the auditing of these accounts by independent auditors, and for inspection of companies' accounts and records by the Registrar of Companies or by other inspecting officers appointed by the Central Government. These provisions are in fulfilment of one basic aim of the Companies Act, viz. compelling company management to disclose maximum possible information about the company. They are codified in Sections 209-233A. The maintenance of accounts in accordance with accepted methods is considered to be one of the primary duties of management. Sections 234-251 confer on the Registrar and other prescribed Government authorities very wide powers to call for information and inspect a company's records. There is also provision for ordering investigation by the Central Government in certain circumstances (Sections 235 and 237). These provisions are intended to check malpractices and fraudulent activities in the company management.

The Board of Directors is required by the Act to present before every annual general meeting of the shareholders the following documents:

(i) a balance sheet for the year

(ii) a profit and loss account

(iii) a report by the directors indicating (a) the state of the company's affairs

(b) the amount in the balance sheet which is proposed to be carried on to any reserves

(c) the amount, if any, which they recommend as dividend, and

(d) material changes and commitments, if any, affecting the financial position of the company.

The Companies Act also protects the statutory auditors from the whims and arbitrary action of the directors and virtually makes them agents of the shareholders and the watch-dogs of their interests. Today, while the auditors' foremost duty is to check the accuracy of accounts, they are not to confine themselves merely to the risk of verifying the mathematical accuracy of the balance-sheet, but to go into the correct state of affairs and to report to the shareholders accordingly.

Section 408 enables the Central Government to take certain actions to protect the interests of minority shareholders and also to appoint as many Government directors on the company as is necessary in order to effectively safeguard the interest of the company, or of its shareholders, or the public interest. The Central Government may issue appropriate direction on such company, and also obtain reports from the Government directors. Section 409 also gives the Central Government some drastic powers to take corrective action after there have been representations from the shareholders of a company or its directors that there has been a change in the shareholding of the company which can be prejudicial to the interests of the company or to public interest. When an order under Section 409 is passed there cannot be any change in the Board without Central Government's approval and the voting rights are frozen. It should be noted that reliefs and remedies from High courts against mismanagement and oppression are also available under Sections 397 and 398 of the Companies Act.

The various measures indicated above are only illustrative and not exhaustive. But they do make it clear that our Company Law seeks to achieve certain socio-economic objectives enshrined in our Constitution. It also seeks to provide for certain degree of ultimate control of the shareholders, over some very important matters, to democratise company management, and also to prevent certain known malpractices in company management. The Act of 1956 imposes certain measures calculated to dispel concentration of economic power and also to reduce inequalities of income and wealth. These follow the Directive Principles of our Constitution and also the priorities of the Five Year Plans and the objective of Socialist Pattern of Society. It is with these ends in view that in the administration of the Act attempts have been made not only to restore the authority of the shareholders and the Board of Directors and to democratise company management, but also to promote some measure of corporate ethics professionalised management and to assert the responsibility of joint-stock enterprise towards larger interests like the community and the State and the public interest.

## The Companies (Amendment) Act, 1999

The capital market required immediate morale boosting efforts on the part of the government to promote investors' confidence. The economy also needed certain impetus for promoting inter-corporate investments considering slow inflow of funds in new investments. With a view to promoting investors' confidence in capital market and to promote the climate for inter-corporate investment, it was felt that the companies should be permitted to buy-back their own shares, to make investments or loans without approval of Central Government, to provide for nomination facility to the holders of shares or debentures and also to make provision in law for establishment of Investors Education and Protection Fund etc. Keeping these objectives in view Companies (Amendment) Bill, 1999 was passed in Parliament to effect amendments in the Companies Act, 1956. The salient features of the Companies (Amendment) Act. 1999 are as follows:

(i) The Infrastructure Development Finance Company, a company formed and registered under the Companies Act has been included as a Public Financial Institution for the purposes of the said Act.

(ii) Shareholders/debenture holders and depositors have been permitted to make nominations.

(iii) Companies have been permitted to buy back their own shares or other specified securities subject to certain conditions.

(iv) Companies have been permitted to issue sweat equity shares subject to fulfillment of certain conditions.

(v) An Investor Education and Protection Fund would be set up from amounts which remained unclaimed and unpaid for a period of seven years from the date they became due for payment in the (a) un-paid dividend accounts of companies.

(vi) Certain new institutions such as the Security and Exchange Board of India (SEBI) which were not envisaged by the earlier Act have now been recognised in the new Act.

   (b) application moneys received by companies for allotment of any securities and due for refund

   (c) deposits with companies as have matured

   (d) debentures of companies that have matured with interest that have accrued thereon, grants and donations given to the fund by the Central Government, Sate Government, companies or any other institutions for the purpose of the Fund, and interest or other income received out of the investments made from the Fund, is to be credited to the Fund.

(vii) A National Advisory Committee on Accounting Standards to be constituted to advise the central government on formulation and laying down of accounting policies and accounting standards for adoption by companies or class of companies.

(viii) Companies have been permitted to make inter-corporate investments or give loans to other body corporates without prior approval of the Central Government. The Companies Act, 2000.

### The Companies Act, 2000

The comprehensive Companies Bill, 1997 was introduced on 14th August, 1997. Thereafter the Government felt that it was essential to bring in further changes in the Companies Act, in order to provide certain measures for good corporate governance and protection of investors. The government, therefore introduced The Companies (Second Amendment) Bill, 1999 in the Lok Sabha on 23rd December, 1999. It has been passed as the Companies Act, 2000. There is proposal to bring yet another amending bill in order to simplify the provisions on liquidation of companies with a view to speed up liquidation proceedings.

A massive amendment of the Companies Act is now under consideration to remove some of the extreme restrictive provisions and to bring the Act in line with the new environment of the economic reform. These are on the basis of recommendations by an Expert Committee headed by on J.J. Irani. Interestingly, the government has in recent years made a large number of controls operate the rough E-governance.

## COMPANY LAW BOARD

The Central Government under S. 10-E of the Companies Act set up an independent Company Law Board to exercise many of the powers of the Central Government delegated to it. The Board, a quasi-judicial body, is not subjected to the control of the Central Government and has the powers to regulate its own procedures and act in its own discretion. But it also exercises certain independent powers conferred on it under Section 17, 18, 19, 58-A(9), 79, 113, 141, and 186 of the Companies Act. It also exercises the powers of the Central Government under 52A of the MRTP Act, 1969 and S.22A(4)(c) of the Securities Contracts (Regulation) Act, 1956. The Board consists of a Chairman and two members and has four Benches, one each at Delhi, Calcutta, Bombay, and Madras.

### An Overview

All that has been stated above will go to show that in its evolution in the last four decades Indian Company Law has moved spectacularly away from its earlier dependence on British Law with a 'traditional reluctance to analyse and rationalise the effect of social changes on contemporary law'.[1] It has become in conjunction with industrial licensing and the MRTP Act one of the major instruments of Government policy towards corporate business. Under its provisions Central Government has assumed in larger public interest very wide powers of intervention in large areas of what in orthodox view till the other day were) preserves of decision-making by corporate management. But it should also be noted that this is also in keeping with the recent trends in company or corporation law in the entire West. Ever since the publication of the epoch-making study of corporations in modem society by Berle and Means[2] the separation between corporate ownership and corporate management in a typical modem joint-stock enterprise has been understood, From this came a realisation of the minimal role of shareholders in a modem corporation with its widely dispersed share-holding and hung number of shareholders and an awareness that in to-day's context the shareholders is neither the owner, nor the manager, but only the supplier of the risk capital, or an investor. The position of the shareholders in a modem corporation is picturesquely described by John Kenneth Galbraith: "As stock-holders cease to have influence, however, efforts are made to disguise this nullity. Their convenience is considered in selecting the place of meeting. They are presented with handsomely printed reports, the preparation of which is now a specialised business. Products and even plants are inspected. During the proceedings, as in the report, there are repetitive references to 'your company'. Officers listen with every evidence of attention to highly irrelevant suggestions of wholly uniformed participants and assure them that these will be considered with the greatest care. Votes of thanks from women stock-holders in print dresses owning ten shares 'for the excellent skill with which you run your company' are received by the management with well-simulated gratitude. All present show stern disapproval or critics. No important stock-holders are present. No decisions are taken. The annual meeting of the large American corporation is, perhaps, our most elaborate exercise in popular illusion."[3]

From this general recognition of the shareholders's powerless position arose in sequence an awareness of the importance of management,[4] the rise of professional management, the concept of modern corporation's social responsibility, and a general acceptance of the idea that corporate management is accountable not only to the shareholders but to a host of other interests like the workers, the consumers, the community and the government.[5] Traditional company law is held utterly inadequate for achieving these broader objectives. As Goyder states: 'Indispensable to the democratic process is the condition. that decision-making few shall be accountable to the many affected by their decisions. Yet the Acts at present governing the creation and administration of the Acts at present governing the creation and administration of limited liability companies do not provide for the directors or managers to heed—still less to be accountable to—the workers employed in them, the consumers of their goods and services, or the community in which they operate. These are not even mentioned in company law."

Two other major dimensions are of great importance to our understanding of the changed basis of company law: the growth of big corporate business, and the rise of multinational or transnational corporations. The first reflects what may possibly be an irreversible trend towards large size or scale on account of technology. But, it also brings in its wake problems of concentration of economic power or monopoly. Inevitably company law has to concern itself with these developments. Similarly it also has a concern with the spread of multinational business, another consequence of modem international commercial relationships. Some of the recent developments e.g., the Verdam Commission in the European Economic Community, the move towards a European Company Law, and the interest being taken by the U.N. and international bodies like the Organisation of Economic Corporation and Development (OECD), the setting up of the U.N. Commission on I.N.G. of a code of conduct for National Corporations and the negotiations for international agencies for regulating the multinationals and World Trade Organisation (WTO), have added a new dimension to company law. All these developments, and above all, and awareness that a joint-stock enterprise is not a private association, but a public, socially responsible body have made for greater and greater public, social or governmental control over these enterprises, and India is no exception. Then again, one has to recognise that the Indian corporate sector is still dominated by Government Companies. In 1951-52 the Government companies accounted for only 7 per cent of the total corporate sector's equity capital. Today they account for about 68 per cent. If we add to this the share of public sector institution in the share capital of the private sector companies the over-all government interest in the corporate sector appears overwhelming. The government companies are a new hybrid organisation partly independent juristic entity and partly extension of the government itself.[6] Company law will have to concern itself increasingly with these large, wholly public, industrial companies, as with the large, private but socially responsible and professionally managed industrial companies. The difference between the two is fast disappearing. This will be all the more so as the announced and on-going policy of the Central Government selling some of its shares in government companies to mutual funds, employees, public etc., progresses. Finally, we have to accept that some of the provisions in the present Act appear to have been outdated by the great changes in the corporate sector in recent years. Indian corporate sector today is such larger, much more diverse and integrated with global economy than what it was in 1956. It is no longer family-dominated as in those days. Professional managers have come into the corporate scenario very prominantly replacing owner-managers. The share holding population has increased enormously. There is an urgent need to .improve the corporate governance. Our company law needs to shed off some of its earlier prejudices. Many things have been done but many more are yet to be done in line with the sweeping policy changes in the direction of deregulation, debureaucratisation and globalisation.

## Impending Changes in the Companies Act

The Companies Bill currently before the Parliaments has brought in elements of law that work will in other markets, such as accepting the changes related to the digital age by allowing the use of video conferencing for board meeting, electronic voting in general meetings, electronic filings shelf registrations, exit options for minority shareholders, etc. as well as a few elements that make it contextual for India. The new Bill has consolidated many sections of the previous Act and appears to be relatively lean, with 470 clauses and 7 schedules as against 658 sections and 15 schedules in the existing Companies Act, 1956. The fundamental premise of this Bill is to present a law that is modern and relevant while incorporating global best practices and balancing the complexities and realities of operating in India. The Bill is particularly powerful in the areas of oversight, protection of minority shareholders, management and business conduct and overall governance.

This new Bill includes many provisions that recognize the changing times and includes affirmative actions for the protection of small investors, defining revised roles of directors to make them more effective and accountable, enhancing responsibilities of auditors as gatekeepers and laying down provisions that include severe punishment for fraud, false evidence or known misconduct for every person who has a duty of trust towards a company.

The Indian system was plagued by a delayed system of enforcement. This Bill envisages a quick redressal mechanism by constituting that tribunals, special courts and even high courts delegate some of their responsibilities to lower courts for a quicker delivery of justice.

However, the success of the proposed Bill with enhanced protection to society is largely dependent on the quality of implementation irrespective of how good the intent of legislature is in its design and objectives.

There are significant changes in the role, independence, appointment, rotation, evaluation and responsibilities of independent directors and the code of conduct by other directors. The current Bill requires that all resolution in a meeting convened with a shorter notice should be ratified by at least one independent director. This could create an element of veto power by these directors, which will be unique to India. The other clauses on directors' responsibility statements, statement of social responsibilities, and the directors' responsibilities over financial controls, fraud, etc. will create a more transparent system brought about through better disclosures. The Bill also proposes inherent principles of anti-self-dealing, whereby any undue gain made by a director by abusing his position will be disgorged and returned together with monetary fines.

The additional provisions and proposals that foster corporate governance include regulating related party transactions, consolidation of all companies within the group, self declaration of interests by directors along with disclosures of loans, investment and guarantees given for the businesses of subsidiary and associate companies, which may be outside of normal disclosures.

The Bill proposes an enhanced investor protection framework by bringing in proposals for class action suits, empowering small shareholders who can restrain management from actions that they believe are detrimental to their interests of circumstances when such shareholders can exercise an option of exiting the company when they do not concur with proposals of the majority shareholders. The new Bill also proposes tighter norms for raising money from the public and makes insider trading, impersonation, etc a criminal offence. These norms in isolation do not constitute a paradigm shift but, when aggregated these changes are structural and fundamental.

However, in the quest for creating an environment of independence, laws can become restrictive for an enterprise. A case in point is the clause that requires that companies need select independent directors from a database maintained by the government or explain why they have not used such a database. A board is a unit of management and oversight of an enterprise whose primary objective is to maximize returns for its shareholders. In such a case, having independent directors—who may have significant dissimilar views on the running of a company—could create significant barriers to decision-making, especially when they could collectively exercise veto powers. The jury is still out on whether having activist individuals on a board creates better value for the minority shareholders.

Recent financial frauds have sullied the image of the Indian corporate environment and to restore confidence in the legal framework governing Indian corporate and the capital market, this Bill has proposed radical revisions in the roles of gatekeepers.

Statutory auditors now have onerous duties and responsibilities as whistle-blowers to formally report any fraudulent acts of the management. They are subject to compulsory rotation and are expected to adhere to strict independence standards. They hold their position in a fiduciary capacity, are subject to periodic rotation and this Bill has proposed restrictions on accepting no-audit jobs. In case of a failure to act diligently or in a case of fraud, the proposed law prescribes civil, criminal and monetary fines, in proportion to the quantum of fraud that is later detected.

The oversight mechanism apart from the audit committee will also include a statutory body, the National Financial Regulatory Authority with powers of a civil court empowered to notify accounting and auditing standards and monitor compliance of such standards, including regulating the professionals who are required to comply with them. The Serious Fraud Investigations Office (SFIO), will be another agency enforcing governance with statutory powers to prosecute. The oversight framework for auditors is now moving away from the principles of self regulation of the Indian Institute of Chartered Accountants to a government body with the powers of a court. This change may alter the way accounting in India is carried out.

Indian companies usually do not differentiate between CSR and corporate philanthropy and hence no distinction is made between strategic spending and donations. A compulsory spend of 2 per cent of profits by companies of a certain size for causes approved by the government also works against shareholders rights and entitlements as this spending is not aligned to the company's strategy and hence is not sustainable.

The freedom of choice to determine how much and the manner to spend on CSR should be left to the company. From the point of view of the beneficiaries, how they get affected in a year of a loss or low profits is a matter of concern as the investments of earlier years may be lost if funding is not sustained over the life of a project.

The Bill will have a significant effect on the amount of loans a company can take, or give guarantees in the case of a loan by another subsidiary, for acquisition or other purposes, which will impede their ability to leverage their balance sheets. The new provisions, stating that acquisitions by Indian companies overseas will not be allowed to be layered beyond two entities, may affect complex and structured transactions.

## REFERENCES

1. Friedmann—*Law in a Changing Society.*
2. A.A. Berle (Jr) and Gardiner C. Means—*The Modern Corporation and Private Property, 1933.*
3. Galbraith—*Modern Industrial State.*
4. James Burnham—*The Managerial Revolution.*
5. George Goyder—*The Responsible Company.* Also see S.C. Sen—*The New Frontier of Company Law.* N.K. Sengupta—*Corporate Management in India.* Neil Jacobi—*Corporate Power and Social Responsibility.*
6. *Op.cit.*, p. 17.

## CHAPTER 5

# Trends in Corporate Management Since Independence

Independent India inherited a structure of corporate management which was dominated organisationally by the managing agency system, and entrepreneurially by some particular business communities, and among them again, by a group of families or houses. Some other features which characterised it, were:

(i) a phenomenal expansion of the corporate sector in response to the needs of the war-time economy, during the Second World War;

(ii) an increased domination of big industrial house over the economy as it expanded and diversified;

(iii) a brazen misuse of the provisions of the Companies Act and of other laws during the years immediately preceding independence by some businessmen and financiers in control of companies to serve their own ends and the consequent unsavoury image which corporate management in general, and management in the large-scale sector, in particular, acquired in the eyes of the public; and

(iv) the preponderance of European business houses in the manufacturing sector of the corporate economy.

In sketching the developments in the field of corporate management in the last twenty-five years, we may divide this into three dearly marked periods, namely, 1947 to 1956, 1956 to 1969 and 1969 to date.

### FIRST PHASE: 1947 TO 1956

During the War and in the years following it, there was a phenomenal rise in both the number of companies and the volume of paid-up capital. In March 1948, there were 22,675 companies with a paid-up capital of Rs 570 crores as against only 11,114 companies in 1939 with a paid-up capital of Rs 290 crores. But, along with this expansion, the quality of management started deteriorating and the evils of consciously practised dishonesty, mismanagement and malpractices also started dominating the corporate scene. Inevitably, therefore, there was much public clamour for reforms in company management and the tightening of the Government control over the functioning of corporate management. A committee was appointed in 1950 under the chairmanship of Shri C.H. Bhaba, to suggest amendments to the Companies Act. But the situation became so critical that without waiting for the committee's report an ordinance was promulgated in 1951, followed by an amending law for bringing about certain very urgent reforms in corporate management.

On the whole, the 1951 reforms were based on the assumption that managing agency was still necessary for the country's economy. The Government intervention was, however, restricted only to extension of the terms conditions of managing agents wherever there was an intention to extend these terms or to transfer the office to another person. In several important respects, the reforms of 1951 can be said to have culminated in the Companies Act, 1956. They also marked the beginning of the Central Government's assumption of very extensive powers of control and regulation over the working of corporate management.

During these years, the corporate management in the large-scale sector was characterised by the concentration of ownership and control in the close-knit family groups or business associate groups. One factor, which accentuated this trend, was the acquiring of the controlling interest by large Indian houses in companies which were formerly European-owned or European-managed. It is, however, interesting to note that until 1950-51, few Indians held directorships in the foreign-controlled segments of the corporate economy. There were, in fact, two distinct corporate sectors, one dominated by foreigners and the other by Indians. The other notable trends, during this period, were a general movement among managing agency houses to change over from partnership to private companies and again from private companies into public companies; the beginning of change in the ownership of some European business houses and the consequent partial Indianisation of some of these houses; and a general scramble among bigger houses, European and Indian, to absorb smaller houses.

## SECOND PHASE: 1956 TO 1969

The Companies Act 1956, based on the recommendations of the Bhaba Committee, was said to have "for the first time attempted to bring about some changes in the law by superimposing on the traditional legal concept a system of partial social control in the public interest." In brief, this Act attempted to restore the eclipsed authority of the board of directors and shareholders, and to subject management to a large degree of government control, including the power of intervention in certain circumstances in order to uphold public interest. Implicit in the whole scheme of the Act is a recognition that the shareholders are the ultimate source of authority in company management but they cannot exercise the powers of actual management which must therefore rest with the board of directors which is statutorily recognised as the top management body in a company. There could be direct management of a company by the board. But board can also manage indirectly through anyone from among the categories of corporate managers, such as (1) Managing Agents, (2) Secretaries and Treasurers, (3) Managing Director, and (4) Manager.

The various forms of corporate management, which prevailed during 1956 to 1969, can be illustrated in the following diagram:

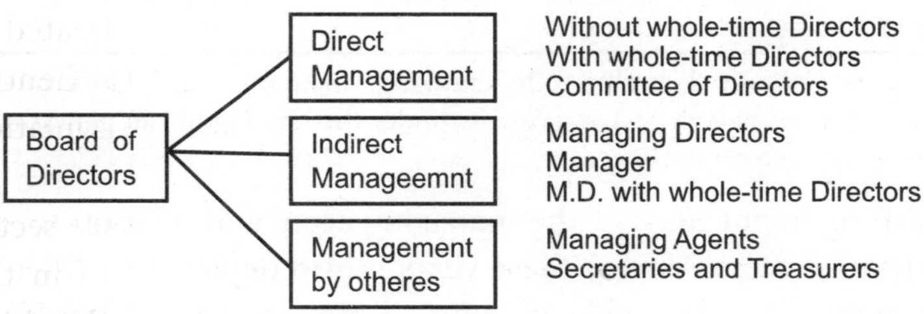


The 1956 Act also took a number of significant steps in order to reduce the concentration of managerial control in fewer hands and in general, to improve the quality of management and remove mis-management. The quality of corporate management was sought to be improved by making it responsive to shareholders, providing a built-in mechanism through the widest possible disclosure of the company's working and financial position and also by providing not only for judicial remedy but also direct Government control over a very large area of the functioning of corporate management. The objective of these regulatory provisions is to impose a degree of discipline on regulatory management so as to ensure a clean administration for the benefit of shareholders and of the community, and also to provide a proper code of conduct under which an enlightened top management is able to achieve the highest standard of performance.

The intention of the 1956 Act as clarified by Shri C.D. Deshmukh, the then Finance Minister, seems to have been that *the managing agency system/ at a future date—not a very distant future—will be abolished. But the time/ place and the manner of its abolition are left to the Government.* With this end in view, the Act put the managing agents under a code of rigorous discipline within the overall control of board of directors and in a way put this institution on a sort of grace period pending its eventual extinction. Between 1954-55 and 1968-69, the managing agency system was steadily declining both in terms of the number of managed companies and their paid-up capital. This is illustrated by Table 1.

Table 6.1: Decline in the Number of Managed Companies

| | 1<br>Total No. of public companies | | 2<br>No. of companies managed by M/As | | 2 as % of 1 | |
|---|---|---|---|---|---|---|
| 1954-55 | 1978 | (616.6) | 4091 | (439.0) | 44.6 | (71.2) |
| 1960-61 | 5688 | (826.0) | 1049 | (391.7) | 18.4 | (47.4) |
| 1962-63 | 5477 | (1076.1) | 1149 | (409.8) | 21.0 | (38.1) |
| 1963-64 | 5607 | (1187.1) | 1121 | (523.9) | 20.0 | (44.1) |
| 1964-65 | 5639 | (1236.3) | 1090 | (509.4) | 19.3 | (41.2) |
| 1965-66 | 5609 | (1255.0) | 800 | (487.5) | 14.3 | (38.8) |
| 1966-67 | 5543 | (1309.4) | 683 | (493.0) | 12.3 | (37.7) |
| 1967-68 | 5452 | (1375.4) | 642 | (584.8) | 11.7 | (42.5) |
| 1968-69 | 5432 | (1402.3) | 568 | | 10.4 | (4.1) |

Note: Figures in Column 1 exclude the banking, insurance and Government companies which could not have Managing Agents under the law. Figures in parenthesis indicate paid-up capital in crores of rupees.

The diminishing importance of the managing agency in relation to the developing corporate sector during these years is also depicted in Table 2, indicating the number of registered companies during the years 1956-57 to 1967-68, those amongst them who actually applied for managing agency from of management and the number of such actually approved by the Government.

The controversy over the abolition of the managing agency system gradually became intense in the sixties, particularly after the publication of the finding of the Vivian Bose Inquiry Commission. A new dimension now added to it was its relationship with the growth of concentration of economic power. A Managing Agency Inquiry Committee was appointed in 1965 under the chairmanship of Dr. I.G. Patel. The Committee confined its enquiry into five well established industries, such as sugar, cotton textiles, jute, cement and paper and recommended the abolition of the system in sugar, cement and cotton textiles. But the Central Government went beyond the balanced recommendations of this Committee and decided to abolish the managing agency system in all the five industries with effect from April 2, 1967. The final coup de grace given to this institution was the companies (Amendment) Act of May 1969 which compulsorily abolished existing managing agencies and secretaries and treasurers with effect from April 3, 1970. This meant not only the end of the historical institution of managing agency which had been anachronistic survival from India's colonial past and which was in fact losing its functional significance but also the termination of the institution of secretaries and treasurers, a legislative innovation of the Companies Act 1959, deliberately introduced with a view to enabling companies to accept professionalised group management without the evils of the much abused institution of managing agency.

Table 6.2: Diminishing Managing Agency System

| Year | Total No. of registered Companies | No. of companies which cam up for approval to managing agency form | No. of cos. where approval was given | % of col. 3 to 2 | % of col. 4 to 2 |
|---|---|---|---|---|---|
| 1956-57 | 848 | 10 | 10 | 1.2 | 1.2 |
| 1957-58 | 961 | 11 | 10 | 1.1 | 1.0 |
| 1958-59 | 1095 | 1 | 1 | 0.1 | 0.1 |
| 1959-60 | 1452 | 6 | 5 | 0.4 | 0.3 |
| 1960-61 | 1683 | 15 | 13 | 0.9 | 0.8 |
| 1961-62 | 1614 | 20 | 19 | 1.2 | 1.2 |
| 1962-63 | 1497 | 18 | 13 | 1.2 | 0.9 |
| 1963-64 | 1227 | 11 | 6 | 0.9 | 0.5 |
| 1964-65 | 1366 | 6 | - | 0.4 | - |
| 1966-67 | 1039 | 1 | - | 0.1 | - |
| 1967-68 | 1044 | 1 | - | 0.1 | - |

In retrospect, the compulsory legislative abolition of the managing agency system in 1970 should be considered as a somewhat hasty step. It would perhaps have been better had the Patel Committee's suggestion for a unit or company wise approach been adopted. Operationally this would have meant non-renewal of the existing managing agencies and non-approval of any fresh appointment as managing agents. This would have avoided a certain amount of dislocation which followed the compulsory abolition of the institution in 1970. But on the whole, there was very little murmur and the company management in the corporate sector directly effected it as an inevitable and unalterable measure and the overall impression remains that such a momentous event did not lead to any severe dislocation in industry or in the economy as a whole as had been forecast by the protagonists of this system. After the abolition of managing agency, the following forms of corporate management are permissible under the law:

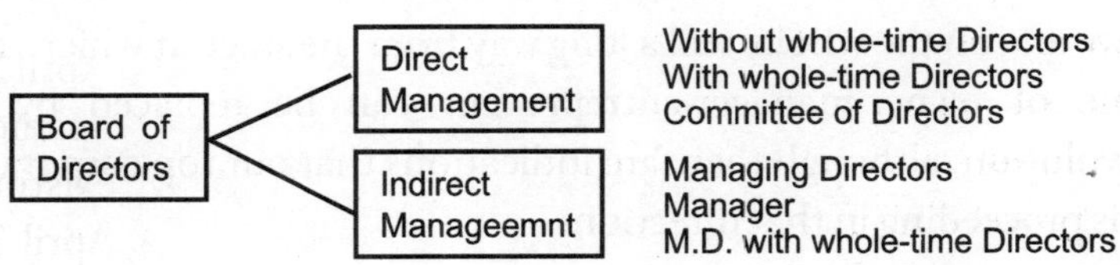

On the basis of a study of the pattern of management in the public limited companies with paid-Up capital of RS 1 crore and above as on April 1, 1968, it seems that on that date, 141 among them were under the management of managing agents (including even secretaries and treasurers), and 176 had other forms of management. An analysis of the forms of management in these 176 companies would indicate the following break-up:

| | Companies |
|---|---|
| Managing Director (with or without whole-time directors) | 105 |
| Board of Directors | 96 |
| Authorised Controller under Industries (Development and Regulation) Act | 1 |
| General Manager | 1 |
| Total | 176 |

A detailed analysis of the management pattern in the 105 companies having managing or whole-time directors reveals the following patterns:

| | Companies |
|---|---|
| Persons educationally qualified as well as professionals | 81 |
| Persons educationally qualified but not professionals | 9 |
| Persons who are professional managers but not educationally qualified | 3 |
| Persons neither educationally qualified nor professionals but ordinarily having substantial financial stake | 7 |
| Details not immediately available | 5 |
| Total | 105 |

It will be seen that the number of companies led by professional managers in the widest sense of the term was surprisingly large. Others were led by large investors and yet others represented a compromise between the two. One reason why professional management seems apparently to be in such a dominant position is that in India professional management is very often equated with non-proprietary management. But the available data do indicate that we are, on the whole, still a long way from the stage at which the ancient regime of owner-manager-entrepreneur can be replaced by a managerial revolution, although there are indications that our top corporate management is proceeding in that direction.

The management, structure and pattern in the large public companies in corporate management between 1956 and 1969 had several other interesting features. First, Indianisation of the top management on a very significant scale was undertaken in the companies owned or managed by foreign enterprises. Another significant change was the decline in both volume and proportion to the total equity of direct shareholding by the directors. The data furnished by some of these companies in response to a questionaire indicated that whereas in most of these companies directors themselves owned a substantial bloc of shares at the time of incorporation, by 1968-69, in the majority of cases, directors were just holding qualifying shares. A casual observer of the corporate scene may get an impression that this indicates a gradual process of replacement of proprietary management by professional management. But the real picture seems to have been quite different. In the great majority of the cases, the domination of the Board by the entrepreneurial class having a financial stake in the fortunes of the company hardly gave way, although the sheer complexity of modern business very often necessitated the handing over of day-to-day management excluding finances to technical personnel with seats on the Board.

It also appears that in most of these companies, shareholding does not bear any significant relationship to management control. Traditionally, the shareholder has been content to entrust the control in the hands of those in whom he has confidence, and does not take any interest whatsoever in the company's management so long at least as he gets his annual dividend. It is only in recent years that he has started showing a very half-hearted degree of interest. It is thus possible for a family or a combination of a few families or a group—at times a professional group—to control the affairs of companies where their own shareholding may be as little as 10 per cent. As Merchant observers: "Unless one belongs to the *charmed circle* of the family or friends of the existing management which, more often than not, has only a minor share interest in the company, one has no chance whatsoever of becoming a director, however competent one might be. Hence, the only legitimate method available to anyone to crash into management is by buying up the requisite number of shares." The controversies over National Rayon and Synthetics and Chemicals indicate the struggles for management control between two groups, each claiming to represent the mute shareholders. When control thus passes from one group to another, the new management, even though called professional, still retains most of the obnoxious features of the old system, specially the characteristics of being a family preserve. This has stood in the way of our large companies going under truly professional management, or developing along the lines of the giant corporations of the West.

There is in fact no indication as yet that this family or group management control is withering away on any significant scale. The distinction drawn by some writers between an entrepreneurial Board and an executive Board is unreal in the Indian context except in the case of some foreign companies. Even the foreign equity holders in some of the latter type is known to have preferred reliance on particular Indian families to direct participation by themselves in the management of companies. However, it cannot be said that all Indian business houses have remained unchanged: in fact, one finds both modern and traditional social skills side by side with modern technology. Also the younger members of the Indian business class are showing great inclination towards modern methods and techniques in working with men. All these have come about from a genuine conviction of the need for change in technology and social skills. Their success will, no doubt, influence many non-changers in the class in no time. However, the process of growth in which technology and social skills can move with modern thinking has been still slow."

It would thus appear that today we are face to face with two forceful trends coming up against each other. On the one hand, the operational complexities of corporate business are so compelling that the chief executive team will have to maintain a close liaison with the line managers and top executives. On the other hand, the Board, as the top policy-making body, should devote more time to the factors affecting the national or international economy. However, compromise between the two positions has been found in the U.S. by making the Board an "organ", as described by Peter Druker, and leaving the actual management to the executives designated as Presidents or Vice-Presidents who usually constitute an informal team. But perhaps an even more ideal arrangement is the German system of two-tier management.

A study team of the Administrative Reforms Commission on Company Law Administration also suggested the adoption of this pattern of two-tier boards in Indian Company Law on the German model. This German practice can be said to have reconciled "the professionalisation and growing entrepreneurial role of executives leading to their increasing self-reliance and independence of judgement, with the increasing pressure and control exerted by interested groups, such as employees, the State or the reviving forces of shareholders,"[8] the Executive Board symbolising the former and the Supervisory Board symbolising the latter. And, in keeping with the general trend in the Continental countries, some companies in India seem to be entrusting actual management to groups of employee-directors, if not formally, at last.

Finally, with an increase in size and the growing complexity in corporate business and the need for professionalisation even at the board level, there has been a marked shift of appointing whole-time executive directors to functional boards to be in charge of specific functional areas like production, marketing and finance. Indeed, the great majority of the newly formed companies during the years 1956 to 1968 seem to have preferred the board of directors form of management. Thus, in 1966-67, nearly 70 per cent of the newly incorporated companies opted for direct management by the board and only 28 per cent preferred to have managing directors. This was in contrast to the pattern adopted by the erstwhile managed companies which changed to alternative forms during this period. A majority of them seem to have preferred to have managing directors. Thus, in 1964-65, 230 such companies opted for managing directors and 120 for direct management by the board. On the whole, the abolition of the managing agency system and the 1969 guidelines paved the way towards functional boards and also the induction of professional managers in the higher echelons of company management in India.

## THIRD PHASE (1969 TO DATE)

It is possible to indicate the following emerging trends since 1969. The abolition of managing agency did not really mean the end of the system of group management or the end of domination by large industrial houses over vast industrial territories. In a large number of cases, the erstwhile managing agents entered into various types of service agreements with their former managed companies under which the services of the former were available to the latter in such fields as administrative services, financial services, management consultancy and secretarial work. In some cases, the old managing agents served as secretaries to the formerly managed companies. Some of the managing agency houses have converted themselves into consultancy organisations. In several cases, this represents a genuine effort to break new grounds. The Tatas, for instance, set up a management oriented modern consultancy organisation. Similarly, members of the former managing agency firms or the controlling families have been appointed as managing directors or whole-time directors in the companies formerly managed by them. In some cases, the managing agency houses merged with the former managed companies, thus retaining their control. For instance, the six companies of the Binny group got themselves merged into one company at the end of 1969. Thus, today there is, indeed, a growing trend towards mergers and amalgamations in the corporate scene.

An overall impression is that the old managing agents, by and large, retained the hold over their former managed companies. One should, however, pause to remember that the managing agency was not the cause but really the effect of concentration of economic or industrial power in certain families and houses. It existed in India even before Company Law was introduced and also flourished for about half a century before it was taken note of by Company Law and for about four decades more, it was brought under effective control by the 1956 Act. From this point of view, it may appear that the mere deletion of the provision in the Companies Act on managing agency by the 1969 Amending Act simply meant a relapse into the pre-1913 state of affairs. That is to say that so long as the conditions which had favoured managing agency remained, some sort of group management or control mechanism would also be there perhaps in a different name, but without the discipline imposed on managing agents by the Companies Act, 1956.

From an analysis of the proposals received by the Central Government from former managed companies during 1969-70, it appears that the great majority of them switched on to management by managing directors. But this does not necessarily show a marked preference for Board management, but only that the majority were undecided about the appropriate form of corporate management they should finally adopt.

The dominance of the old managing agency houses and families started getting eroded from the late 70s on account of several new factors. The foreign houses by and large stagnated without expansion or diversification and eventually made their exit through disinvestment to Indian houses, or just stopped business forcing the government to take over. Many of the great old names (e.g. Andrew Yule, Forbes and Campbell, Bird, Balmer Laurie, Duncans) fall in this category. Many of the Indian houses went through family feuds or partition resulting in the emergence of several separate clusters. In some cases, after the passing away of the old patriarchs, there was no unifying control any more, and the successors carved out their own domains. This was the pattern in houses such as the Birlas, the Goenkas and the Singhanias. Also, very often business was becoming so diversified and complex that professionals had to be entrusted with full management control over enterprises, and there was no room for the kind of control the old managing agents exercised. To take one example, to-day's Tata Steel, Tata

Engineering or Tata Chemicals are totally separate companies with virtually nothing in common except the name Tata, and the shared history and traditions. These developments, coupled with the growing enlargement of the equity base of own companies, the rising percentage of the shares held by financial institutions in private sector companies and the influence exercised by the latter in the management of these companies considerably accelerated the drive towards professional management in the corporate sector.

Indian corporate management suffered some critical challenges during the decade of the 1970s on account of several government policy interventions such as the MRTP Act, introduced in 1970, the FERA of 1973, and the general anti-large house stances of government policy. Many old well-known managing agency houses disappeared or dwindled into insignificance. Many familiar foreign names also disappeared because the foreign shareholders sold off their stocks to Indian houses straight forwardly, or sometimes in covert manner through dummy foreign registered corporate bodies. The movement of professional management steadily developed fostered by the management schools, the universities and managen1ent associations. Many of the old family-managed companies slowly inducted professional managers to their board rooms. Some of the scions of the traditional business families also turned professionals through acquiring formal management training or other types of professional education. Family dominance which characterized India's corporate management all along started disintegrating during the 1980s. There were amicable partitions among family members. Also, there were violent and noisy family splits. As a result most of the old family conglomerates disappeared. Some of them got regrouped. This process helped the growth of professional management. Also, many of the old family managed companies were turning into widely held modern corporations. The phenomenal expansion of the capital market during the 1980s added another new dimension to corporate management. As more and more companies through public issues became public limited companies or vastly enlarged their share-holding base they acquired the characteristics of the modern Western corporations with large number of shareholders and controlled by professional managers with little or no share-holding interest. The size of the corporate sector also grew in a phenomenal manner during the 1980s.

Following the phenomenal deregulation there was another sea change. First the emergence of countless entrepreneurs, managers who carried S Indian Corporate Business to dizzy heights. Second, India's Corporates also became globalized.

In carrying on the dialogue between Government and Business an important interfacing role is played by industry bodies popularly known as the Chambers of Commerce as also industry specific bodies such as fertilizer industry association or hotelier association or steel producer association. Apex Chambers of Commerce are three: FICCI, ASSOCHAM and CII. FICCI has come to be accepted as the representative of Indian owned trade bodies. It has several important constituent bodies such as the Indian Chamber of Commerce, Calcutta or the PHD Chamber of Commerce, Delhi. The ASSOCHAM originated in Calcutta out of the Bengal Chamber of Commerce and became known as representing the European largely English Companies. With the grating transfer of interest by European owners to Indian owners it became primarily the non-owner management body. It has powerful constituents like Bengal Chambers of Commerce, Bombay Chambers of Commerce and Madras Chamber of Commerce. The latest entrent in the CII. Initially there were the Calcutta based Indian Engineering Association and the Bombay based Engineering Association of India. These two merged to form the Confederation of Engineering Industries (CEI) which later on got transformed into the CII, a broad association of professional manager, which took the name of Confederation of Indian Industries.

There is also a Standing conference of Public Enterprises (SCOPE) which plays a similar though not identical role for CPSE's in voicing their common grievances to the Government.

Apart from these three apex bodies, there are very effective industry associations such as Indian Jute Mills Association, Indian Cotton Mills Federation, as also regional bodies such as the Bengal Chamber of Commerce and Indian Chamber of Commerce in Calcutta, the Indian Merchant Chamber and the Bombay Chamber of Commerce in Bombay, the Punjab, Haryana and Delhi Chamber of Commerce in Delhi, and the Madras Chamber of Commerce in Madras. Also, more specialised bodies such as the very active and effective Association of Indian Engineering Industry (AIEI) now renamed Confederation of Indian Industries, are serving a useful role as professional forum in Government business dialogue, and in the dialogue between Indian industry and international industry.

Happily, the interfacing between the Chambers on the one hand and Government agencies on the other has improved qualitatively in recent times. In today's environment some people are questioning the wisdom of having so many Chambers of Commerce to represent their interests. They would like all these apex bodies to merge and the regional bodies to work in unison.

The separation between corporate ownership and corporate management has become an acknowledged phenomenon in the West ever since Berle and Means came out with their pioneering work. There can be no doubt that the future development of corporate management in India will also reflect this trend. Some of the key factors, which will accelerate this trend, are growing size and complexity of modern corporations, the wide diffusion of shareholding, the growing interest taken in management by the public agencies holding shares in companies, the need for professionalising top management, and last but not the least, the declared Government policy of systematically trying to broad-base the equity-structure of companies which are closely held by families or groups. Increasingly company management will have to be "a sort of government of best minds, ultimately responsible to a community consensus which sets up general objectives, standards of performance, and results." Corporate managers will have to hold top positions in the company hierarchy, not because of their shareholding, or because of their family, caste or community background, but because of their education, ability, experience, and managerial skill. Such managers will be responsible not only to the shareholders, but to a number of other interests—the employees, the consumers, the community around and the State.

Indeed, the corporate management all the world over is today in quest of a new business ideology. In the great debate now going on in the West over the concept of social responsibility in which very eminent people like Galbraith (*The New Industrial State*), George Goydar (*The Responsible Company*) and Jean-Francois Revel (*Without Marx or Jesus*) have taken part, the central issue is the imperative need for the general acceptance of the concept of social responsibility of business. This implies giving due priority to the interests of the society, and treating the business corporation as a face for social change. In our country, there are only a few isolated ripples in this direction. Corporate management by and large is still to accept it.

Corporate management in India has to strive to create a proper image for itself consistent with the social environment in which it operates. Its image in the eyes of the larger public is still very hazy. Unfortunately, the corporate business has collectively done little to dispel these impressions, to bridge the great gulf between itself and the larger public, or to create a proper image of itself. It has to learn to operate in the environment created by the Government policy in response to the people's aspirations. It is also expected to conform to the broader social and economic goals accepted by the country, and to play its role as an agent for achieving these goals. Indeed, it would be correct to say that the awareness of the Government policies and responsiveness to them constitutes one of the crucial resources for corporate management today. Once our corporate management accepts this basic philosophy and a business ideology consistent with It, it will be possible to evolve a new social milieu in which, in place of the present suspicion between the Government and business, there will be a happy understanding and sense of partnership between the two, based on mutual appreciation of each other's role. This will elevate the government-business relationship in our country to the level of which it is in Japan or Korea, This has become all the more important in the new deregulated environment of today when government policy has been fast moving away from the excessive interventionist role of yesteryears on to deregulation, shrinking of government's omni presence and giving a much larger role to private sector initiative. True managerial revolution is establishing itself as a pervasive way of life in our corporate sector at long last.

Incidentally, every since the publications of the Cadbury Commission Report on the corporate governance in the U.K. there has been redoubled emphasis on how to make corporate governance responsive and responsible. Special emphasis has been paid to concepts such as the presence of independent directions on company boards creating separate audit committee in every company board and the duties and responsibilities of Chairman and directors. The SEBI has also championed this concept and Article 49 of the SEBI listing Regulations makes it obligatory for every limited company to have a separate audit committee. Also there must be a few independent directions. These changes were directly improved by the newly brought U.S. laws following the scams of Enron, World Com. Etc. Also there is general acceptance of corporate social responsibility C.S.R). In the public sector system using two percent of the profits for C.S.R has been accepted. This is likely to be the standard for the private sector under the ongoing companies Amendment Bill.

## REFERENCES

1. Reprinted from Administrative Staff College of India, Journal of Management, Vol.2 no.2 (March 1973) pp. 71-82. Article by N.K. Sengupta.
2. According to a study conducted around 1950-51, 600 industrial concerns were controlled and managed by 36 managing firms in 1951. Of them, more than 250 were managed by nine leading British managing agency houses-Andrew Yule, Mcleod, Martin Burn, Bird, Jardine Henderson, Duncan, Octavius Steel, Gillanders

Arbuthnot, and the British India Corporation. The leading Indian managing agency hours were the Tatas, the Birlas, the Dalmia-Jains, the Singhanias, The Thapars and the Goenkas, controlling 26 24, 38 and 14 companies respectively. The nine leading Indian families held nearly 600 directorships. 100 persons held 1,700 directorships. 30 held as many as 860 directorships. This illustrates to what extent multiple directorships prevailed—Mehta M.M., combination Movement in Indian Industry, 1951, pp. 5-26.

3. India, Administrative Reforms Commission, Report of the Working Group on Company Law Administration, Delhi, Manager Publications, 1968, p.35.
4. It imposed a ceiling of 20 directorships in public companies to be held by an individual at any time to reduce the scope of multiple directorships. Further, it was provided that no one could be a manager (as defined in the Act) or managing director in more than two public companies without the Central Government's approval.
5. Merchant, K.T., Management Change in Companies, Economic and Political Weekly, 19705(23), 921-3.
6. Das Gupta, A., Indian Business and Management, University of Delhi, p. 28.
7. See The Company, edited by Charles de Houghton-PEP, London 1970, pp. 141-163.
8. PEP, Companies Beyond Jenkins, p.61.
9. Interviews.

## CHAPTER 6

# Control of Monopolies and Restrictive Trade Practices: Advent of Competition Law

The Monopolies and Restrictive Trade Practices was passed in 1969. Chapter III of the Act, occupied a crucial position in the corporate legal structure between 1970 when it came into force and 1991 when the Chapter except three sections was repealed as an important part of the ongoing economic reform and restructuring programme. Since its enactment in 1969, this legislation came under heavy fire. Broadly, the criticism come from two opposite directions. On the one hand, it was argued that this Act seriously inhibited economic growth and hence was unnecessary for, and irrelevant to, the present economic development. On the other hand, it was termed as an ineffective instrument, not going far enough to control the concentration of economic power and monopolies. Inevitably, a certain amount of folk-lore, based not on the real provisions of the Act, but on beliefs and guess work, came to be associated with this Act. Most have been carried away by such folk-lores, while few attempted to understand its actual contents and its implications. A popular notion was that the Act intended to stop all large business houses, more popularly· known as monopoly houses, from further growth.

The MRTP Act had three objectives: (1) to control and regulate the concentration of economic power to the common detriment; (Chapter III of the Act); (2) to control monopolies and monopolistic trade practices (Chapter IV); and (3) to prohibit restrictive trade practices unless any of them can be justified to be in the public interest (Chapter V and VI). The MRTP Amendment Act, 1984 introduced a fourth objective, i.e., regulation of unfair trade practices by inserting Part B to Chapter V of the Act containing Sections 36A, 36B, 36C, 36D and 36E which empowered the Commission to enquire into such practices as if they are restrictive trade practices. However, there has been no corresponding amendment of the preamble of the Act to include unfair trade practices.

It is important to emphasize that Chapter III of the Act had no parallel among monopolies or anti-trust legislations of other countries. In their scope and application! the provisions of this Chapter, in particular Sections 21 and 22, impinged the area of industrial licensing and almost introduced a parallel system of regulation through licensing applicable to a fairly large cross-section among industrial entrepreneurs. It had its own administrative apparatus distinct from the administrative apparatus for industrial licensing, its own statutory advisory body in the form of the MRTP Commission, its own assumptions and principles, distinct from those guiding the industrial licensing, and indeed, its won terminology. For entrepreneurs who were covered by these provisions, it was not enough to have a letter of intent or industrial licence for the implementation of any programme of substantial expansion or the setting up of a new undertaking. They must also have the Central Government's approval under, Chapter III of the MRTP Act, before they can go ahead with these proposals. Similarly, the mergers amalgamations or takeovers in which such companies are involved also require prior approval. The rationale for these restrictive provisions was a growing realisation that over and above the system of industrial licensing, another mechanism was needed by which entrepreneurs belonging to large industrial houses or dominant undertakings must submit to some special requirements of national policy before they could implement their expansion programmes.

Chapter VI, consisting of Sections 31 and 32, deals with monopolistic trade practices. Whenever it appears to the Central Governmet that any monopolistic trade practices. Whenever it appears to the Central Government that any monopolistic undertaking—one which by itself or with others produces or controls 50 per cent or more of the market in any goods—in indulging in any monopolistic trade practices or that monopolistic trade practices are prevalent in any industry, it has to refer this to the MRTP Commission for a full-scale inquiry. On receipt of the Commission's report, the Central Government was required to pass remedial orders. As in the case of chapter III, there is automatic reference by Central Government of every case to the Commission for inquiry.

Chapters V and VI dealt with what were by far the most important provisions of the MRTP Act. For, these provisions, for the first time in our legislative history, have tried to cover an area where legal control has been notoriously absent and yet there is the all too well-known phenomenon of restrictive trade practices indulged in by our business men. On the other hand, chapter III only provides the Government with an additional control in a field where, thanks to industrial licensing, there was already an immense volume of Government control over further growth of industry. Restrictive trade practice is defined in section 2(o) as a trade practice which results in preventing, distorting or restricting competition in any manner and which, in particular, tends to obstruct the flow of capital or resources into the stream of production or to bring about manipulation of prices or conditions of delivery and thus, impose unjustified costs or restrictions on the consumers. The importance of this definition was emphasised by the Supreme Court in its famous judgements in the TELCO case (AIR 1977 SC 973) and the case of Mahindra & Mahindra (1970) when it laid down that the tests contained in section 2(o) must be satisfied before the MRTP Commission could go into the question of whether an agreement which confronted to any of the types listed in section 33 could be considered as being prejudicial to public interest—prior to the TELCO judgement the Commission had been following the general line of considering agreements almost entirely in the light of section 33(1) and pronouncing them as contrary to public interest whenever they confronted to the descriptions in that section. But the Supreme Court cautioned against it, and upheld the company's contention that even if an agreement contained clauses with regard to area allocation or exclusive dealership, these were not restrictive trade practices within the meaning of section 2(o) as long as they did not have, or were not likely to have the effect of preventing, distorting or restricting competition, or imposing on the consumers unjustified cost or restriction etc. This same position was reaffirmed in the Mahindra & Mahindra.

(a) The substantial benefits or advantages conferred on purchasers, etc. by the agreement or any arrangement arising out of it.
(b) The need for counteracting measures taken by any person, not a party to the agreement with a view to preventing or restricting competition.
(c) Enabling parties to the agreement to negotiate fair terms for the supply of goods.
(d) Adverse effect of the withdrawal of the agreement on the general level of unemployment.
(e) Possible reduction in the volume of earnings of the export business.
(f) The necessity of the restriction for maintaining another restriction found by the Commission to be not contrary to the public interest.
(g) Insignificance of the relevant restriction for purposes of restricting or discouraging competition.

These eight circumstances, described in English law as "the eight gateways of escape" can always be invoked by anyone to justify before the

Commission that a particular agreement is not against the public interest and is to that extent justifiable. They should be carefully studied by business with reference to the rich case laws on them in Britain so that appropriate case laws are also built up in our country in this very new field of legislation.

In 1991-92, faced with unending criticism the Act was drastically amended deleting most of the provisions on concentration of economic power. The MRTP commission was also abolished soon. Incidentally none lamented the passing away of the MRTP Act.

The provisions of the MRTP Act on restrictive trade practices and unfair trade practices still remained. Unfortunately they have to compete with another new law that has come into existence viz. the Consumers Protection Act, 1986 under this Consumer Fora have been established Aggrieved consumers have the right to approach a Forum with his complaint to them and the Forum can issue redressal orders to any provider of goals and services if the complaint is a established. There are State Level Consumer Disputes Redressal Commissions are also a National Consumer Disputes Redressal Commission with appellate jurisdiction.

**Competition Act, 2002**

The Competition Act, 2002 is the latest entry to the scene. A Competition Commission of India has already started functioning with a Chairman and six members.

## INTRODUCTION

The Competition (Amendment) Act, 2007 (the Act) follows the philosophy of modern competition laws and aims at fostering competition and at protecting Indian markets against anti-competitive practices by enterprises. The Act prohibits anti-competitive agreements, abuse of dominant position by enterprises, and regulates entering into combinations (consisting of mergers, amalgamations and acquisitions) with a view to ensure that there is no adverse effect on competition of India.

## ABUSE OF DOMINANCE

Dominance is not considered bad per se but its abuse is. Abuse is stated to occur when an enterprise or a group of enterprises uses its dominant position in the relevant market in an exclusionary or/and an exploitative manner.

The Act gives an exhaustive list of practices that shall constitute abuse of dominant position and, therefore, are prohibited. Such practices shall constitute abuse only when adopted by an enterprise enjoying dominant position in the relevant market in India.

Section 4(2) of the Act specifies the following practices by a dominant enterprises or group of enterprises as abuses:

(i) directly or indirectly imposing unfair or discriminatory condition in purchase or sale of goods or service;

(ii) directly or indirectly imposing unfair or discriminatory price in purchase or sale (including predatory price);

(iii) limiting or restricting production of goods or provision of services or market;

(iv) limiting or restricting technical or scientific development to the prejudice of consumers;

(v) denying market access in any manner;

(vi) making conclusion of contracts subject to acceptance by other parties of supplementary obligations which, by their nature of according to commercial usage, have no connection with the subject of such contracts;

(vii) Using its dominant position in one relevant market to enter into, or protect, other relevant market.

## INQUIRY INTO ABUSE OF DOMINANCE

In exercise of powers vested under section 19 of the Act, the Commission may inquire into any alleged contravention of section 4(1) of the Act that proscribes abuse of dominance. Section 19(4) gives a detailed list of factors that the Commission shall consider while inquiring into any allegation of abuse of dominance. Some of these factors are market share of the enterprise, size and resources of the enterprise, size and importance of the competitors, dependence of consumers, entry barriers and social obligations and costs in the relevant geographic and product market.

The Commission, on being satisfied that there exists a prima facie case of abuse of dominance, shall direct the Director General to cause an investigation and furnish a report. The Commission has the powers vested in a Civil Court under the Code of Civil Procedure in respect of matters like summoning or enforcing attendance of any person and examining him on oath, requiring discovery and production of documents and receiving evidence on affidavit. The Director General, for the purpose of carrying out investigation, is vested with powers of civil court besides powers to conduct 'search and seizure'.

## POWERS OF THE COMMISSION

After inquiry the Commission may pass inter-alia any or all of the following orders under section 27 of the Act:

1. Direct the parties to discontinue and not to re-enter such agreement;
2. Direct the enterprise concerned to modify the agreement;
3. Direct the enterprises concerned to abide by such other orders as the Commission may pass and comply with the directions, including payment of costs, if any, and
4. pass such other orders or issue such directions as it may deem fit.
5. Can impose such penalty as it may deem fit. The penalty can be up to 10 per cent of the average turnover for the last three preceding financial years upon each of such persons or enterprises which are parties to bid-rigging or collusive bidding.

## Appeals

The Competition Appellate Tribunal (CAT) has also been is established under section 53A of the Act, to hear and dispose of appeals against any direction issued or decision made or order passed by the Commission under specified sections of the Act.

An appeal has to be filed within 60 days of receipt of the order/direction/decision of the Commission.

Already this Commission has made its mark by giving an adverse verdict against the National Stock Exchange on a complaint accusing it of abusing its dominant position. Also in another case it has imposed a stiff fine on D.L.F. the leading estates company in India for abusing its dominance.

According to recent press reports there are proposals to amend the Act in order to give power to the Competition Commission to enter into selected areas such as insurance and telecom where specific bodies such as Insurance Regulatory Authority and Telecom Regularity Authority existed in order to prevent the growth of monopolies.

The Competition Commission has already made its presence felt in several significant cases, e.g. questioning the fixation of price by three foreign owned cement companies, i.e. ACC, Ambuja and Lafarge, its orders on National Stock Exchange and the DLF and the reported move to prevent cartelisation and profiteering by the airways companies.

## CHAPTER 7

# Government and Foreign Direct Investment

Since Independence the policy of the Government of India towards private foreign investment and collaboration, has moved from cautious encouragement through a brief spell of near 'open door' in the fifties, a long phase of rigorous selectivity from 1968 to 1991 on to the current post-1991 policy of open encouragement of foreign direct investment specially in priority areas even with 74 per cent participation in equity. Independent India started with a legacy of well-established foreign capital and all the fear and prejudice associated with it. While the overwhelming thrust has all along been towards the goal of a self-sufficient economy and of freeing national economic and industrial policy from the dictates and manipulations of foreign capital, the compulsions of an economy of scarcity and the chronic foreign exchange deficiency also had an effect in shaping official policy towards foreign investment and foreign collaboration. During the seventies and eighties official view has been inevitably influenced by the controversy the world over on the role of multinational corporations in relation to the third world countries. Based on the exposure of a series of misdeeds perpetrated on some third countries by some of the multinationals like International Telephone and Telegraph Corporation (ITT), United Fruit, Union Miniere and Lockheed, criticism welled up against the MNCs in the Indian Parliament and outside. On the other hand there was also a realization that all foreign enterprises operating in India should not be tarred with the same brush and that there were some amongst them who were performing a useful role in the economy by their import-substituting or export-oriented operation, or by making valuable contribution to the technological skill and capability of our country. Official policy after several years of oscillation settled down to one of allowing foreign private investment or collaboration on a selective basis in only priority, export-oriented operation, or by making valuable contribution to the technological skill and capability of our country. Official policy after several years of oscillation settled down to one of ollweing foreign private investment or collaboration on a selective basis in only priority export-oriented or sophisticated technology-based industries, of disallowing them in any other area, and of permitting existing foreign investment in these non-priority areas to operate in future only on the basis of up to 40 per cent of equity holding. A general xenophobia had throughout been the backdrop of India's foreign investment policy.

## ARGUMENTS AGAINST AND FOR FOREIGN INVESTMENT

The various grounds of objections to the import of foreign capital may thus be summerised: First, the historical exploitative character of foreign investment as a partner of colonialism naturally arouses deep-rooted nationalist sentiments and suspicions. Secondly, there is a wide-spread belief based on sufficient empirical evidence that foreign capital is essentially interested in low technology but high profitable consumers' goods, and not in technologically difficult, long gestation industries which are of high priority from the point of view of the host nations. Thirdly, in trying to interpret direct foreign investment as a capital movement economists have often found that investors do not generally take money with them to the host country, but raise capital locally from profits out of sale of their own imported goods or by borrowing in the local market. Thus there is only gross capital movement, not net, through patents, technology or machinery etc. against equity claims etc. and through reinvestment of profits with the so-called outflow rarely matched by earnings on past investment, and not through the normal transfer of funds through the foreign exchange market. The clue to direct investment lies not in physical movement of capital from a developed country to a less developed country, but in capital formation in the latter country through the local operation of a multinational corporation based on the former. Fourthly, foreign capital has historically been accused of an attitude of discrimination against employment of local nationals in high-salaried jobs and against local transport, insurance or credit organisations. Fifthly, the development caused by foreign investment tends to have an 'enclave' character. That is to say, it only creates small pockets of affluence isolated from the main stream of the host country's state of social and economic development.[5] Sixthly, the foreign enterprises by virtue of their financial strength and general competitive efficiency inevitably obstruct and stifle the growth of indigenous industrial entrepreneurship. Seventhly, the cost of foreign capital for the host country tends to be very high. According to the well-known Reserve Bank of India Study Census of Foreign Assets and Liabilities, published in the 60s, the weighted average of the return on U.S. capital invested in India was 19.2 per cent and that of Canadian capital was 33.3 per cent. How costly this tends to be becomes clear when it is understood that a normal return of 10 per cent or so on U.S. domestic investment would be considered attractive. That such costly capital imposes a very severe strain on the host country's foreign exchange can easily be understood by comparing the quantum of capital inflow excluding investment profits with the quantum of foreign exchange outgo on account of capital and profit remittances. Finally, there are questions of political strings attached sometimes to foreign capital, of the inevitable stranglehold that foreign governments gain over important sectors of the host country's economy and the uncertainty of stay of foreign capital and skill. The recent history of the third world countries is replete with such instances.

As against these, there are three major economic arguments which have been reiterated again in favour of allowing unrestricted flow of foreign private capital for the private sector under the ongoing companies Amendment Bill:

(i) It would supplement inadequate domestic savings and capital formation.
(ii) It would increase the foreign exchange resources of the country and reduce strain on balance of payment.
(iii) It would facilitate the transfer of modern and sophisticated technology not otherwise available from advanced countries.

It is interesting to note that during the three successive phases of the evolution of the Indian Government's policy towards foreign capital since 1949 each one of these arguments has been successively emphasised. Another consideration sometimes advanced is that foreign private investment in India is too small to be a threat to the Indian economy occupying as it does a bare 9 per cent of the total capital employed in the corporate sector .

## GOVERNMENT POLICY TILL 1968

Until the early 50s foreign investment was welcomed with reference to the first argument. The policy of cautious welcome to foreign capital was briefly reflected in the Industrial Policy Resolution of April 1948. This was subsequently amplified by Prime Minister Nehru in his statement to Parliament on April 6, 1949 which for a very long time remained the only major policy statement. He declared that the stress on the need to regulate, in the national interest, the scope and manner of foreign capital arose from past association of foreign capital and control with domination of the economy of the country. But circumstances today are quite different. The object of our regulation should, therefore, be the utilisation of foreign capital in a manner most advantageous to the country. Indian capital needs to be supplemented by foreign capital, not only because our national savings will not be enough for the rapid development of the country on the scale we wish, but also because in many cases scientific technical and industrial knowledge and capital equipment can best be secured along with foreign capital. The Prime Minister further added that the Government of India would expect all undertakings, Indian or foreign, to conform to the general requirements of their industrial policy. In return he assured them that there would be no discrimination between Indian and foreign interests. He proceeded further to say that 'as regards existing foreign interests Government do not intent to place any restrictions or impose any conditions which. are not applicable to similar Indian enterprises. Secondly, foreign interests would be permitted to earn profits, subject only to regulations common to all. Thirdly, if and when foreign enterprises are compulsorily acquired, compensation will be paid on a fair and equitable basis.... The Government of India have no desire to injure in any way British or other non-Indian interest in India and would gladly welcome their contribution in a constructive and cooperative role in the development of India's economy.' He assured foreign enterprises that there will be no restriction on remittance of profit or withdrawal of foreign capital investment subject to normal foreign exchange considerations. If any foreign concern was to be compulsorily acquired Government would provide reasonable compensation.

During the Second Plan period the accent was on increasing the foreign exchange resources of the country and increased foreign investment was encouraged in order to finance import of required plant and equipment. There was a clear shift of emphasis around 1957, although there was no formal pronouncement to this effect. This was due to two immediate factors: (i) a massive industrialization programme under the Second Plan and (ii) the acute foreign exchange situation from 1956-57 onwards. The need for external finance and know-how became all-important, and even imports were allowed on condition of securing foreign partnership. The Birla Mission was sent abroad in 1957 with the specific object of encouraging foreign industrialists to invest in India. Both the Indian private sector, till then totally opposed to foreign capital, and the Government became strong votaries of the doctrine of foreign capital being essentially complimentary to Indian capital. For several years foreign investment and know-how were almost indiscriminately allowed even in non-essential areas.

By the mid-60s the manufacturing base of the economy had considerably broadened and there was a greater availability of domestic resources and technical 'know-how'. Official policy, therefore, came to relate the role of foreign capital to its capacity to bridge important technological gaps in the country, in particular with reference to import substitution and increased export. A high degree of selectivity came to be exercised in allowing private foreign investment and collaboration proposals. Such investment came to be allowed only when it was considered to be essential and of high priority from the point of view of techno-economic considerations and where the technology was of an advanced kind not indigenously available. Since this policy came to be crystalised around 1968 outright purchase of technology or a limited duration royalty agreement was generally favoured. Foreign equity participation was normally been limited to 40 per cent save in exceptional cases involving substantial export, import substitution or sophisticated technology which cannot be secured by any other means.

## PROCEDURAL AND POLICY CHANGES OF 1968

1968 was a landmark in the evolution of the foreign investment policy of the Government of India. For the first time after Nehru's statement clear guidelines were issued regarding Government of India's policy with regard to foreign investment and collaboration. There were also big procedural changes.

The Foreign Investment Board was set up in December 1968 as a single agency within the Government to deal with all matters relating to foreign investment and collaboration. The Board itself was not a statutory body, but its powers to approve foreign collaboration agreements are derived from the Foreign Exchange Regulation Act 1947, which requires all remittances of foreign exchange to be approved by the Government or the Reserve Bank of India.

Since 1973, under the new industrial licensing procedure when an applicant submits composite application for both industrial licence and approval of foreign investment or technical collaborations such composite cases were decided by the Projects Approval Board (chaired by Secretary, Ministry of Industrial Development, and do not go to the Foreign Investment Board).

With the establishment of the Foreign Investment Board, the Government also laid down clear guidelines for foreign investment in respect of the areas in which they would be allowed, in what forms, and the conditions to which they would be subject as regards royalty, lumpsum payment etc. Three illustrative lists of industries were issued which showed three broad categories:

(i) Industries in which foreign investment would be permitted.
(ii) Industries in which only technical collaboration would be permitted.
(iii) Industries in which neither foreign investment nor technical collaboration is to be permitted.

These lists were subject to review from tih l e to time.

A general decision was taken to limit foreign equity participation to less than 40 per cent except in cases where the required technology was highly sophisticated, or the project was export-oriented. There is nothing mystical about this 40 per cent which came to be established as the norm because the Foreign Investment Board had powers to permit foreign investment only upto 40 per cent. But this 40 per cent survived through many years and acquired a special sanctity after it was recognised by the FERA guidelines, 1973 as the normal permissible foreign equity ceiling in a company operating in non-priority areas.

## REMITTANCES AND CAPITAL REPATRIATION

India has always freely permitted remittances of profits and dividends. There was never any obstruction even in India's trying times. Limits are set on royalties for use of foreign technology (as described above). Foreign investors have to pay income tax on dividends and royalties, and other income earned in India at rates varying from 24.5 per cent to 70 per cent. Interests on foreign loans granted to companies with Government approval are not subject to taxes nor are there any obstacles to the repatriation of foreign capital.

## THE FOREIGN EXCHANGE REGULATION[1] (AMENDMENT) ACT, 1973

The Foreign Exchange Regulation Act of 1947, the basis law of exchange control also become the main legal instrument for controlling the operation of foreign-controlled companies in India. Its preamble states that "it is expedient in the economic and financial interests of India to provide for the

[1]Recently replaced in the year 2000, and replaced by the Foreign Exchange Management Act, 2000.

regulation of certain payments, dealings in foreign exchange and securities, and the import and export of currency and bullion." The Act empowers the Reserve Bank of India to ensure that the foreign exchange earned by exports or otherwise is properly accounted for or released, and that the acquisition and holding of foreign exchange in any form and the making of payments in foreign exchange are controlled. Section 18 prohibits without the Reserve Bank's approval (1) the transfer of business from the control of residents to non-residents (2) the transfer between two non-residents of an interest in business in India and (3) the transfer to a non-resident of any business in India by a resident. An Indian company cannot make investment outside India without the Reserve Bank's approval. The Foreign Exchange Regulation Rules framed under the Act contain detailed and fairly drastic regulations for declaration of full value of all exports, all remittances and receipts to prevent devices such as undervaluation of exports, overvaluation of imports and building up hidden foreign exchange reserves.

In 1973 the Government felt it necessary to review the entire gamut of private foreign investment, in particular investments which occurred in the remote past when controls were non-existent, and determine on a selective basis, in the light of current licensing and foreign investli l ent policies, the nature and extent of foreign investment that may be permitted. The FERA was therefore substantially amended.*

The Sections in the amended Act which were relevant for our purposes are 28 and 29. According to the provisions of Section 28, non-residents, branches of foreign companies, and Indian companies having more than 40 per cent shareholding, will require the permission of the Reserve Bank of India before they can accept an appointment in India as an agent or technical or management adviser.

Under Section 29, the permission of the Reserve Bank of India will further be necessary for the above categories of individuals and firms if they seek to carry on or establish in India any activity of a trading, commercial or industrial nature, and also if they propose to acquire in whole or in part any Indian undertaking engaged in a trade, commerce or industry. Under the Act individuals and companies holding appointments as agents or advisers who are engaged in any trading, commercial or industrial undertaking, prior to the commencement of the Act will be required to apply to the Reserve Bank of India for permission to continue to act, or carry on business, whatever the

*The 1973 amendments were almost wholly repealed by an ordinance on January 8, 1993 which virtually restored the pre-1973 situation.

case may be, within a period of six months after the commencement of the Act.

To avoid the tremendous pressure that these applications would impose on administration certain guidelines were issued which clearly laid down the terms and conditions the Government wished to impose on various forms of foreign capital engaged in different types of activities.

The main principles of the FERA guidelines are given below:

(i) If the activities of a company under Appendix I together with activities requiring sophisticated technology and exports, account for not less than 75 per cent of its total annual turnover, such a company will be allowed to continue its activities subject to the condition that it will increase Indian participation, within a specified period, to not less than 26 per cent of the equity capital of the company. This will also apply to tea plantation companies engaged in exports.

(ii) If the activities of a company under Appendix I together with activities requiring sophisticated technology and exports account for not less than 60 per cent of the total annual turnover, such a company will be allowed to continue its activities, subject to the condition that it will increase within a specified period, Indian participation to not less than. 49 per cent of the equity of the company. In such cases a condition will be stipulated that the company concerned should undertake to export a minimum of 10 per cent of its total annual turnover within a period of two years commencing from the date of approval by the Reserve Bank of India.

(iii) If the exports of a company account for more than 40 per cent of the total annual turnover, such a company will be allowed to continue its activities subject to the condition that it will increase, within a specified period; Indian participation to not less than 49 per cent of the equity of the company.

(iv) Cases of companies coming with proposals for substantial exports could be considered, on merits, for higher level of equity participation, provided such participation is in the overall interest of the economy of the country.

(v) The ceiling of 25 per cent of the ex-factory value of the annual production for permissible trading activity by multi-activity companies will be raised to 40 per cent and 60 per cent respectively in the types of cases mentioned in (b) and (c) above.

(vi) All branches of foreign companies except airlines and shipping companies have to convert themselves into Indian companies.

*Notes:*

(a) The item treated as being covered by Appendix 1 or sophisticated technology will not be again counted towards exports while clubbing the three together in (a) to (c) above.

(b) The above clarification and amplification of the guidelines will not be applicable to the drug industry.

The misapprehensions and doubts that the 1973 FERA changes aroused in certain quarters both in India and abroad were not justified. There was no warrant for the belief either that foreign investment is no more welcome or that the existing foreign investments must invariably be brought down in all cases to 40 per cent. Nowhere does the Act hint at the sell-off of foreign investments, or of the prohibition of further inflow of foreign capital. The declared industrial policies with reference to Prime Minister Nehru's 1949 declaration, the Industrial Licensing Policy of 1973 and other pronouncements still remained valid, and the general policy of selectivity continues. All that happened was that Government took the power of review[7] of all pre-1970 cases of existing foreign investment (over 40 per cent in a company) which by and large took place before the policy of selectivity came to be crystallised, to allow continuance of majority foreign holding in those cases where it would have normally been allowed under the present policy, and to bring down foreign holding in other cases to 40 per cent.

All the companies where foreign shareholding was more than 40 per cent were made to change their capital structure or their product-mix in order to conform to the FERA guidelines. A majority seemed inclined to meet the requirements of the guidelines by partially bringing down the foreign shareholdings, but retaining a majority holding by diversifying into Appendix 1 areas and by stepping up the exports to the stipulated level during the period of two years allowed to them from the date of the approval by the Reserve Bank for complying with the FERA guidelines. There was a pronounced trend among the majority not opting for expansion in the core or high technology sectors, but rather for low technology sectors with high export potential e.g. canned meat or food products, (Brooke Bond), sea food processing (Union Carbide, ITC), hotels (ITC).

Another visible trend was that nearly all the foreign companies with high reserves capitalised huge amounts from the reserves before they went for new public issues to the Indian public. This was due to restrictions on the repatriation of earnings, the changing value of currencies, and also the anticipated difficulty in obtaining too high a premium on fresh issues, and in getting equities with high premia subscribed in the depressed capital market at that time.

The process of corporate restructuring under the FERA was completed. between 1975 and 1980. Nearly all the branches except shipping, airlines and banks were either transformed into Indian companies or closed. Also, the process of restructuring of the shareholding of the foreign companies according to the permissible limits of 74 per cent, 51 per cent or 40 per cent, as the case may be was completed except for about 20 drug companies whose cases were considered separately. In this process there was very substantial increase in Indian shareholding in these companies, a spectacular upsurge of the Indian stock market and significant increase in export activity. Close to 1.3 million new stock-holders were added and the volume of fresh capital issued to them was of the order of about Rs 583 millions. The forced diversion of some of the companies with their managerial strength and financial ability from low technology, consumer products areas into Appendix I industries was a standing gain for the Indian economy. Also important was the stimulus given to exports by the concerned efforts of some of the companies with their marketing skill and international linkage.

For so many years foreign companies in India were suffering from some kind of stagnation. They made large profits and built up huge reserves. But they were not allowed to expand in the existing usually non-essential lines of production where they were often dominant. The new FERA rules with their linkage between expansion and dilution gave them an opportunity to use their reserves, and also raise fresh capital for expansion programmes in areas of national priority, and thus to resume a process of corporate growth after years of stagnation. Some foreign companies diversified into areas of high profitability such as hotels, fisheries, food processing and detergents. Some of them chose to expand into exports. Over time, however, most of even those companies who had initially sought to retain majority foreign holding found it to their corporate long-term advantage to reduce foreign holding to 40 per cent or less so as to go out of the FERA requirements imposing special restraints on their activities such as internal trading, acquisition of property and diversification. This led to a new wave of dilutions during the early 1980s, no longer compulsory but voluntary. The cases of the foreign drug companies were delayed, as the Central Government waited for the Hathi Committee Report on drug industry, and announced a new drug policy only in 1978. Under this policy, only the manufacture of basic drugs was to be treated as Appendix I activities, and not mere formulation activities as hitherto. The process of FERA exercise for foreign drug companies on this basis was completed by 1982. It is important to note that between 1973 and 1983, as a result of the FERA process, the number of foreign majority companies came down sharply. In 1985, there were only 142 FERA companies of which only 84 were dear foreign subsidiaries.

In two significant cases, viz., IBM and Coca Cola which were required to bring down non-resident holdings to 74 per cent and 40 per cent respectively but declined to comply with these requirements, the Government directed the two companies to close their business in India. Significantly, after the liberalisation from 1991 onwards, Coca Cola has returned to India, and IBM is in the process of returning. Most of the foreign companies took steps to comply with the FERA guidelines through disinvestment or fresh issue of capital, and only a few chose to wind up their business. It is important to note that in the wake of the structural adjustment process from July 1991 and the great importance given by the Indian government to the inflow of foreign direct investment a new foreign investment policy was announced. By an ordinance issued on January 8, 1993 the 1973 changes in the FERA were almost wholly repeated. This virtually restored the pre-1973 situation making it much easier for foreign companies to operate in India.

## FOREIGN EXCHANGE MANAGEMENT ACT, 2000

This new Act has replaced the earlier FERA with a view to recast the countings law on foreign in line with the on-going globalisation process and to facilitate the process of foreign direct investment. Foreign investment is no longer unwelcome in our country, and the provisions have been liberalised and simplified. The new law is reproduced in Appendix after this chapter. But another new law to prevent and paralise money-laundering is also on the anvil.

From 1980 onwards the climate for foreign collaborations improved distinctly. Not that there was much change in the announced foreign investment policy. But a clear enthusiasm was noticeable for speedy disposal of collaboration proposals and for approving them when they confirmed to the policy requirements, This was illustrated by the steep growth in the number of approved collaboration proposals from 1980 onwards, each year thereafter setting a new record (590 in 1982, 673 in 1983 and 752 in 1984). U.S.A. seems to have become the largest source of technology followed closely by U.K. and West Germany.

## RECENT LIBERALISATIONS

In sharp contrast to the pervasive anti-MNC feeling in the world during the 1970s and early 1980s, the outlook changed dramatically in the late 1980s.

All developing and erstwhile socialist countries appeared to vie with one another in courting foreign direct investment as a means of bringing new technology, investment capital and reducing pressure on balance of payments.

The tidal wave of Industrial Policy changes announced by the Indian Government in 1991-92 signifies a phenomenal opening up of the traditional restrictive policy regime in this country so far as direct foreign investment is concerned. The process has been continued. The following are the key changes to the date.

(i) There are two modalities for FDI approval: automatic approval by RBI; and secondly, the Foreign Investment Promotion Board (FIPB) / Government approval;

(ii) In February 2000, Government took a major decision to place all items under the automatic route for FDI/NRI/OCB investment except for a small negative list, which includes the following: (i) items requiring an industrial license under the Industries (Development and Regulation) Act, 1951; (ii) foreign investment being more than 24 per cent in the equity investment, being more than 24 per cent in the equity capital of units manufacturing items reserved for small scale industries; (iii) all items requiring industrial license in terms of the locational policy notified under the New Industry Policy of 1991; (iv) proposals having previous venture/tie-up in India with foreign collaborator; (v) proposals relating to acquisition of shares in existing Indian company by foreign/NRI/OCB investor; (vi) proposals falling outside notified sectoral policy/caps or under sectors in which FDI is not permitted and/or applications chosen to be submitted through FIPB rather than automatic route by the investors. This is an important step to dispense with case-by-case approval procedure and to impart greater transparency in the process of foreign investment;

(iii) Furthermore, subject to sectoral policies and sectoral caps the automatic route would be available to all foreign and NRI investors with the facility to bring in 100 per cent FDI/NRI/OCB investment. All proposals for investment in public sector units, as also for EOU/EPZ/EHTP/STP units would qualify for automatic approval subject to the aforesaid parameters;

(iv) The activities requiring approval of FIPB/Government, FIPB endeavours to dispose of applications for FDI within a time-frame of 30 days;

(v) At present FDI is not permissible in sectors such as agriculture (including plantations), housing and real estate, domestic trading, print media, defence and strategic industries etc;

(vi) The foreign equity proposals need not necessarily be accompanied as in the past by foreign technology agreements;

(vii) Liberal access to foreign technology is available through the automatic route which permits lump sum payments up to US$2 million and royalty@5 per cent for domestic sales and 8 per cent for exports (subject to a total payment of 8 per cent on sales) for a period not exceeding 7 years from the date of commercial production. Cases not falling under the automatic route approval are considered by FIPB or Project Approval Board (PAB) depending on whether it is a composite application for financial and technical collaboration (FIPB) or an application for technical collaboration only (PAB);

(viii) Comprehensive guidelines for the consideration of FDI proposals by FIPB have been notified with a view to lending greater transparency to decision making;

(ix) Full repatriation of original investment and returns is allowed except for dividend balancing and foreign exchange neutrality conditions in certain sectors, however, later on dividend balancing condition is removed;

(x) The access given to the small-scale industries sector to foreign technology tie-up and even to limited volume of foreign investment (upto 24 per cent);

(xi) Easy access to domestic debt is available. to Foreign companies which invest in India who can leverage domestic debt from domestic financial institutions;

(xii) Liberal external commercial borrowings (ECB) and debt servicing norms have been notified and no ceiling has been placed on raising Global Depository Receipts (GDRs)/American Depository Receipts (ADRs)/Foreign Currency Convertible Bonds (FCCBs);

(xiii) The Government have, inter-alia, taken steps to simplify foreign investment procedures, allowing foreign investment in new activities such as Global Mobile Personal Communication Systems and bringing FDI up to 100 per cent in power sector, roads and highways, ports and harbours, vehicular tunnels and vehicular bridges, etc. under the automatic route; and

(xiv) Considering the enhanced opportunities of Indian software companies for expanding globally, operational norms governing their overseas investments and mode of financing acquisition of overseas software companies have been liberalised.

These are very important sign posts. These measures together with the abolition of industrial licensing except in 6 industries, the reduction of the number of industries reserved for the State sector from 29 to 3 the abolition of the requirement of pre-entry scrutiny of investment decisions under the MRTP Act, the repeal of the FERA restrictions and the announced intention of closing down chronically sick public sector enterprises which cannot be made viable do open up new visit a for direct foreign investment in India.

They signify that India made virtually a U turn from the negative foreign investment policies that prevailed during the last three decades and is entering into a foreign investment friendly regime. Gone are the days of strict selectivity for permitting foreign investment which was viewed not as a substitute for domestic savings, but only as a vehicle for acquiring technology when a technology was needed and could not be acquired except through foreign investment. Also, gone are the days when multinationals were viewed as camp followers of Western Colonialism not essentially interested in the development of the third world countries, but only in exploiting their market and cheap labour. Also over is the almost theological preference for permitting to foreigners not more than 40 per cent of equity and permitting foreign majority only in very exceptional cases. During the 1970s India earned a certain amount of notoriety in the global foreign investment market on account of the FERA (Foreign Exchange Regulation Act, 1973) exercises when the existing foreign companies were compelled to go down to 40 per cent of foreign equity by a variety of means except in some cases where their engagement in export oriented activities or sophisticated technology justified higher level of foreign shareholding. This policy culminated in the withdrawal from India of IBM and Coca Cola, two Chair leaders among MNCs. That lead to a general fear psychosis for foreign investment in India. It was on account of this negative policy that the total volume of direct foreign investment i.e., foreign equity participation in India increased only marginally from Rs 1.4 billion in 1960-61 to Rs 2.07 billion in 1964-65 and Rs 3.06 billion in 1969-70. Also the share of foreigners in the equity of the foreign companies steadily declined. All these are now things of the past and India has clearly decided to opt for the general global trend covering both developing countries and former socialist countries of trying to woe direct foreign investment as a means of accelerating development efforts and bridging the growing balance of payment difficulties.

From the point of view of foreign investors. India is indeed a land of great promise. The following are some of the positive inducements for foreign investment in this country:

(i) India is ranked seventh among the top 20 economies in the Asia Pacific region for FDI Inflow, as per World Investment Report, 1999 published by the United Nations in 1998.

(ii) India's huge market potential. Even if we were to exclude from the currently estimated population of one million those who are below the poverty i.e. around 30 per cent or taking a more realistic point of, view, even if we were to assume that only 25 per cent of the Indian population are able to buy products of modern industry, that would constitute a market almost equal in size with the markets of Western Europe and North America. It is observed that in the long run it is not so much the incentives offered by most countries as the market opportunities that attract foreign direct investment.

(iii) The remarkable record of profitability of the Indian companies in the private sector, in particular, the so-called foreign controlled companies, would itself provide sufficient inducement. The studies made by organisations such as the Indo-US Business Council would provide eloquent support. According to the study of 34 Indo-US joint ventures in India for the period 1976-81 the combined sales of all these companies grew at an average annual compound rate of 17.9 per cent. Net profit grew at 20.3 per cent, profit before tax at 15.6 per cent, dividends at 14.8 per cent and retained earnings at 22.8 per cent. Equity capital grew at an annual rate of 21.5 per cent. Gross fixed assets grew at an annual average compound rate of 13.4 per cent and total assets at 17 per cent. Some of these rates were higher than those of their US principles.

(iv) India's impeccable record of honouring international payment obligations. Even in her most critical foreign exchange crises like the one in the late 1950s or the one during the opening year of 90s India always honoured her international payment obligations and never sought to put restrictions on the right of foreign investor to repatriate the profits earned or to disinvest whenever he chose to do so. This contrasts sharply with the records of most other third world countries.

(v) The existence of a vibrant private sector in this country is itself an inducement and a protection for direct foreign investment. There is a solid industrial base that contributes significantly to the GDP.

(vi) India has built up a huge and diversified capital market during the 1980s. Introduction of screen based trading has increased significantly the scope of the market during recent years. This market comprising 25 stock exchanges is capable of raising Rs 10,000 to Rs 15,000 crores a year. It is also opened to foreign investors to raise parts of their project financing. The country has an impressive savings record, and a fast growing number of people turning from savers to investors.

(vii) India is the world's third largest pool of scientific and technological skill and manpower.

(viii) One of the widespread banking and insurance networks ill the third world decades. There is a well-spread system of management education which can compare with the best in the world, and Indian managers have proved their worth the world over. This, along with India's traditional entrepreneurial capability, must be considered great assets unlike in most third world countries.

(x) India has been following a stable democratic regime since her independence and there is a general rule of law which also means non discriminatory treatment of foreign companies vis-a-vis Indian companies.

All these special inducements must be viewed along with the general positive aspects of the Indian economy like a strong and vibrant agricultural sector, a fast growing services sector which itself indicates a mature economy, one of the most widespread transport systems in the third world including the railway system which can perform fairly efficiently under good management, and dependable private sector truck services.

As against these plus points there are also some negative points.

(i) There is a continuing fear of a long lasting negative policy regime despite the announced liberalisation in recent years. There is even now a pervasive xenophobia in some circles, political and academic, in relation to foreign investment. The recent past imbroglios over Enron's Dabhol power project and Kentucky Fried Chicken restaurant in Bangalore and Delhi, and examples of the Suzuki-Government (Indian) clash over management of Maruti Udyog Ltd., demise of Tata-Singapore Airlines joint venture, and attacks on Monsanto's cotton field trials in Karnataka and Andhra Pradesh, and recent power project's sell-off by Enron and ABB have underscored this.

(ii) The fear of procedural difficulties still remains. Many foreign investors are still not very sure whether what is being brought about by the liberalised policy announcements will not be negatived by bureaucratic and procedural obstacles. Foreign Investment Implementation Authority (FIIA) has been set up recently in order to ensure that the approvals for foreign investment are quickly translated into actual investment inflows and proposals fructify into projects. And also, in all cases where government approval is involved, approval time has been fixed at 30 days. So all this shows government's sincere intentions to remove hurdles in the way of FDI.

(iii) There is a lurking fear of trade union intransigence and industrial unrest leading to loss of production and productivity and failure to be internationally competitive.

(iv) There is perception that in India there is no easy 'exit' for investors, after they have effected investments. These perceptions even if somewhat true in the yester-years are fast losing their validity in the changing scenario of current times. The recent policy and procedural changes have made things easier, faster and much more flexible than before. India's trade unions have shown responsibility and responsiveness to the needs of the time. Even most leftist leaders have shown considerable pragmatism. As regards 'exit' there are clear provisions in our Industrial Disputes Act and Companies Act for 'exit'. These need to be implemented with political will and economic realism.

India has been passing through a policy of adjustment to overcome severe budgetary deficits and the Government has taken a number of significant steps to restore efficiency and speed in the economy. Some of them have really started showing fruits and will no doubt yield more dividend as time passes, if only the nation is able to withstand the populist pressure and does not slacken in its grim determination to overcome the hurdles in the way of adjustments. On balancing the attractions and disincentives there can be no doubt that India is a very attractive destination for foreign direct investment, and foreign investors will have no cause for regret.

Some of the other new policy relaxations are:

(i) The introduction of full convertibility of the rupee on the current trading account and partial convertibility on capital account (for foreign investment).

(ii) Permitting Indian companies to raise equity capital from international capital markets through GDRs/ADRs/FCCBs (GDRs stands for Global Depository Receipts, ADRs for American Depository Receipts and FCCBs for Foreign Currency Convertible Bonds) and listing shares on foreign stock exchanges. Some Indian companies have already raised capital internationally and got its scrips listed on stock exchanges overseas.

(iii) There are no end-use restrictions on GDR/ADR issue proceeds, except for an express ban on investment in real estate and stock markets, however, FCCB issue proceeds need to conform to external commercial borrowing end-use requirements.

(iv) The NRIs and OCBs are allowed to invest in housing and real estate development sector, in which FDI is not permitted.

(v) Permitting foreign currency non-resident accounts as a collateral by a third party for obtaining loan from banks and Institutions.

(vi) Automatic clearance for foreign investment proposals to all items except far a small negative list.

(vii) Even if approval is required, it will be decided within a time-frame of 30 days.

(viii) Dividend balancing is removed.

(ix) Allowing foreign provident funds, pension funds, trusts and similar financial bodies to make portfolio investment in Indian companies. As a matter of fact foreign institutional investors have become significant portfolios investors in India accounting for an aggregate funds folio of U.S. $10 billion.

(x) Introduced of Foreign Exchange Management Act, 1999, which seeks to consolidate and amend the earlier law (FEMA) relating to foreign exchange with the objective of facilitating external trade and payments.

(xi) Massive reduction of customs duties and withdrawal of import restrictions including quantitative (QRs) ones. But while this would no doubt encourage foreign companies. this may also harm India's economy in two ways viz by hurting IndIa's manufacturers and by encouraging foreign companies to import rather than invest.

(xii) Last, but one of the very important point that the FDI policy is continuously reviewed and reformulated to facilitate foreign investment into India. The Foreign Investment Implementation Authority, comprising representatives from State Governments, nodal central ministries for specific projects and entrepreneurs, has also been set up to address the problems faced by the investors and facilitate implementation of projects.

These are highly significant concessions. Overnight all the notorious restrictions of the past on foreign investment seem to have been cleaned up by a giant broomstick, and in that process attempts have been made to integrate Indian economy with the global economy in a way it never was after the 1950s. The massive overhaul of the FERA guidelines, the bugbear for foreign companies of yester-years, will remove the procedural irritants and impediments which have obstructed foreign direct investment and stifled the operation of the foreign controlled Indian companies for well over two decades. Foreign investors can take full advantage of these concessions to submit investment proposals and ensure speedy completion of these projects within a short time to avoid cost and time overrun. In that way they will be able to take full advantage of the huge domestic market and also the potential for larger exports from India. Foreign investment in India so far has been abysmally low, not because of the lack of opportunities, but because of the fact that India never encouraged foreign investment as a part of her planned economic development and by and large relied on domestic savings. India does not even figure in the IMF list of countries with foreign investment. That policy has outlived its time and therefore India has been going all out to woo foreign investment. The prospects of her success will also be affected by the currently prevailing recession in most of the western countries, and the fact that on account of the recessionary conditions the great majority of the multinational corporations may not just have enough of investible surplus. India should therefore tap small and medium companies as well as also the trusts and pension funds etc. which often have enough resources for investment and who do not seek to control the companies where they invest, but look at them only as investment opportunities for steady and handsome returns. Fund Managers for such funds need to be specially addressed to. But for the general recessionary conditions there is no doubt that India could well emulate the performance of several countries like China in attract in sizeable volume of foreign investment.

The question now is whether the recent and on-going policy initiatives, and reforms will succeed immediately in renewing the confidence of foreign investors and MNCs and bring in substantial investment flow. Clearly, the success of these policies will depend on the sincerity with which they are given immediate effect, the skill with which they are marketed abroad and the speed with which the bureaucratic and procedural bottlenecks are removed. Deeprooted among foreign investors and bankers is a fear of the Indian bureaucracy and the image of India being a difficult country. Unfortunately there were even in the announcements aspects which conjure up unpleasant visions of bureaucratic skulduggery. Thus the statement that dividend repatriations from the new investments would have to be covered by exports earnings. Similarly, conditions attached with the import of capital goods were also irksome. However, these conditions were in a way not different from those which the Asian countries or even China have been insisting upon for years. But in the case of India these requirements brought in fear of having to face interminably the bureaucrats, a prospect which the foreign investors would ever detest. However, government has removed these irritants to a larger extent. But there are some that need to be removed if India is to make a policy package which is fully attractive to foreign investors. A little modification can bring in a lot more investment and substantially increase foreign capital.

**Table 7.2 Foreign Investment Flows by Host Region**

(US$ Million)

| Country | 1992 | 1993 | 1994 | 1995 | 1996 | 1997 | 1998 |
|---|---|---|---|---|---|---|---|
| China | 11,156 | 27,515 | 33,787 | 35,849 | 40,800 | 44,236 | 45,460 |
| India | 277 | 550 | 973 | 2,114 | 2,426 | 3,351 | 2,258 |
| Indonesia | 1,777 | 2,004 | 2,109 | 4,346 | 6,194 | 4,673 | -356 |
| Korea, Rep. of | 727 | 588 | 809 | 1,776 | 2,325 | 2,844 | 5,143 |
| Malaysia | 5,183 | 5,006 | 4,342 | 4,178 | 5,078 | 5,106 | 3,727 |
| Philippines | 228 | 1,238 | 1,591 | 1,478 | 1,517 | 1,222 | 1,713 |
| All developing countries including China (LDCs) | 51,108 | 78,813 | 1,01,196 | 1,06,223 | 1,35,343 | 1,72,533 | 1,65,936 |
| Share of India in LDCs (%) | 0.4 | 0.7 | 1.0 | 2.0 | 1.8 | 1.9 | 1.4 |

Source: Economic Survey, 1999-2000.

India has a very large degree of absorptive capacity for FDI. The volume of FDI in India is only around Rs 11 billion which works out to 1 per cent of the GDP and 1 to 2 per cent of the country's aggregate corporate equity capital. India is not even included in the IMF list of countries with foreign investment. Also, fresh foreign investment has been one of the lowest in the world starting with 36.14 million rupees in 1969 reaching 88.26 million in 1980 and only reaching the somewhat respectable figure of 2133.26 in 1988 and2609.08 in 1989. Even that declined sharply in 1990 by 48 per cent reaching 1283.21 million rupees. This was on account of the political uncertainty that prevailed during the year and the fact that the still born foreign investment policies of the two successive Governments also kept foreign investment out. Also there was no improvement during the caretaker Government during the first part of 1991. But it reached to Rs.351 crore in 1991 and continued to grow reaching at Rs. 6720 crore in 1995 and Rs. 9116 crore in 1998. Thus on the whole fresh foreign investment in India from 1969 to 1990 aggregated only to the level of Rs 13400.08 million and from 1991 to 1998 FDI reached at the level of Rs.42173 million. However, it is a very modest figure if compared to the record of many of our neighbours like China or several other Asian countries which recently attracted impressive foreign investment (Table 7.2). China attracted foreign direct investment of the value of US $40 billion in 1996 which was several times the foreign direct investment in India i.e. less than 3 billion dollars in the same year, whereas Indonesia attracted $6.2 billion and Malaysia $5.1 billion in 1996.

A lot more of special promotional efforts and hard-sell would be necessary for undoing the special negative image that India has in the global foreign direct investment market. India needs to do some vigorous global marketing to attract FDI and show some spectacular and visible speed in clearing long pending investment proposals. The demonstration effect of such speed is expected to show foreign investors that the changes are really not make-beliefs. but do signify a new era of pragmatism and reforms. Under the new policy of automatic approval scheme, the proposals for approval are made to the RBI only. And now almost all items are placed under automatic route except for a small negative list. The erstwhile Foreign Investment Board has been abolished so that new investors only need to go either to the Secretariat for Industrial Assistance or to the Foreign Investment Promotion Board. In normal cases investors are not even required to go to the Government, but Reserve Bank of India has been authorised to clear all normal foreign investment proposals falling within the parameters of the announced policy. According to the available figures the actual inflow of foreign direct investment after 1991 reforms amount to Rs. 42,173 crores as against Rs. 1,93,648 crores which has been approved in the aggregate during the same period. The uncertainty over the entry of FDI in retail or FDI in airlines illustrates the problems facing FDI in India. India needs to do much more than what she has done so far in scrapping her notorious procedures and administrative practice in the interest of high speed decisions. The past controversy over Enron's Dahol power project shows the need for greater transparency and secondly, the problems that political factors can sometimes create when a new political group coming to power insists on reopening a contract entered into by a previous government. All this can create much uncertainty in the mind of foreign investors.

The foreign inestment market in the world is huge. In 1992. the share of India in FDIs to all developing countries was less than 1 per cent. It has grown and reached at about 2 per cent in recent years, with an exceptional year of 1998, which is however a worrisome development. True, that nearly 70 per cent of the total cross-border investment was confined only to the developed countries. but if India could attract a fair percentage of whatever portion went from the world to the developing countries, i.e., around $165 billion that itself will amount to several billion dollars. Today countries in the developing and socialist worlds are vying with one another to attract foreign investment. India is almost the last to join the queue. But it is never too late. And given the attractive conditions that India offers. if only she can remove the fears and prejudices which haunt foreign investors—fear of the procedure and of hostile policy—she can easily attract massive investment funds. This will be true even if we take into account the current recessionary conditions in the global economy. in particular the economies of the developed countries which generate most of the foreign direct investment. Indeed, taking into account ail the pluses and minuses of investment in India, there is no doubt that, for foreign investors, investing in India can never be a risk. Not investing in India can be one from their corporate point of view in the long run. Interestingly significant foreign funds are coming through the route of portfolio investment in the stock market by foreign financial institutions besides foreign direct investment. It is sometimes argued, however, that in recent years a significant proportion of FDI has been utilized in the acquisition of Indian companies and not in the creation of new productive assets and as a result FDI has involved only a change of ownership of exiting assets rather than an increase in the productive capacity of the economy e.g. the foreign takeover of companies like Rainbaxy, ACC and Ambuja. Further, it is claimed that this trend may be accentuated in the future, with greater incidence of hostile take-overs of Indian companies, if FDIs inflow is further liberalized.

Some recent policy nuances by the government have been viewed adversely by foreign investors. Examples are proposal for retrospectively amending the tax law to undo the effect of the Supreme Court judgment in the Vodaphone case, the so called GAAR proposals (General Anti-Avoidance Regulations), proposals for reviewing the tax status of Mauritius companies investing in India and precautions over permitting FDI in retails, civil aviation and insurance. Positive steps in these areas should vastly improve the outlook for foreign investment in India. From this point of view the policies announced on 14th September, 2012 to permit foreign investment upto 51 per cent in multi brand retail (although limited to million plus cities in States which are in four of this) and upto 74 per cent in digital broadcasting and 49 per cent in civil aviation, have to be welcomed. Coming as they have done after a long spell of policy paralysis these announcements should vastly improve the outlook for foreign investment in India and also step up growth in Indian economy.

## REFERENCES


1. For a lucid readable account see Louis Turner. *Multinational Companies and the Third World* (Hill and Wang), New York. The author's final conclusion is that foreign private investment is expensive for the recipient third world country, and open to serious abuses for which the answer lies in concerted moves and forms of economic nationalism by the third world countries.
2. Reserve Bank of India-Census of India's Foreign Liability and Assets as on March 31, 1987 published in RBI Bulletin, April 1991. Two tables given here are obtained from this study.
3. These figures are mostly obtained from *Indian Journal of Public Administration,* Vol. XX, July-Sept. 1974, Article by T.N. Chaturvedi entitled Foreign Investment and Collaboration in India.
4. See Charles P. Kindelberger, *American Business Abroad,* Yale University Press. This is a well-argued defence of the multinationals from purely the angle of the economics of direct foreign investment. He strongly recommends the setting up of international organisations and the evolving of international policies to, regulate the growth of international business in order to ensure its most optimum use.
5. This has been very forcefully propounded by the renowned economist Raul Prebisch who has asserted that far from helping developing countries in the process of development, the MNCs only promote the consumption patterns of their home countries to the benefit of a few, and bring technology that does not solve the problem of poverty and unemployment in the developing world. According to him, developing countries should not repeat the process of growth of the industrialised countries, and MNCs are therefore not suitable agencies for third world countries where basic problems relate to economic inequalities and income distribution.
6. It replaced the relevant Defence of India Rules, 1939 which for the first time introduced foreign exchange control in India.
7. Michael Kidron, *Foreign Investment in India,* 1956.
8. Reserve Bank of India.
9. RBI *Foreign Collaboration in Indian Industry,* Survey Report, 1968.
10. RBI *Foreign Collaboration in Indian Industry,* Second Survey Report, 1974.
11. Kidron, *op.cit.,* pp. 250-51, 266.
12. These figures have been obtained separately from the July 1975 issue of the Bulletin of the Reserve Bank, *India's Investment Position 1968-1972.*
13. See Kidron, *Foreign Investment in India,* 1965.
14. Second Survey, *op.cit.,* pp. 132-133.

## CHAPTER 8

# Capital Market, Stock Exchange and the Securities and Exchange Board of India (SEBI)

Securities market—primary (new issues market) and secondary (stock exchanges)—is a big source of business funds. Government regulates this market so to provide adequate funds to the industry and protection to the investors' interests. If so regulated securities market is supplemented with efficient industrial sector, growth of securities market becomes obvious. The Securities and Exchange Board of India (SEBI) is assigned with the job of regulation of securities market. SEBI was set up on April 12, 1988 initially as a non-statutory body. It took almost four years for the government to bring about a separate legislation in the name of Securities and Exchange Board of India Act, 1992 conferring statutory powers. The Act charged to SEBI with comprehensive powers over practically all aspects of capital market operations.

Indian securities market has undergone a complete transformation during the liberalised decade of 90s in terms of market micro-structure, market practices and volumes, driven as much by market forces as by policy initiatives. The recent past has witnessed dramatic increase in dematerialised settlement of securities, introduction of rolling settlement, internet trading and trading in derivatives of securities. With these large and fast changes in the market, responsibilities of the regulator ha ve also increased to enable domestic market take the benefits of globalisation and not become a playground of the mere global forces.

### NEW ISSUES MARKET

Prior to 1992 Capital Issues Control was a major instrument of Central Government's intervention over corporate business. With the repeal of this Act on May 29,1992 the issue of securities and their pricing have been placed under the discretion of companies subject to guidance from merchant bankers who will operate with recognition from Securities and Exchange

Board of India (SEBD and within SEBI's guidelines. Also the prospectuses to be issued by companies before capital issues are compulsorily required to be vetted by the SEBI.

Capital Issues Control was introduced at first under Defence of India Rules 1943, purely as a war-time measure, with a view to restricting the use of scarce resources for non-essential purposes. After the war this control was retained as a purely temporary legislative measure in 1947 and was continued from year to year. it was only in 1956 that the Capital Issues (Control) Act was permanently put on the Statute Book. Another law of the same year closely related to the operation of capital issues control was the Securities Contracts Regulation Act (1956) which governed the working of the stock exchanges. The main object of capital issues control was to ensure that investments in all sectors of economy are according to the priorities laid down under the national policy. Indeed prior to the MRTP Act, 1969, this was the principal tool in the hands of the government for regulating the financial aspects of various projects for which industrial licences were being issued. Furthermore, this control was administered through the Ministry of Finance (Department of Economic Affairs) under which the Central Government appointed the Controller of Capital Issues who was invested with the powers conferred on the Central Government by this Act.

## Capital Issues Control Abolition and other Recent Developments

Capital Issues Control became one of the first casualties of the Indian Government's economic reform and restructuring programme of 1991-92. Thus the Capital Issues (Control) Act, 1947 was repealed. The office of the Controller of Capital Issues (CCI) was subsequently abolished. With the abolition of CCI, prior government permission was no longer needed by companies to access the capital markets. Companies were free to approach primary capital market after clearance of the prospectus as finalised through merchant banking by SEBI (established in 1992). Control over price and premium of shares was removed .Companies were required to disclose all material facts and specific risk factors associated with their projects while making public issues. Through the notification issued under the Securities Contract (Regulation) Act, 1956 the power to regulate stock exchanges was delegated to SEBI.

The phenomenal growth of the capital market, the advent of the SEBI and the burgeoning of the merchants banking had made the capital issues control apparatus redundent and counter productive. The Central budget for 1992-93 announced the decision to abolish capital issues control.

Shortly after this, by Ordinance No.9 of 1992 followed by a one line legislation, the Capital Issues (Control) Act was repealed on May 29, 1992 and companies were declared as competent to issue capital including rights issues and bonus issues provided they did so through merchant bankers within the guidelines announced and subject to the superintendence and monitoring by the SEBI. In theory the issue of shares and their pricing have been freed. But companies have to go through the merchant bankers who have been placed under the SEBI's supervisory authority. Also, companies must comply with the SEBI's disclosure and investment protection norms as given in its announced guidelines. They are also required to get the draft prospectuses vetted by the SEBI. The sudden abolition of capital issues control, in particular permitting companies to price their own shares, led to a certain amount of abuses by unscrupulous company promoters and merchant bankers.

But the fact remains that the abolition of capital issues control in 1992 was premature and hasty. The country was not prepared for the introduction of free, pricing of issues. The small investor who, under the C.C.I. regime was the main player in the market was literaly placed at the mercy of dishonest company promoters and greedy merchant bankers who contrived to float any number of issues in the market with fancy prices. The common investors, after buying those shares on false and misleading assurances, lost heavily and thereafter simply left the market. The deterioration of the primary market was accelerated by the developing crisis in the secondary market after the 1992-93 'scam' and the arbitrary and sudded imposition of the ban of forward trading by SEBI in 1994.Thus both the primary and the secondary markets started declining very fast. As a result the primary market suffered heavily. Whereas under the 8th Five Year Plan very huge amount was expected to be raised in the capital market (to the tune of Rs.50,000 crores per annum or so) in actual practice primary issues just become a trickle. There were several quarters in recent times when not a single primary issue is raised from the market. The continuous slack of the primary capital market since 1994-95 must be considered to be a tragedy for economic development for contemporary India just as a spectacular rise in the decades of the 70s and 80s was considered to be great achievement.

## Growth of the Capital Market

Capital market was, by and large, in a state of boom from the 1950s following the rising tempo of industrial growth. If the funds raised from the capital market declined after the mid 60s, the explanation lies in factors such as deterioration of the investment climate; the highly restrictive industrial licensing policies, the regulatory legislations such as the M.R.T.P Act, the ban on forward trading in the stock market in 1969 and the restriction on payment of dividend in 1974. The revival of the capital market began in the late 1970s with the new issues made by the FERA companies which were forced to dilute their foreign share holding. It enjoyed boom from 1980 to early 90s. The bear phase began in October 1994 due to which Market continued to remain dormant.

Indian capital market had an unprecedented and phenomenal quantum jump during the period 1980-92. Indeed, there would be few comparable developments in our economic development annals after independence. Between 1947 and 1979, Indian companies annually raised only Rs.58 crores on an average. But starting with Rs 120 crores in 1980, this figure jumped to about Rs 27,632 crores in 1994-95 but it fell thereafter and reached the figure of 5,587 crores in 1998-99. There was both a deepening and a widening of shareholding structure. Our capital market from having been confined to only the cities of Mumbai, Calcutta, Delhi, Chennai and Ahmdabad got extended to many newer areas of the country and also reached new nontraditional sections such as agriculturists, the middle class investors and non-resident Indians. As against only about 5 to 6 stock exchanges which operated a few years ago, today there are 25 of them. In the olden days, an issue of Rs 2 to 3 crores was considered to be a big issue, but in bull years there had been any number of cases of companies raising staggering volumes of thousand of crores in single issue. At the same time, many more companies became broadbased. While until 1981 the company with the largest number of shareholders had only about 80,000 of them, but till early 90s there were any number of companies with several lakhs of shareholders. In a way, these Indian companies, widely held and professionally managed, have been becoming similar to the modern public corporations of the west. This happened largely because of the general improvement in the investment climate and the consciously through the government policy, relentlessly persued from 1980 onwards, of compelling M.R.T.P. companies, whenever they sought permission for expansion, to raise substantial portion of the cost of the project from the market through shares or debuntures rather then relying almost wholly on long term institutional finance as they had been doing till then. The demonstration effect of several such cases of successful public issue during the 1980s and early 1990s was phenomenal. Convertible debentures became the main instrument of these issues. It gave investors both a good return from the beginning and certainty of conversion into risk capital by the time company will have reached the stage of profitability. Convertible debentures, therefore became a highly popular instrument and mainly did the trick. From 1982 onwards, after the government had announced a package of policies to make a non-convertible debuntures attractive, nonconvetible debuntures also became popular. A parallel market in debuntures was thus created side by side with the share market. Many more companies, aware of the then newly found strength of the capital market, and the fact that public response was expected to be overwhelming if they had business reputation and if the project in question was sound, went to the public, and the public responded overwhelmingly. A number of industrial houses which throughout the 70s had been sitting on the sidelines and not gone in for any expansion for fear of the convertibility clause followed suit with new project and concommitant public issues. Indeed, a new horizon had been created for the corporate sector. At the same time pressure on the Government financial institutions substantially eased, as companies were no longer dependent on them for raising their requirement of long term capital.

Encouraged by the growth of the capital market, the Government also permitted public sector companies to revise resources through non-convertible debentures. Such debentures were given some fiscal concessions, and were also listed on the stock exchanges. Many companies e.g. I.T.I, H.M.T successfully floated such debentures. The guidelines issued by the Ministry of Finance regarding flotation of Bonds by Public Sector Undertakings in the Telecommunications and Power Sector in September 1985 were significant. Following this several Public Sector Enterprises went to the capital market and raised non-convertible bonds including tax-free ones. It should be highlighted that in the post-1991 scenario of globalisation many Indian companies have successfully tapped the overseas capital market by issuing Global Depository Receipts (GDRs) and American Depository Receipts (ADRs), which are regularly quoted and traded in the leading World stock market.

The bull phase of 80s and early 90s was followed by the bear phase that began in October 1994. Relatively tight domestic liquidity and a slowdown in FII inflows were thought to be the immediate causes of the fall of this phase. Since then market is charatersied by falling trend, weak sentiments, almost withdrawal of small investors, great volatility and playing up by FIIs and mutual funds and alike fectors. Several measures, even by SEBI, have been taken to improve the capital market —for widening and deepening different segments of the market and for promoting investor protection and market development. These consisted of the reforms in primary and secondary, and foreign institutional investment. But despite reforms the market continued to remain dormant, the primary market remained depressed with substantial decline in number of issues and amount raised e.g. from Rs 27,632 crores in 1994-95 to mere Rs.5,587 crores in 1998-99, the secondary market kept witnessing declining prises with subdued market sentiments and the net investment by FIIs reaching at the similar low levels of its starting period of 1993-94 during 1997-98 (US$ 1.6 billion) after touching the high level of about US$ 2.4 billion in 1996-97. For the whole of 1999, the FII investment stood at $1.47 billions.

## Causes of the Depressed Situation in the Seventies

Besides political instability, overall slow down in the national economy and international economic problems especially in East Asian countries, vanishing companies basic deficiencies in the capital market may also be seen as a major cause for the depressed developments. Moreover, like the stock market scam in the short fun, these deficiencies may shed even worse long term effects if these are not corrected. What happened in the past—with the deregulation of the share market through the closure of the CCl and the establishment of the SEB1, and greater freedom being given to promoters for determining the premium on equity issues, there became a general tendency to overpricing the shares. This was even permitted by booming secondary market and outgrowing naive small investors. Under the CCI regime the premium for a share that could be fixed only on the company's track record (net asset value and profitability). But in the new environment, many companies, even when their reserves and dividend records did not justify it, and even new companies fixed up high premia on the basis of projected growth and profitability. This uncritical acceptance of such a basis for prices of new issues by relatively ill-informed investors led to the phenomenon of pervasive over-pricing. The result of it has been the considerable loss of confidence among the small investors, who have lost fairly substantially in the recent past on account of insufficient secondary market transactions in most scrips and the consequent lack of liquidity in the over-priced shares. As an inevitable reaction the SEBl appointed a committee (the Malegam Committee) in order to recommend corrective measures. This report, inter alia, suggested the forbidding of premia on the basis of projection.

Apart from merchant banking, another beneficiary of the new system of free pricing of shares was mutual funds industry. Under the new directions of the SEB1, between 1991 and 1995 the percentage of shares for the general public in a new issue was drastically reduced and the percentage of preferential allotments to corporate bodies sharply raised. This considerably helped the growth of mutual funds. Available statistics indicate that the aggregate of such schemes registered an average growth of 3.89 percent in 1994-95 over 1993-94 for all schemes against a growth rate of minus 13.71 per cent for the 30-share Bombay Stock Exchange Sensitive Index (Sensex) and minus 12.24 percent for the 100-share national index. Thus mutual fund industry initially outperformed the market indices spectacularly in generally depressed conditions, but thereafter became a victim of the general depression of the stock market from 1993 onwards with sharp fall in the quoted value of their shares. But the SEBI's most recent decision to limit the share of Indian mutual funds upto 20 per cent in the proposed total issue may be seen as a step to check the overplay of these mutual funds.

While we need not reintroduce the CCI guidelines to check the adverse developments like over-pricing and over-play by the few market players, institutional arrangements have to be set right. The SEBI has clearly and correctly indicated that it would not perform the function of determining the issue price of shares and that this should be determine by more market based arrangements. The principle tasks to be performed by the SEBI are to ensure investor protection through transparency in the capital markets and full disclosure by the promoters and to prevent market manipulations. While transparency and diaclosure are undoubtedly essential, they only provide the information base which, combined with strong analytical skills, enable a proper determination of the issue price. The appropriate institutions for this purpose would be the merchant bankers and the issue managers, who are not only responsible for advising the clients but also for ensuring that the issue is picked up by the market or that the underwriting functions are carried out smoothly. Unfortunately their track record on this account is not particularly good. In order to bring greater discipline into the primary issues market it is suggested that the condition for recognition of lead merchant bankers and their supervision be made more stringent. This role would have to be carried out by SEBI and appropriate institutional arrangements would have to be made for expeditious and rigorous implementation of enhanced panel provisions. The other source of discipline is issue pricing. The major financial institutions could act as the intermediary for the small investors. In the Indian case, however neither the banking system nor the development financial institutions are involved in any significant manner in the primary issues market. A number of mutual funds were set up in the earlier 1990's in order to play this intermediary role. These too could not effectively perform the disciplining function and most of them withdrew from the primary market and started focussing excessively on the secondary market and in debt instruments. With the decline in the stock market, most of the mutual funds have suffered serious erosion in their net asset values (NAVs). The involvement of mutual funds in the primary issues market, however, is essential for the healthy growth of industry and revival of investor confidence. Earlier efforts at encouraging mutual funds were centred around tax concessions. While these are useful, they are not a substitute for demonstrated expertise in investment appraisal and asset management. It is suggested that tax incentives should be granted primarily to encourage greater focus on primary markets and approved institutions should possess the necessary skills.

In order to revive confidence in the equity market a number of steps need to be taken. First, the tendency to list new issues immediately on the major stock markets needs to be checked. Shares should be quoted on the major stock exchanges only after they have established adequate track records in terms of trading behaviour. The existing classification system of grading shares adopted by most major bourses may not be adequate for this purpose, unless distinct indices are developed and publicised for each category, and every new issue is placed in a specific category by the concerned exchange and ratified by SEBI. Another methodology would be to have a distinct exchange for new issues with well defined graduation criterion for listing in the major exchanges. The Over the Counter Exchange of India (OTCEI) was established essentially for this purpose, but remained more or less non functional due to the lack of adequate market-making efforts. This institution needs to be revived and energised, and all new issues should be listed first with the OTCEI and should be allowed to graduate to the major exchanges only on the establishments of a minimum track record. This would have the advantage of bringing a certain amount of discipline in the matter of setting issue prices. In order to energise the primary market and the operation of the OTCEI it is suggested that market-making efforts be broadened by encouraging further participation of the major financial institutions, including banks. Furthermore, in order to increase the level of liquidity, foreign portfolio investments should be permitted freely in these two segments over and above the limits placed on their activity in other markets and instruments. In addition, the restrictions on forward trading activities such as "Badia" and other derivatives should be less stringent in the OTCEI than in the major exchanges. Another method to bring rationality into issue pricing would be to introduce "Issue Houses", which would have to take responsibility for providing equity funds even before the shares are sold to the public.

## STOCK EXCHANGES BEFORE INDEPENDENCE

From scattered and haphazard beginnings in the late 18th century India's stock exchanges have today developed into a respectable-sized multi-centred stock exchange system through spells of total non-regulation, self-regulation, half hearted government control, and in the recent past close government supervision. Capital market has two branches, the primary or the new issues market, and the secondary or the stock market. The second provides to investors a market for buying and selling of existing securities, viz. equity shares, preference shares and debentures. Both the primary and the secondary markets are inter-dependent and indivisible, and one cannot exist without the other. Indeed the capacity of a nation to channel savings into long-term equity financing is central to the maintenance of a free enterprise market economy system. Stock markets and stock exchanges are the mechanisms for such financing. The effectiveness of these mechanisms depends upon the degree to which certain conditions exist: a stable political environment; reasonable and successful fiscal and monetary policies; reliable accounting and financial reporting standards and procedures, the ready availability of timely and accurate financial information; existence of short and long-term financial instruments that attract household and corporate savings and meet the risk/reward requirements of savers and borrowers; a secondary market for such instruments; and a legislative and regulatory infrastructure that includes the means to administer in through regulatory agencies. The last of these conditions is a major factor in determining the amount of confidence it is a major factor in determining the extent to which investors will channel their savings into long-term equity financing. *Investor confidence is thus the key to smooth and successful operation of the market system.*

Stock exchange is an essential pillar of the private sector corporate economy. It discharges three essential functions in the process of capital formation and in raising resources for the corporate sector. First and most important, the stock exchange provides a market place for purchase and sale of securities viz. shares, bonds and debentures etc. It therefore ensures the free transferability of securities which is an essential basis for the joint stock enterprises system. Private sector economy cannot function without the assurance provided by the stock exchange to the owners of shares and bonds that they can be sold in the market at any time. At the same time those who wish to invest their surplus funds in securities for long-term capital appreciation or for speculative gain can also buy scrips of their choice in the market. Secondly, the stock exchange provides the linkage between the savings in the household sector and the investment in the corporate economy. It mobilises savings and channelises them as securities into those enterprises which are favoured by the investors on the basis of such criteria as future growth prospects, good returns and appreciation of capital. The importance of this function has remained undiminished in spite of the prevalence in the Indian scene of such interventionist factors as industrial licensing, provision of credit to private sector by public sector development banks, price controls and foreign exchange regulations. The stock exchange discharges this function by laying down a number of listing regulations which have to be complied with while making public issues e.g. offering at least the prescribed percentage of capital to the public keeping the subscription list open for a minimum period of three days, making provision for receiving applications at least at the centres where there are recognised stock exchanges, allotting the shares against applications on a fair and unconditional basis with due weightage being given to the applicants in lower categories, particularly those applying for shares worth Rs 500 or Rs 1,000, etc. Members of stock exchanges also assist in the floatation of new issues by acting as managing brokers/official brokers of new issues in which capacity they, inter alia, try to sell these issues to investors spread all over the country. They also act as under-writers to new issues. In this way the broker community provide an organic linkage between the primary and the secondary markets. Thirdly, by providing a market quotation of the prices of shares and bonds—a sort of collective judgement simultaneously reached by many buyers and sellers in the market—the stock exchange serves the role of a sort of barometer not only of the state of health of individual companies, but also of the nation's economy as a whole. It is often not realised that changes in share prices are brought about by a complex set of factors, all operating on the market simultaneously. Share values as a whole are subject to secular trends set by the economic progress of the nation, and governed by factors like general economic situation, financial and monetary policies, tax change, political environment, international economic and financial developments, etc. These trends are influenced to some extent by the periodical cycles of booms and depressions in the free market economics.

A fact which needs to be emphasised is that the Stock Exchange in India also serve the joint sector units as also to some extent public sector enterprises. There is substantial private participation in the share capital of a number of government companies such as Balmer Lawire, Andrew Yule, Gujarat State Fertilisers Corporations, Gujarat Narmada Fertilizer Corporation, Hyderabad Allwyn, Polymers Corporation of Gujarat and M.Y.E.F. of Karnataka. In recent times some of the Central public sector companies have gone in the public debentures through the stock exchanges. Also, some public sector companies have in recent years opened a part of their share capital for public subscription.

Another important function that the stock exchanges in India discharge is in providing a market for giltedged securities i.e. securities issued by the Central Government, State Governments, Municipalities, Improvement Trusts and other public bodies. These securities are automatically listed on the stock exchanges when they are issued and transactions in these take place regularly on the stock exchanges. Also the Reserve Bank of India conducts market operation in governmental securities.

The beginning of trading in securities started in India towards the close of the 18th century when buying and selling of securities of the East India Company were going on in both Bombay and Calcutta. In Bombay the brokers used to gather under a banyan tree and in Calcutta under a neem tree. However, real beginning of stock exchange could only come after the introduction of joint stock companies and limited liability during the 1850s. The 1860s witnessed feverish dealings in share business on scrips like those of Port Canning in Calcutta and Back Bay Reclamation in Bombay (being quoted with premium of Rs 11,000 and Rs 50,000 over their paid-up value of Rs 1000 and Rs 50,000 respectively). Reckless speculations invariably led to a disaster. It was in the wake of it that the Bombay share brokers came together in July 1875 to form the first formally organised stock exchange in the country viz. The Bombay Stock Exchange. This was followed by Ahmedabad and Calcutta where stock exchanges were set up in 1894 and 1908 respectively. Stock exchanges also come up subsequently at Indore in 1930, Madras in 1937, Hyderabad in 1943, Delhi in 1947, and Bangalore in 1957. The corporate forms were different at different places. At some places the exchange took the form of a joint stock company. In other places it took the form of an Association. For a very long time, there was no regulation whatever by the Government and the stock exchanges were entirely guided by their own rules, regulations and bye-laws.

The beginning of the First World War brought activity and wealth to members of the Bombay and Calcutta Exchanges. The value of a card or seat on the Native Stock and Share Brokers' Association exchange went from Rs 2,900 in 1914 to Rs 48,000 in 1921. During this period there were no established trading rules. The public was not prohibited from entering the trading floor, where clients often transacted business among themselves. In 1918-19 some brokers manipulated the price of two highly traded stocks, Standard Mill and Madhavji Mill resulting in a crash. Fourteen brokers defaulted, forcing the exchanges to sell off their cards. The public criticism that followed the manipulative practices and the market slump of the early 1920s moved the Bombay Legislative Council to create a committee to look into the activities of the Bombay Exchange. Sir Wilfred Atlay, previous Chairman of the London Stock Exchange, was chosen to head the Committee. In its report the Committee stated:

The most sinister manifestation of speculation in Bombay is the frequent occurrence of corners in the market, and the policy and practice of the Association with regard to corners appears to us to constitute the head and front of their offending.

The Securities Contracts Control Act of 1925 was passed by the govern ent of Bombay. It annulled all trades unless made in accordance with rules approved by the Bombay Government. The exchange submitted a complete set of rules and regulations which gave itself the power to intervene in cases of manipulation and cornering the market. Although these rules were sanctioned by the Government in 1927, they were never effectively implemented.

The Second World War witnessed an enormous increase in trading. As usual this also meant a sharp increase in illegal conduct by brokers. Restrictions imposed on forward and options trading forced brokers to leave the exchange and to transactions in the adjacent streets. Nine out of ten deals in Calcutta in 1945 were rumoured to have taken place in the "Katai" market, just outside the Calcutta Stock Exchange. During the war years companies mushroomed and public issues multiplied. Many gullible investors were duped by the false promises offered, and came to ruins when many of these companies went into liquidation, or stock market prices crashed.

## AFTER INDEPENDENCE

After independence the Central Government appointed a Committee headed by A.D. Gorwala to report on the prevalent situation. The report of the Committee, submitted in 1951, led to the passage of the first Central Law, viz. its Securities Contracts (Regulation) Act of 1956 and the Securities Contracts (Regulation) Rules of 1957. This act gives the Central Government power to recognise stock exchanger, to approve their bye-laws etc. to issue directives to the stock exchanges on their functioning and to approve the appointment of Presidents and Executive Director in major stock exchanges. Initially, the 8 existing stock exchanges were recognised. Subsequently, following some promotional work done at the initiative of the government, 5 new stock exchanges were incorporated, viz. Cochin, Kanpur, Poona, Ludhiana and Gauhati these in total number of 13 stock exchanges.

Several other legislations also deal with the regulation of securities in India in a major way. The Companies Act of 1956 regulates the incorporation of companies and their periodic financial and other reporting requirements. Until May, 1992 the Capital Issues (Control) Act of 1947 strictly controlled the issue of securities. Now the SEBI. Act 1992 has assumed an important role. To a lesser extent, several other laws also affect the regulation of securities viz., the Foreign Exchange Regulation Act of 1973; the Banking Regulation Act of 1949; the Unit Trust of India Act of 1963; Indian Trusts Act; Reserve Bank of India Act of 1934; the Income Tax Act of 1961; the Estate Duty Act of 1953; Wealth Tax Act of 1957; Gift Tax Act of 1958; Public Debt Act of 1942; and the Indian Stamp Act of 1899.

### Securities and Exchange Board of India

However, now SEBI has assumed the role of regulatory authority which was earlier done by Central Government. The Government promulgated an ordinance, on 25 January, 1995 to amend the Securities and Exchange Board Act, 1992 so as to arm SEBI with necessary authority and powers for regulation and reform of capital market. Accordingly, through a notification issued under the Securities Contract (Regulation) Act,1956 the power to regulate stock exchanges was delegated to SEBI. This includes recognition, rules, articles, voting right, delivery contracts, stock exchange listing and nomination of public representatives. Under these functions many important developments have taken place, some of these are:

(i) Merchant banking brought under SEBI regulatory framework and a code of conduct issued.

(ii) SEBI notified regulations for primary and other secondary market intermediaries bringing them within the regulatory framework.

(iii) The 'Banker to the Issue', brought under purview of SEBI for investor protection.

(iv) SEBI's autonomy reinforced by allowing it to issue regulations and file suits without prior approval of the Central Government.

The preamble to the Securities Regulation Act states that it is "an act to prevent undesirable transactions in securities by regulating the business of dealing therein, by prohibiting options and by providing certain other matters connected therewith." This Act provides for the direct and indirect control of virtually all aspects of securities trading and the running of the stock exchanges. The Act makes every transaction in securities in any notified state or area illegal and punishable by fine and/or imprisonment if it is not entered into between or with members of a recognised stock exchange in the state or area. It also makes very much securities contract void.

After the advent of the SEBI that body has taken over the Central Government's functions in relation to the Stock Exchanges. It is the SEBI which now accords recognition to stock exchanges, approves their bye-laws, appoints public representatives on the Boards and, in general, supervises their working in general. In practice, actual administration of the provision of the Securities Regulation Act and of its rules is left to the exchanges themselves.

The first major intervention by the Central Government after 1956 Act was the complete ban imposed in 1969 on trading in shares for clearing, or forward trading in popular language, by a notification dated June 27, 1969. this was at a time when prices of essential commodities had registered appreciable rise and forward trading in commodities was suspected to be the major factor behind it. There was also reckless speculation going on in the share market and Government came out with a heavy hand along with the number of other measures to make forward trading in shares illegal. Under the Stock Exchange Rules, there can be three types of transactions:

(i) Spot delivery.
(ii) Hand delivery i.e. delivery of the script within 14 days.
(iii) Trading in "cleared" securities through the Clearing Houses under which it is possible to carry forward contract indefinitely on payment of only the difference between the contract price and the prevailing price.

It was the third type of transaction which was completely banned by the 1969 Notification. This had a very adverse effect on the stock market. Prices of shares in the Stock Exchanges nosedived, and there was a crisis. Shortly after that the Central Government appointed a Committee headed by Shri Anjiah to review the situation and recommend appropriate remedial measures. The Committee recommended the revival of forward trading subject to certain safeguards. However, the Central Government could not take any decision on this report, and forward trading remained ever since. This situation was further aggravated by the 1974 restriction put on payment of dividend by companies as part of the package of anti-inflation measures. The stock market generally remained depressed until after 1976 when many of the foreign companies were forced under the FERA to issue fresh capital to the public. But it was eventually the boom witness from 1980 to early 1990s which revived the share and put it on a glorious surge-forward

However, reckless speculation also revived its head and created considerable problems. The difficulty was that along with the ban on forward trading, the regulatory powers which the Exchange authorities had under the Rules for checking excessive speculation and forward trading also remained suspended. Initially, under the directions of the Government, the Stock Exchange Authorities did try to control the situation by ad-hoc measures, such as the imposition of margins on share brokers, who had been reporting unusually large volumes of activity. But this was not able to control the situation. In 1982, the Bombay Stock Exchange passed through three successive payment crises the first one over Reliance shares, the second over Century and the third over TISCO. Now, a certain amount of speculative activity is essential for the operation of the share market. However, the volume of speculation and of the informal forward trading which had always been going on must bear a relationship with the volume of actual transfer of securities. When speculation runs riot and the actual physical transfer of securities lags far behind, there is inevitably payments crisis.

From 1974 onwards, under a scheme first evolved by Bombay Stock Exchange and thereafter accepted by Calcutta, Delhi and Ahmedabad, a certain informal type of forward trading was revived. This was done by carrying forward the delivery contract beyond 14 days in an informal manner by concluding the earlier contract and entering into a new contract without any actual delivery, but merely the payment of the balance between the contracted price and market price, between the buyer and the seller. This system was being continued in an extra-legal manner without anyone questioning its legality. Obviously, this system could not stand the strain of the excessive speculative activity that carne about around 1982 and started escalating leading to payment crises one after another. The Central Government had to intervene repeatedly by forcing the Stock Exchanges to declare some leading members as defaulters or expelling them from membership, by increasing the number of Government nominees on the Boards of the leading Stock Exchanges and by forcing the imposition of stringent margin money and rigorous inspection. Also, on several occasions the financial institutions particularly the Unit Trust of India intervened by buying or selling thereby arresting market trends towards steep rise or steep fall of the price level. But this could not really deal with the basic crux of the problem. In 1983, Government at long last proceeded to face the real problem by permitting the revival of a limited volume of forward trading. This was done not by reviving the previous practice of trading in cleared securities as in the past, but ,by permitting carry-forward of contracts beyond 14 days up to a total period of 3 months. This was coupled with several other measures, such as providing for compulsory audit of the books of accounts of stock broking firms. This was resisted very much by the broking community. But Government struck to the ground. At the same time, Government also made enabling provision for membership of Stock Exchanges by private limited companies, and not merely by partnership firms of brokers which had hitherto been the practice. Steps were also taken to increase the number of non-broker Government representative in the Boards of Stock Exchanges on the ground that Stock Exchanges were no longer to be viewed as private checks of the brokers, but as public bodies in which Government, industry and the public at large were keenly interested. There were also other serious problems.

The phenomenal expansion of the market from 1980 brought out in sharp focus the infrastructural and legal inadequacies in dealing with large volume of business. There are company law restrictions on transfer of shares and transferability of shares which had been alright when Indian share market largely meant the Metropolitan towns and a few other centres. They are hopelessly inadequate to deal with the vastly enlarged number of shares and shareholders covering the length and breadth of the country. According to one estimate, the total number of shareholders in India in 1983 was about 15 million (Stock Exchange Foundation Bombay—Present Position of the Stock Market in India, Page 14). These shareholders are now scattered all over the country. Surely, in such a spread-out market, the limitation of 2 months or so for the validity of the transfer deeds is totally unsuitable. Similarly, the existing Stock Exchanges Regulations, the Banking Regulations, the conditions of postal delivery, and the F.E.R.A. Regulations relating to non-resident Indian shareholders are totally inadequate to deal with the tasks and responsibilities which have been imposed on the Stock Exchanges by the vastly increased market size. It has, therefore, become urgently necessary to examine the entire infrastructure, legal and physical and to introduce necessary changes wherever necessary. It is also essential to computerise Stock Exchanges operations as soon as possible.

The upsurge of the primary market in the 80s and early 90s created serious problems of interfacing with the secondary market, viz., the stock exchanges which still by and large, continue to the same old infrastructure and ways of working which suited the very narrow base of the capital market in the yesteryears but are totally out of time with the vastly grown size of the market and the desired tempo of work. It was this imbalance which facilitated the 'scam' of 1992 caused by reckless speculation, rampant dishonesty and fraudulent manipulation of the banking system. Unless the secondary market is re-oriented so as to discharge the new responsibilities cast on it by the recent developments and the means ramifications, this will act as a drag on the future growth of the primary market itself. Investors who are anxious to buy new securities are bound to get disenchanted if they face serious problems while trying to buy or sell scrips.

Majority of the stock exchange members until recently were old-fashioned lacking in both modern education and spirit of service to the clients. Many of them need to graduate from their role as pure stock brokers into a newer role as investment counsels or investment brokers. They are reluctant to permit new members and want to retain all control. There needs to be substantial enlargement of the number of brokers in major stock exchanges, such as Bombay, Calcutta and Delhi. Further, some of the existing brokers were engaged in reckless speculation. For over a decade, forward trading was not recognised by law and yet permitted in the major exchanges through extralegal means over which our laws and regulations had no control. Some year back, the Bombay Stock Exchange passed through several severe payment crises largely because of reckless speculation and over trading when deals were entered into trading without even a minimum volume of scrips bring available. However, introduction of trading in derivatives will practically solve the problems. But the basic question remains one of having a hard look at the existing rules and regulations, whether under Company Law or Stock Exchange Regulations or F.E.R.A., to find out how many of them have outlined their utility and are, by and large, anachronistic in the context of the sea changes that has taken place in the capital market.

Time has come when Stock Exchange Boards should no longer be just private clubs of the stock brokers but must be viewed as guardians of public interest. Essentially the stock exchange is a public institution in which Government, the industry and the public are vitally interested. Thus, there should be representatives from all these interests on the Boards. Indeed, such representatives should constitute a majority which at present consists of the elected representatives of the stock brokers who very often find it difficult to distinguish between their own private interests and the larger public interest. There should be uniformity of working hours amongst the Stock Exchanges in India. They should be linked up with one· another through computer terminals. In fact, there is a strong case for greater computerisation in our Stock Exchanges. Another consideration is that our secondary market still has very narrow base where two or three government institutions, viz., U.T.I., L.I.C. or G.I.C. have a commanding influence. Of late FIIs seem to have taken over this job. When they start buying, prices automatically go up. When they start selling, prices immediately go down. A market can be said to exist only when there are hundreds and thousands of independent decision-makers. Our stock market is still handicapped on account of the fact that decision-makers are few. Trusts and Provident Funds should be permitted to buy and sell stocks upto a small percentage of their funds—say one or two per cent. Also, the commercial banks which have been, by and large, absent from the market since 1969 should be allowed to utilize a small percentage of their funds to buy and sell shares.

Despite the phenomenal growth of the primary market, there is a dearth of floating stock in the secondary market. There should be concerted effort to induce and motivate closely held companies to make more and more of their shareholding available on the stock market. Public sector companies with an established record of profitability should sell up to 24 per cent of the shares to the public and get enlisted on the stock exchange as some of them have already done.

Our capital market as it has developed in the last decade has immense potential for attracting the savings of the community to corporate investment both for the Government and non-Government sectors. But this will not materialise unless we exercise a constant vigilance to discipline the working of the secondary market, viz., the Stock Exchanges. It should be ensured that genuine investors and traders in securities have opportunities for growth and the activities of pure speculators in the market are kept under strict control and discipline. In fact, much of the so-called boom in the market was due to the activities of the speculators and did not necessarily reflect the true worth of some .of the scrips. We should continue to be vigilant to see that there is adequate disclosure by companies, that there is no 'insider' trading, that there is free and hassleless transferability of shares by ordinary share-holders, and that genuine investors are not duped.

## FUTURE PROSPECTS

After rising to dizzy heights the stock market prices started crashing from 1992-93 onwards after the so-called 'scam'. Huge funds were fabulously withdrawn from Public Sector Enterprises and banks and invested in the stock market on the expectation that prices would further rise making possible for these institutions to make good profits. This did not happen on account of unearthening of scam and resultant downwards swing of prices. The, small investors, so long under protected umbrellas of Controller of Capital Issues. lost heavily and withdrew from the market causing general depression of prices. The stanglehold of FIIs had established on the market and made itself felt when they tried to book their profits and losses on large scale. In this situation SEBI thought it fit to ban 'badia' transactions (1993) which had already subjected to serious allegations of malpractice and auspicious speculation. This led to further depression in the market which has not been recovered even now after 5-6 years. Inspite of the SEBI's reintroducing legitimate forward trading with proper ckecks in recent years there has been no impact on the market where sentiments are absent and prices are still not recovering the early 90s level. Recent legislation for setting up depositories and the establishment of National Securities Depository Limited for carrying on share custodial is a step in the right direction.

The establishment of the NSE (National Stock Exchange) with screen based trading in 1993 was a major development. The NSE with its branches in other major centres and with hundreds of brokers with terminal facilities all over NSE has in a short time made its appearance felt and established itself as the leading stock exchange in the country. During 1999-2000 NSE accounted for 41 per cent of total turnover in equities and 51 per cent of turnover of government securities in the country. The NSE and BSE have made great strides in the computerised and electronic data processing. Some other sophisticated instruments have also been launched in recent years. One such institution is the National Securities Depository Limited (NSDL) which is responsible for dematerialisation of share scrips and has made possible paperless trading of share scrips under its auspices, significant number of companies have already entered into the arrangement with its incorporation. One more institution is Stock Holding Corporation which serves as a common custodian of share scrips, helped by the Financial Institutions (FIs).

But with all these changes most of the earlier stock exchanges have ceased to exist except on paper. With both the NSE and BSE accepting screen-based trading, nearly every broker has accepted screen-based trading under the NSE or the BSE. But a new stock exchange has now been reorganized by the SEBI viz. the MCX-MX Stock Exchange at Andheri which is expected to provide tough competition to the NSE and the BSE.

In recent years, computerisation has made significant progress in our stock market. Many rationalisation measures have been introduced such as the introduction of uniform working hours in all stock exchanges. A number of new institutions are also in the field, such as mutual funds, venture capital firms, credit rating corporations, the stockholders corporation, a corporation for over-the-counter trading, offshore growth funds like the India Fund, and the Security and Exchange Board of India (SEBI) in 1987. The decision in 1992 to permit overseas institutional investors to make portfolio investment in Indian companies subject to registration with the SEBI was a welcome move. In fact ever since the opening of our stock exchanges to the Foreign Financial Investors (FIIs) there has been excellent response. The FIIs bringing together around 10 billion dollars for portfolio investment in Indian stock market. Interestingly, this has proved a larger source of foreign funds flow than direct foreign investment in recent years.

Another welcome move is the partial privatisation of the government's development banking institutions which did play an invaluable role in the recent decades, but have somewhat outlived their utility on account of sweeping changes in the economy. IFCI, ICICI and IDBI have substantial private shareholding today turning them into joint sector companies. These development institutions together with the three investment institutions of LIC, GIC and UTI today hold a large percentage of equity in the private corporate sector. At times they even have majority of controlling shareholding in some of the major private sector companies. The question is whether they should continue to block their funds in shareholding in companies indefinitely or whether they should follow a systematic policy of selling some of these shares at the market price or at negotiated prices unlocking their funds and using them for assisting new worthwhile projects. It should be borne in mind that the object of development banks is not to control private sector companies or run them but to assist new ventures just as the object of investment institutions like LIC, GIC and UTI is to give their clients a good return and provide other special services.

## Some Recent Institutional Devices

Along with the Security and Exchange Board of India (SEBI) which has more or less taken over the regulatory functions of the Controller of Capital Issues, a number of new specialised agencies have been created to introduce much more sophistication than before in the stock market. These are:

(i) National Stock Exchange (NSE) has now replaced BSE as the largest stock exchange till recent past in terms of volume of transactions.

During 1999-2000, NSE accounted for 4 per cent of total turnover in equities and 55 per cent of turnover of government securities in the country.

(ii) Screen based trading all over India with brokers and dealers from various centres participating in trading Over the Counter Exchange of India (OTCEI) for small companies.

(iii) The National Securities Depository Limited(NSDL), the first depository tool in India, keep custody of shares of its members in a dematerialised form and provide for the paperless trading. BSE has also launched a depository, CSDL, in competition with NSDL.

(iv) Stock Holding Corporation that provides custodial services to the share portfolio held by the public financial institutions.

(v) National Securities Clearing Corporation Ltd. (NSCCL) incorporated to bring and sustain confidence in clearing and settlement of securities; to promote and maintain short and consistent settlement cycles; to provide counter-party risk guarantee, and to operate a tight risk containment system.

(vi) Several credit rating agencies viz., Credit Analysis and Research Ltd.(CARE) floated by IDBI, Investment Information and Credit Rating Agency of India (ICRA) by IFCI, and Credit Rating Information Services of India (CRISIL) floated by (ICICI) for rating debt instrument.

(vii) India Index Services and Products Limited (IISL), a joint venture between NSE and CRISIL, set up to provide indices and index services.

(viii) In the face of the strict competition provided by NSE and BSE, other major stock exchanges like Calcutta, Delhi have also introduced electronic data processing and providing screen based trading on an all India basis.

(ix) NSE.IT, a 100 per cent technology subsidiary of NSE, incorporated with overall goal of harnessing latest technology for optimum business use.

(x) MCX.MX Stock Exchange has appeared as a new stock exchange competing with the NSE and the BSE in equities and derivatives.

The advent of Foreign Institutional Investors (FII) on a very significant scale from 1992 onwards has also introduce a new situation in Indian stock market. They represented enormous buying and selling powers and their influence of the price to the great extent to date. Indian companies have also been permitted to go to global market through the issue of Global Depository Receipts (GDRs), American Depository Receipts (ADRs) and

Foreign Currency Convertible Bonds (FCCBS). But on th. whole the fact remains that after the introduction of free pricing the small investors, the prince of the market, was very inversely affected as a result of manipulation by dishonest company promoters and greedy merchant bankers and generally left the market. This is the main reason for continuous depression in the market, longest and unprecedented. We have to make very serious efforts with a view to woo him back to the market.

All these changes should be viewed against several other prospective developments like sweeping changes in the investor's profile covering both resident and non-resident investors, a remarkable increase in the variety of instruments and an immense growth in market liquidity, a tremendous improvement in the information provided to the investors to help them in making investment decisions; introduction of many modern trading techniques; introduction of demat securities, rolling settlement internet trading, derivatives trading, buy-back of shares; emergence of bodies of trained professionals and the growth of advisory services and the ongoing and irreversible processes of de-regulation of the hitherto government controlled economy and growing exposure to international capital market through current policies such as permitting off-shore funds to make portfolio investment in Indian companies; permitting Indian companies to raise capital outside; and the new joint venture guidelines permitting repatriation of capital for setting up joint ventures outside.

The National Stock Exchange promoted by the I.D.B.I. as a company has been functioning successfully. In fact, it has been considered the catalyst for much of the transformation in the securities market. The standards set by NSE in terms of market practices and technology are being followed by other exchanges. It is also working on a number of ideas: Overseas Trading terminals (so that its trading members be allowed to open trading terminals abroad); Debt market (for replicating trading framework of equity market to debt market); and rolling settlement for all securities (so far select securities are allowed).

Notwithstanding the current depression and gloom prevailing in the market, there is no doubt. that the capital market which played a very significant role during the decade of the 1980s will play an even greater role in the coming decades. Many companies in recent times have financed their projects very largely through funds raised from the market indicating the market's enormous potential. But market capitalisation is still only 10 per cent of GNP as against 23 per cent for the USA, 65 per cent for the UK and 134 per cent for Japan. The average profit earning ratios are still lower than in the UK, the USA and Japan. Capital market instruments constituted only 7.2 per cent of the total household financial savings as against 40.4 per cent for bank deposits. All these would indicate that there is tremendous scope for making use of household financial savings through the capital market during the Ninth Five-Year Plan. But in facing the challenges of the 21st century, serious and immediate attention must be given to the persisting problems of interfacing between the primary and secondary markets and the prevalence of rampant speculation. Finally, it must start functioning effectively as an effective watch dog policing against the ongoing reckless speculative and attendant evils like insider trading, gambling on the kerbs, manipulations with the unofficial premia. These tasks must be given utmost priority if the Indian stock market is to continue to be a barometer of economic progress. To turn to Keynes again, "speculations may do no harm as bubbles on a steady stream of enterprise. But the position is serious when enterprise becomes the bubble on a whirlpool of speculation."

The SEBI has been set up on a statutory basis not only as the main watchdog for the secondary market, but with substantial regulatory powers over the primary market. However, amendments in this Act from time to time empowered SEBI to regulate the capital market more effectively.

## Recent Developments in Securities Market

After a 4-5 years' slowdown year 1999-2000 saw a momentum in the Indian security market. In the primary market equity constituted 61 per cent of total resource mobilisation during April-December 1999-2000 as against a much lower share of 18 per cent in the same period of 1988-99. Prolonged uptrend movements in share prices during 1999-2000 also reflected the revival of the secondary market. Although three sectors, called golden triangle, consisting of information technology, pharmaceuticals and fast moving consumer goods largely contributed to this up trend in share prices. The SEBI continued its regulatory reform to further strengthen investors' protection and modernise the capital market through new measures, systems and instruments. The following changes are instable:

(i) The Securities Laws (Amendment) Ad, 1999 passed by the Parliament in December 1999 expands the definition of securities to include derivatives and units of Collective Investment Schemes. This will allow the introduction of index futures and other derivatives and strengthen the legal framework for regulating Collective Investment Schemes.

(ii) SEBI notified the draft Regulations for Collective Investment Schemes.

(iii) The Securities Laws (second amendment) Act, 1999 amends the SCRA, 1956, the SEBI Act, 1992 and the Depositories Act, 1996 to empower the Securities Appellate Tribunal to dispose of appeals under these Acts.

(iv) The requirement of "actual payment" of dividends before an Initial Public Offer (IPO) was replaced by an "ability to pay" criterion.

(v) The "par value" concept was abandoned so that companies can now issue shares of any value. Companies with demat shares can alter the par value indicated in the Memorandum and Articles of Association. Existing companies with shares of Rs. 10 or Rs. 100 can avail of this facility by consolidating or splitting these shares.

(vi) SEBI issued Regulations for Credit Rating Agencies.

SEBI also considered and accepted a system envisaging the use of he existing infrastructure of stock exchanges for marketing IPOs. Though the secondary market has not been free from price volatility, the strong margining system and other risk containment measures could ensure the safety of the market and the payment system.

Another factor which has qualitatively changed the capital market receives is the central Governments disinvestment policy in respect of central public sector enterprises. In a large number of central PSE's the government has issued new shares to the public. Through these successive Initial Public offers handled by the Disinvestment Department of the Union Ministry of Finance companies like Coal India, BHEL and ONGC have substantial public shareholding today. Although government holds more than fifty per cent and will continue to hold it. Today around fifty CPSE's are listed on the Bombay Stock Exchange, but they account for around one-third of the capitalized market value. The foreign institutional investors (FIIs) control very significant market capital today.

## CHAPTER 9

# Government Control over Distribution and Price of Essential Commodities

Government Control over the price and the distribution of essential commodities has emerged as a very important sector of India's economy, and the performance of the public agencies will be a critical factor in the future overall industrial growth. Production, however efficient becomes purposeless if the goods produced are not delivered to the final user at the right time, in right quantity, and at the right price by an equally efficient distribution network. Unfortunately, the existing private sector trade channels in India, although claiming to operate, on a very low margin, one of the most economical distribution systems in the world, have also acquired in public estimation a certain notoriety on account of their well-known malpractices and a general proneness to take advantage of scarcity situations Adulteration, short-weight of goods, hoarding, manipulated scarcity, profiteering, blackmarketing, unduly excessive rates of credit and other anti-social and unethical practices not only create public disaffection, but also saddle the economy with very high costs. It is said that consumers in India pay several hundred crores of rupees every year on account, of short-weighted goods alone. While public distribution system is an answer, it has its limitations and cannot in any case fill the vacuum caused by the dismantling of the traditional retail and wholesale trading system over the length and the breadth of our vast country. Thus there is need on the one hand for greater vigilance over the existing distribution net-work, and on the other hand for organising public distribution agencies in the more vulnerable sectors, and more encouragement to consumers' cooperatives in other areas to provide growing competition and the effect of demonstration to private business. Apart from its relevance to the society as a whole, distribution also acquires a great importance in a developing economy like India on account of its employment potential, and also for the fact that a substantial number of industrial raw materials are in short supply and need to be distributed fairly and equitably among competing users.

## LEGAL FRAMEWORK OF COMMODITY CONTROL

A system of commodity control came into operation during the Second World War under the cover of the Defence of India Rules. Statutory rationing of food grains was introduced in a number of large cities (e.g. Calcutta) and distribution and price control were also imposed over a large number of items like steel, cement, kerosene and C.I. sheets. Although, after the War, the Central Government through various temporary measures, continued to exercise many of these controls, there was some hesitation about giving them a permanent statutory base. It was only in 1954 that Entry 33 in List III of the Constitution was amplified into its present shape by the Third Amendment bringing within the purview of Central legislation, in addition to the products of 'scheduled' industries as defined in the Industrial (Dev. and Reg.) Act, such other commodities like imported goods, foodstuffs, cattle fodder, raw cotton and raw jute etc. as would be necessary. Thus Parliament was empowered to make laws controlling production supply or distribution of any or all of these commodities. The basic legal frame for commodities control is provided by:

(i) the Essential Commodities Act, 1955, and

(ii) Section 18(g) of the Ind. (Dev and Reg.) Act, 1951 relating to the products of 'scheduled' industries.

There are also a number of other specific laws covering specific industries in the field of commodity control, e.g. the Coffee Act, 1952; the Tea Act, 1953; the Rubber Act, 1947; the Coir Industries Act, 1953.

The Essential Commodities Act provides in the interest of the general public for Government control over the production, supply and distribution of or trade and commerce in certain essential commodities which are listed. These commodities fall into three broad categories:

(i) Food items;

(ii) Raw fitlaterials for industries;

(iii) Products of the centrally-controlled industries.

This list of commodities is not exhaustive and Central Government has the power to declare any commodity as an essential commodity for purposes of the Act, if it is a commodity with respect to which Parliament has power to make law under Entry 33 of List III. Hence the list is changed from time to time according to the exigencies of the situation.

Section 3 of this Act confers wide powers on the Central Government to issue orders regulating or prohibiting the production, supply or distribution of any essential commodity if it is of the opinion that it is necessary or expedient to do so for maintaining or increasing supply of an essential commodity or for securing its equitable distribution and availability at fair prices. There can also be delegation of this authority to the State Government or to any authority under a State Government. Under this considerable authority is delegated to authorities such as the District Collector in matters like compulsory procurement of food grains or the enforcement of levy on farmers. This section gives the Central Government practically an unlimited authority with regard to the policies of control it may follow from time to time in respect of various commodities. To make this authority even more complete, it has been provided that an order made under Section 3 is to be effective even if it is inconsistent with any statute or any statutory instrument. Thus, the authority of the Government agencies under the Essential Commodities Act is nearly absolute. Distribution control under this can include things such as specifying distribution margins, allocating products on the basis of State-wise or area-wise consumption or class of consumers and :restricting inter-state, inter-zone or even inter-district movements.

It should be noted that under this Act, all powers emanate from the Central Government, and the State Government or the authorities subordinate to it acts as a delegate of the Centre within the scope of the authority assigned to it and subject to any conditions imposed or directions given by the Central Government regarding the exercise of the delegated powers. This enables the Central Government to keep an overall control over various State Governments and also create some sort of uniformity of practices all over the country. From the very nature of things, there has to be regular consultations between the Centre and the States, and the Centre shapes its policies in the light of these consultations.

Under the Essential Commodities Act, a large number of orders have been issued covering a wide variety of commodities. Large discretionary powers have been conferred on administrative officers in many cases and a very large body of administrative procedures and rules have also come into existence. Apart from their writ jurisdiction, courts have for practical purposes, very little to do in this field of bewildering complexity, Parliamentary control through the Committee is Subordinate Legislation, is also marginal. Rules and Regulations not only multiply at a very fast pace, but are also often subjected to amendments without adequate notice to the public leading to confusion and uncertainty. The entire field has become highly administration dominated.

Section 18 (g) of the Industries (Development and Regulation) Act, empowers the Central Government to regulate supply and distribution of and trade and commerce in any article relatable to a scheduled industry which means both finished products and also imported articles of the same nature and description as the articles manufactured. A number of orders have been promulgated under this Act. e.g. Cement Control Order, 1961; Commercial Vehicles (Distribution and Sale) Control Order, 1963; Motor Cars (Distribution and Sale) Control Order, 1963; Motor Cars (Distribution and Sale) Control Order, 1960 etc. There seems to be a good deal of overlapping between Section 18 (g) of the 1 (D and R) Act and the essential Commodities Act, 1955. This tends to create some confusion and it should be considered whether, after the passing of the Essential Commodities Act, 1955 which covers a much broader area, there is any more necessity for Section 18 (g) of the 1 (D and R) Act, which was added to the act in 1953 to continue.

Act 1986 also offers some safeguards to the consumers through some quasi-judicial tribunals. This comprehensive law which came into force on April IS, 1987 also seeks to give due recognition to consumer organisations and consumer movement and to provide speedy redressal and compensation to the consumers. The Annexure to this chapter gives a summary of the provisions of this Act.

## DISTRIBUTION OF FOODGRAINS

The Government of India inherited from the colonial government a structure of public distribution system hurriedly organised during the war years covering very largely the urban centres. Although this was dismantled in 1954 following Rafi Ahmed Kidwai's policy of decontrol, the Government remained all along alive to the significance of distribution of essential commodities. As early as 1950-51 the Planning Commission observed that "our knowledge of the present distribution mechanism, its composition and distribution and the ways various links in the system are related is at present inadequate ... before decision can be taken, there is need for clearing up factual position regarding the amount of capital involved, profit margins, costs of operation, number of people employed and related aspects of the question. "The subsequent plan document have always reflected a growing awareness of the importance of and the need for equitable distribution of essential commodities, especially to more vulnerable sections of the population. With the developing shortage of food grains from the Second Plan onwards there started a process of abandonment of de-control and rebuilding of the public distribution system. This reached its climax in 1965-66 when formal statutory rationing covering all the big urban centres was reinforced and a system of informal rationing was sought to reach out to the rural areas. The Ministry of Agriculture was the administrative ministry at the centre for food grains procurement and distribution. Now the Department of Public Distribution under the Ministry of Consumer Affairs and Public Distribution is given this responsibility. The Department is concerned with the formulation of policies concerning the food grains sector— procurement, storage, movement and distribution. The Department implements the scheme of minimum support price to the producers of wheat, paddy and coarsegrains and the distribution of food grains from the Central Pool. A close watch is kept on the stock and price levels of food grains and efforts are made to ensure their adequate availability at reasonable prices in different parts of the country.

The distribution of foodgrains in urban areas represent one of the best examples of the complementary nature of private trade and Government agencies. The number of fair price shops in the country steadily increased and rose from 2.33 lakh at the close of 1975-76 to about 4.6 lakh in 2000. For a long time Government as part of procurement strategy experimented with arranging 'surplus' States and 'deficit' States into various zones among which movement of foodgrains except on Government account or with Government approval was not allowed. For the next few years the strategy was to treat each State as a single rice zone or wheat zone, but to allow free movement of inferior types of food grains.

But a very significant change was made on April 12, 1977 when the Government decided for 1977-78 to treat the entire country as a single wheat zone and abolish all restrictions on the inter-state movement of wheat. Movement of wheat products was already free. The only restriction was on roller flour mills who could not purchase wheat in the open market, but only from government stocks. The other key aspects of this new price and procurement policy were the increase in the procurement price; the abandonment of procurement target; discontinuance of procurement of wheat levy on producers or traders; and the reliance on a price support programme rather than a procurement drive; a procurement target and a procurement price have become meaningless in the present context of plenty. The announced procurement price would therefore really be the support price.

The prices at which Government agencies will purchase rice and wheat respectively are announced every year by the Central Government on the basis of the recommendations made by the Agricultural Prices Commission, a quasi-government but autonomous body appointed by the Central Government. There are always heated controversies on this issue on account of the powerful farmers lobby from states like Punjab and Haryana seeking to get enhanced prices, and the deficit states seeking to push down the purchase price to protect consumers' interests. The Central Government has to balance these two conflicting interests in announcing the price.

In 1972 the Central Government took a decision to nationalise wholesale trading in foodgrains all over the country. But this policy was abandoned after a while in 1973 largely on the ground of the administrative constraints and financial strains and also partly under severe pressure from private business. The wheat policy of 1977-78 sought to place considerable reliance on the private trade to supplement the efforts of the State Trading Agencies. The Government agencies like the Food Corporation of India reeling under the pressure of a huge buffer stock will welcome the relief offered by the purchase of a sizeable quantity by the private trade. The competition offered to the inflexible giant sized Food Corporation of India is also likely to be welcomed by the small and middle farmers. As the new single-zone wheat policy for the first time makes a distinction between average and superior quality wheat, private trade can also play a role by supplying high income urban consumers with superior quality wheat where the margin of profit is higher, and which is not usually offered by the public distribution system.

## FOOD CORPORATION OF INDIA

The Food Corporation of India set up in 1965 under a Parliamentary legislation has now emerged as the Government's chief agency for internal procurement of foodgrains, handling imports, storage and distribution of food-grains and for implementing the national food policy. It is also to act as a countervailing force to contain the speculative activities of certain sections of private trade and safeguard the interests of the producer and the consumer. It has among its other objectives the primary objective of ensuring reasonable prices to the producer protecting the interests of the consumers, and attaining the commanding position in the foodgrains trade. The Corporation may also with the previous approval of Central Government,

(i) promote by such means as it thinks fit production of foodgrains and other food stuffs;

(ii) set up or assist in the setting up of rice mills, flour mills and other undertakings for the processing of food grains and other food stuffs; and

(iii) discharge such other functions as may be prescribed or as are supplemental, incidental or consequential to any of the functions conferred on it under the Food Corporations Act 1964.

After the teething troubles of the initial years the Food Corporation of India became the main procurement agency in surplus States. The F.C.I. has now built up an impressive inventory of foodgrains. This national buffer stock has acted as the major anti-inflationary force in the economy of the country. But it has also imposed tremendous strain on the Corporation for its storage and maintenance. This forced the Corporation to adopt various unconventional methods of storage apart from utilising the available god own space to the maximum extent, e.g., obtaining unused and abandoned airstrips and strong grains in polythene covers; encouraging private parties to construct god owns on guarantee of occupation by Food Corporation of India. The Government assists the Food Corporation to maintain price stability by reimbursing the difference between the Central issue prices and the economic cost including the cost of storage. Every year the Central budget makes handsome provision for this subsidy. The food subsidy steadily increased over the years. In the post-1991 budget exercises serious efforts were made to reduce the huge fiscal deficit by among other things substantial reduction in the food subsidy. But there has been little sucess in the face of strong political opposition to such structural adjustment at the cost of the beneficieries of the Public Distribution System. Incidentally, the final GATT treaty contains specific footnotes to remove fears that this treaty may be used to abolish food subsidies and exempts developing countries from the disciplines involved in "Public stock-holding" and foodaid operation. Thus our PDS, including procurement and distribution is not in any way affected by the GATT. In any case it is a subsidy for the consumer, not for the farmer. The question is whether we cannot avoid such huge subsidy and the strain on the budget by cost reduction, economy and rationalisation at various levels of handling by the Food Corporation. The Food Corporation has also been taking a series of measures to speed up procurement and streamline distribution of food grains and essential commodities. It acts in coordination with and often as agents of State Government food and supply agencies.

Along with foodgrains, it is also handling from time to time other essential items like sugar and imported edible oil. The Central Government makes monthly allocation to the State Government. Where the State Government handles rationing through its own departmental agencies as in Maharashtra, it transfers the stock from Food Corporation god owns to its own godowns and repacks them into standard weight bags. Ration shops indent their weekly or fortnightly requirements through the wholesalers, usually wholesale cooperative, to whom they send along with the indent the cheques for the cost of the foodgrains. To take one example, there are about 2,100 licensed ration shops in Greater Bombay covering a population of 8.4 millions and providing against about 2 million ration cards specified quantities of wheat, rice, jawar and wheat products (suji, maida) at uniform prices fixed by the Government. Ration cards are issued by the Civil Supplies Department of the State Government through rationing offices. All such cards are registered with one of the licensed ration shops. Thus there is an interesting admixture of the Central Government agencies (Food Corporation of India), the State Government Food and Civil supply agencies, private traders and cooperatives. In most of the States the Food Corporation has now taken over the role of handling and storing agents on behalf of the State Governments with the result that it handles the foodgrains from the stage of procurement on to the point where these are handed over to the ration shops, usually privately owned but sometimes cooperatives for actual disbursements to consumers and sometimes directly to consumers under schemes such as and the recent scheme MGEGA.

A full-fledged Ministry of Consumers' Affairs and Public Distribution has now been set up in the Central Government. It is important that in all such promised schemes there is proper targeting of the truly poor, and that resources are not given away to those who do not strictly need such subsidised support.

## TARGETED PUBLIC DISTRIBUTION SYSTEM (TPDS)

This replaced the restwhile PDS from June 1997. This replacement was necessitated on account of two points: for its urban bias; and its failure to serve effectively the poorer sections of the population. Under the new system a two tier Subsidised pricing system was introduced to benefit the poor. The essential features of TPDS are:

(i) Government of India is committed to making food grains to the States to meet the requirement of food available grains at the scale of 20 kg (from 10 kg, w.e.f. April 1, 2000) per month per family at specially subsidised prices to population falling below the officially estimated poverty line (BPL families).

(ii) The States would also receive the quantity needed for the transitory allocation to Above Poverty Line (APL) population.

(iii) The State governments were to streamline the PDS by issuing special cards to BPL families and selling essential articles under TPDS to them at specially subsidised prices, with better monitering of the delivery system.

(iv) Government originally decided to fix the Central Issue Price (CIP) at 50 per cent of the economic cost for BPL and at the economic cost (earlier it was 90 per cent of economic cost) for APL population, as the non-poor were required to buy at near open market price. However, m practice these percentages went down to about 40 per cent of economic cost (1996-97) for BPL and 80 per cent for APL.

The scheme is now in operation in all states/UTs except Delhi and Lakshadweep.

Keeping in view the consensus on increasing the allocation of foodgrains to BPL population, and to better targetise food subsidy, Government of India has increased the allocation of BPL families from 10 kg. to 20 kg. of foodgrains per family per month at 50 per cent of economic cost and the APL allocation at the economic cost w.e.f. 1.4.2000. The allocation for APL has been retained at the same level which was allotted at the time of introduction of TPDS. It has also been decided that in case any State/UT demands any additional quantity of wheat or rice over and above their normal monthly allocation, it will be allotted at economic cost in view of comfortable stock position in central pool.

## OTHER ESSENTIAL COMMODITIES

Some of the State Governments are handling through their Civil Supplies Departments commodities like cement, kerosene, edible oil and sugar. From the 60's there was much public clamour to which Government could not be unresponsive that it should organise an efficient public distribution system to ensure that the common man, the vulnerable one, was able to get minimum of goods of everyday need at reasonable prices.

In considering the options for distribution of essential articles we have to bear in mind a few very important factors, viz.,

(i) The malpractices and deficiencies which were found in the past in the distribution of essential articles were a result of shortages in supplies and are not inherent features of the existing distribution system. In fact this has been well proven by the fact that with the restoration of supplies the malpractices have disappeared. Soap, vanaspati, cars, tyres, battery cells and a host of other products have all become competitively available and the trade is not only unable to charge any premium but has to work hard to get sales. Therefore, the real remedy is to improve supplies so that distribution becomes a competitive activity.

(ii) In designing a Distribution System for essential articles we should be clear about the group it is aimed for. It is of no use producing Janata cloth for the masses without finding out what the masses need or whether the masses can afford it. Therefore, we should realise that the Distribution System everyone is so concerned about is at present meant for the urban population (i.e., people living in towns with population over 5,000) which constitutes about 20 per cent of our total population.

(iii) The existing Indian trade channels provide one of the most efficient and economical Distribution Systems in the world, because it is able to operate on very low margins (provided the product is adequately supplied and temptations are not placed in its way). If it is to be displaced by a bureaucracy the steep increase in cost to the consumer has to be reckoned with.

Against this background we may have options open for distribution of essential commodities to the urban population.

**State Owned Stores**

The overhead costs of operating emporia owned by the State are so high in terms of salaries that these can be operated in very large cities only where there is a concentration of consumers in a small radius with cheap transport. Apart from the cost, the service in such emporia and the problems of controls in inventory, on finance and on staff etc., will pose disproportionate problems.

It is also unfortunately true that most of these institutions gradually become bureaucratic as they have to be moulded to conform to the Government agencies which control their activity. This not only increases overheads but also deprives them of the attitude of service. For example, the State-owned Distribution System in a metropolitan city in India supplies consumer products to about 2,000 Fair Price Shops. In the same city our products are distributed to 7,000 outlets through trade channels at less than one-fifth the cost. This comparison gives some idea of the disparities in overhead costs.

Furthermore, the State emporia utilise in urban areas funds which have been collected from the tax payers with the primary objective of economic development that should benefit the less affluent majority of populace in the non-urban areas.

Therefore, while a few such State emporia may exist in metropolitan cities they do not present a suitable model for distribution of essential articles even to the urban consumers.

### Consumer Co-operatives

The other option to be examined is that of co-operatives in several fields, which have had a chequered history in our country from the beginning of this century. We are concerned only with co-operatives in the field of distribution of consumer goods and not to several other types of co-operatives which have a remarkable record of success as in the case of the Kaira District Co-operative for milk.

The consumer co-operative system has a three-tier structure consisting of a Federation in each State at the apex, Central Wholesale Societies at the intermediate level and the primary consumer stores at the base. While the State Federation covers, the whole State, the Wholesale Societies cover all or part of a district (Greater Bombay has 8) and their membership could be of individuals or of primary consumer co-operatives which have only individual consumers as members at their location.

The apex Federation mainly provides part of the capital through equity participation in the Central Wholesale Societies. These Wholesale Societies act as procurement agencies for the consumer co-operatives which are financed through loans from district co-operative banks.

Taking into account the strengths and weaknesses of consumer co-operatives, one could conclude that they have a definite place in the urban market, if only as contingent channels of distribution of essential articles in short supply. When products are in plenty, co-operatives will find it difficult to compete with the normal retail trade and can survive only with heavy Government subsidy which is a costly diversion of public finance, that is meant for development. The Kendriya Bhandar, launched as a government effort in Delhi region has achieved moderate success, but it is heavily dependent on government's financial and managerial support.

### Retail and Wholesale Trade

The third option is to make use of the traditional channels of trade and attempt to correct their deficiencies. Companies like Hindustan Lever have used these trade channels over the decades with great success.

Under the present public distribution system the essential goods of daily use are distributed through fair price shops. consumer cooperatives and private retailers who are issued licences for the purpose. There were about 4.6 lakhs fair price shops in 2000 serving a load of 11 crore cards. The Ministry of Agriculture apart from handling foodgrains procurement and distribution, also deals with allied items like sugar and edible oil. The Centre has set up its own Civil Supplies Ministry and the State Governments have their own civil supplies departments to look after the distribution of essential commodities in their respective jurisdictions. The Ministry of Civil Supplies has now been entrusted with the overall responsibility for distribution of essential goods other than foodgrains.

## OTHER RELEVANT GOVERNMENT MEASURES

The Companies (Amendment) Act, 1974 which came into force from January 1, 1975 introduced a new Section 294 AA. According to this, the Centre can prohibit sole selling agents in certain cases and prior sanction of the Government is necessary for the appointment of sole selling agents of any individual, firm or company which has a substantial interest in the employing company. Furthermore, a special resolution and Government's sanction have been made necessary conditions for appointment of sole selling agents in a company having paid-up capital of Rs 50 lakhs or more.

Some recent changes made by the Government in its policy regarding distribution of several essential commodities may also be noted. Both cement and aluminium were decontrolled in 1989. Gold control has also been done away with. With improved availability of steel, the Government announced a new policy for decontrol of distribution and price of steel in 1992. Under this the main steel producers like SAIL, TISCO and IISCO will be free to fix their selling prices and sell them through their own distribution channels. But while the Government has in recent times liberalised its policies for nearly all industries, drugs and pharmaceuticals still constitute one visible area of licensing and price controls. This has resulted in a steady decline of profitability (from a low level of 4% of profit after tax as a percentage of the gross capital employed in 1982-83 to 2.8% in 1990-91). This has driven the industry towards sickness and has seriously obstructed growth and exports and introduction of new drugs by MNCs in the Indian market. Price control in this industry also illustrates the unsustainability of controlling prices of end products without controlling the prices of inputs. The manufacturers are to appoint their representatives at different points, who will call on consumers and book their orders. Thus, easy availability and simplified distribution will help reduce stockpiling by both consumers and producers.

## PRICE CONTROL

Price control, usually under the Essential Commodities Act, but at times even under informal arrangement made by the Government, plays an important role in the regulation, of the entire spectrum of economic activities including production, distribution and consumption. Price controls fall into two categories: statutory and informal. Statutory price control exists in respect of commodities whose prices are fixed by a semi-judicial body such as the Tariff Commission and whose enforcement is imposed by a statute. Examples of such statutes are the Sugar Control Order, the Cement Control Order, the News-print Control Order, etc. The pricing of a product statutorily regulated is· therefore set by the Government, and can only be changed by the Government. Informal price control, on the other hand, is in essence an administrative understanding between the Government and the industry concerned to maintain existing prices to the extent possible, and effect revisions only after obtaining the prior approval of the Government. These prices are not notified in any statute, and to that extent informal price controls do not involve any penalty clause. In actual practice, however, the term "informal" is a bit of a misnomer, because governmental authority is vested with such tremendous controlling powers, that in the eyes of the industry its most informal measures acquire all the solemnity of formal controls.

Having made a distinction between statutory and informal control, mention should also be made of the different levels at which price controls have operated in the past. For some items, notable examples of which are cement and steel, the prices to the producers were statutorily controlled. These are retention or ex-factory prices. At the same time, consumer prices are uniformly regulated throughout the country through an arrangement of freight equalisation. For other items such as petroleum products the concept of ex-factory prices is retained, but consumer prices are determined on the basis of zonal freight costing. In respect of still other products such as fertilizers, drugs etc., price control is exercised only at the consumer level. In short, there seems to be infinite variations in the form of control, each more complex and sophisticated than the other, requiring at every step an elaborate administrative structure to implement them.

Prices are also determined by the changes announced from time to time by administered prices of products controlled by, the Government, the products being energy inputs—petroleum, electricity urea fertilisers. Rises in these prices announced periodically both for raising resources and to make more or less these market-based. Anyway these rises have effect on general price level. Raises or reduction in the rates of central excise, custom and State sales taxes also have a direct effect on the price level of many commodities.

Rigid adherence to price control without proper attention to the supply side can often lead to shortages, quality deterioration, black-money, spurious products and black market. Honest firms can be driven out of business, and a negative image is promoted among international investors. It can at best be a short-term remedy in a situation of emergency like war, and can never be a long-term panacea.

The rationale for price control in the minds of many people is two fold: (a) to contain inflation (b) to enable the vulnerable sections of our population to be able to afford essential supplies. Both these objectives are better met through measures other than price control which will never be able to achieve either of the two objectives.

The only effective means of dealing with or countering inflation is not price control, but a combination of fiscal and monetary policies that reduces money supply and deficits and at the same time stimulates economic freedom and greater competition to increase supply of products. The economies of USA, Japan and Europe do not any more resort to price controls to contain inflation. They have adopted fiscal and monetary policies which have successfully brought down inflation. This can be done by raising interest rates as the UK & USA have done for quite some time and Germany has done in the more recent past. They also reduce government deficits even at the risk of lower economic growth.

When it comes to assisting vulnerable sections of society on a consistent basis, the only way is for government to subsidise directly the supply of essential commodities like food grains, edible oils, kerosene, sugar etc. through a public distribution system as is practised in our country already. It is not by controlling the price given to the producer.

If India had practised price control of food grains, we would never have enabled the Indian farmer/producer to produce increasing quantities to meet the food requirements of our population. Price control would have discouraged the producers. There would have been no Green Revolution and we would have had to import foodgrains which in turn would have made it even more expensive. It was through a well conceived Price Support system the opposite of price control) that India became self sufficient in foodgrains.

Having thus assured adequate availability through incentives to the producer, the best way to ensure supplies at affordable prices to vulnerable sections is through a subsidised public distribution programme based on income of the recipient.

In trying to appreciate the background behind some of the recent price control measures we should note that the recent past has been characterized by (i) rapid international price rises; (ii) domestic price inflation and (iii) stagnation of investment. All teh three phenomena have had an impact on the formulation and revision of price controls. Whereas price controls tend to perpetuate themselves and be forgotten like spiderwebs in dirty corners when the overall price level is reasonably stable, this is no longer so under conditions of rapidly increasing prices. When inflation sets in, price revisions have to be undertaken more and more frequently, especially in a system like India where only a fairly limited number of products have regulated prices. Under these conditions prices of imported or domestic raw materials and inputs increase, investment costs go up, profitability goes down, production stagnates or is diverted into non-controlled generally less essential lines of product (such as the more expensive varieties of products—luxury soaps, vanaspati, art paper etc.) and investment levels fall off.

Spurred by these circumstances the price control system has come under severe attacks in recent times. First of all, the level of controlled prices has had to be revised upwards for these products from time to time, in particular for those items whose prices have fluctuated widely in the international markets. Off handedly it appears that price adjustments have ranged from 3 per cent to over 100 per cent, and were justified either by the increase in domestic inputs or by the rise in international raw materials (oil, fertilizer). In the case of fertilizer, the increase in the domestic sales price was only in part passed on to the domestic producers; the remainder was mopped up to compensate for the even larger price increases, and the losses suffered on the imported fertilizer.

But the recent changes went further than a simple raising of price levels. Because of the widespread and rapid rise in prices, and probably because of the stagnant investment levels as well, the process of rethinking on the price control system which had already set in before, was accelerated and carried further. Having had to adjust the price levels more and more frequently because of inflation, in many cases in the face of a shrunken level of domestic demand and consequently with a largely reduced, and often eliminated, gap between supply and demand, the responsible authorities were forced into wondering whether the game was still worth the candle, and whether it would not be better to get rid of some of the controls altogether. In fact that is what they decided to do. In some of these cases the decontrol was brought about after some previous price rises had been granted. In others the decontrol was effected right away.

In fact "decontrol" is often the wrong word for what happened. Although in some cases there has been pure and simple decontrol and producers are now authorized to set prices as they please (although the Damocles' sword of renewed control is always hanging about their head), in some cases the decontrol is accompanied by a number of (often unpublished) riders and guidelines partly circumscribing the freedom of action of the producers. These riders may include the obligation to produce a certain percentage of cheaper varieties (e.g. the "Janata" soap) or to use only a certain percentage of raw materials input (e.g. groundnut in the case of Vanaspati), in which cases we are really dealing with a kind of production control. In a number of other instances a dual pricing system has been set up, forcing the producer to sell a certain quantity or percentage of his production to Government procurement agencies (as for the steel, paper, sugar and foodgrains) in which case we are in effect dealing with a form of distribution control. In other instances still, the product has been decontrolled, but only after obtaining a promise from the producers that they will distribute their production over the country according to a pre-determined demand pattern (as in the case of truck-tyres). Finally, in some other instances (kept very hush-hush) the Government has let the producers free to set their own prices provided (a) capacity utilization levels are satisfactory, and (b) profit levels remain within certain specified limits.

An efficient and trustworthy distribution system is essential in an economy like ours where marginal shortages can sometimes lead to very disproportionate distortion in prices thereby benefiting only the more privileged sections of the population. In recent years the public distribution system in India has gone on expanding fast and it will, according to all indications, continue to grow. However, In view of the country's vast size and complexities it may not be possible to rely completely on Government agencies and dispense with retail private sector channels altogether. The problem of distribution of essential goods is going to receive an enormous amount of attention from both the Government and the consumers. Distribution employs and has the potentiality of employing a very significant percentage of our population with comparatively much less investment. In view of this, the chronic shortages of essential goods of mass consumption and their rising prices the Government should come forward with a long term distribution policy frame and a concerted plan of action, rather than only reacting to a crisis as it appears and coming out with ad-hoc temporary palliatives. For instance, the recent practice of government with regard to edible oil and vegetables especially onion. In that policy and plan of action Government or semi-Government agencies must necessarily hold the commanding heights, but there should be considerable room for a disciplined private sector specially at the retail level. For with all its known faults the traditional retail and wholesale trading system over the length and breadth of our country can be totally dismantled only at the risk of serious dislocation.

In recent years in quite a number of items government have been following a policy of dual pricing, i.e., charging one price for priority users, and allowing the market price for all other users. The most notable example is suger. Also, the prices charged by the public sector agencies for certain essential products like petroleum, electricity, where they have monopoly or near-monopoly have assumed a very important position. Price rise in these items from time to time in order to avoid government's budgetary support to such undertakings in the face of their mounting losses have a cascading effect leading to general price rise.

## CONSUMER PROTECTION ACT, 1986

This is the latest piece of legislation in an area where there are already several overlapping laws, and yet there is no significant impact on the life of the ordinary people who continue to be exploited by unscruplous traders.

The justification for this legislation was that the earlier legislative measures have been successful to some extent in creating and maintaining competition and protecting the consumers against false or misleading advertisements, bargain sales, bait and switch selling, and other similar unfair trade practices but consumers need to be protected not only from the effects of restrictive and unfair trade practices but also from defective goods or deficient services, over-charging of prices and unscrupulous exploitation. Further, ignorance of the consumer of his rights, lack of consumer movement and lack of due recognition to the consumer organisations have also been some important factors which led to the enactment of the Consumer Protection Act, 1986, (hereinafter referred to as the Act). The Act is a comprehensive legislation with its main thrust on giving speedy redressal and compensation to the consumers. The Act (except Chapter III) came into force on April 15, 1987.

The Act applies to all goods and services unless specifically exempted by the Central Government by notification. For the first time in the history of the socioeconomic legislation of our country, the role of the consumer organisations has been recognised in this Act, and other Acts like the Standards of Weights and Measures Act, the Drugs and Cosmetics Act, the Prevention of Adulteration Act, the Essential Commodities Act, the Agricultural Produce (Grading and Marking) Act, etc. The Act provides for setting up of Consumer Protection Councils at the Central and State levels to promote and protect the rights of the consumers and a three-tier quasi-judicial machinery for redressal of consumer grievances. State includes union territories also, though the union territories may have their own State Council, District Forum and State Commission. The administrators of the union territories of Andaman and Nicobar Islands, Chandigarh, Delhi, Goa, Daman and Diu, Lakshadweep and Pondicherry, and Dadar and Nagar Haveli have been authorised to exercise powers and discharge functions of State Government.

## CONSUMER PROTECTION COUNCILS

The Act, has envisaged the setting up of the Consumer Protection Councils at the Central and State levels, namely, the Central Consumer Protection Council and the State Consumer Protection Councils.

### Central Consumers Protection Council

The Central Government is empowered to constitute the Central Consumer Protection Council (hereinafter referred to as the Central Council) which may consist of the following iso members, namely:

(i) the Minister in-charge of Department of Civil Supplies who shall be the Chairman of the Central Council;

(ii) the Minister of State (where he is not holding independent charge) or Deputy Minister in the Department of Civil Supplies who shall be the Vice-Chairman of the Central Council;

(iii) the Ministers of Food and Civil Supplies or Minister in-charge of Consumer Affairs in States;

(iv) eight Members of Parliament-five from the Lok Sabha and three from the Rajya Sabha;

(v) the Commissioner for Scheduled Castes and Scheduled Tribes;

(vi) representatives of the Central Government Departments, autonomous organisations concerned with consumer interests— not exceeding twenty;

(vii) representatives of the Consumer Organisations or consumers— not less than thirty-five;
(viii) representatives of women—not less than ten;
(ix) representatives of farmers, trade and industry—not exceeding twenty;
(x) persons capable of representing consumer interests not specified above—not exceeding fifteen;
(xi) the Secretary in the Department of Civil Supplies shall be the member-secretary of the Central Council.

The Central Government has notified the Constitution of the Council with 115 members.

The term of the Council shall be three years. The Council may meet as and when necessary, but not less than three meetings of the Council shall be held every year. Each meeting of the Council shall be called by giving not less than 10 days notice in writing to every member, specifying the time, place and agenda of meeting. However, no proceedings of the Council shall be invalid merely by reasons of. existence of any vacancy in or any defect in the constitution of the Council. The Council has the power to Constitute Working Groups.

The findings of such working groups are required to be placed before the Council for its consideration. The resolutions by the Council shall be recommendatory in nature.

## Objects of the Central Council

Section 6 of the Consumer Protection Act provides that the objects of the Central Council shall be to promote and protect the rights of the consumers, such as—

(i) the right to be protected against marketing of goods which are hazardous to life and property;
(ii) the right to be informed about the quality, quantity, potency, purity, standard and prices of goods so as to protect the consumer against unfair trade practices;
(iii) the right to be assured, wherever, possible access to a variety of goods at competitive prices;
(iv) the right to be heard and to be assured that consumers' interests will receive due consideration at appropriate forums;
(v) the right to seek redressal against unfair trade practices or unscrupulous exploitation of consumers; and
(vi) the right to consumer education.

The Central Council may have a significant role in the formulation of the Central Government economic policy. In addition it may respond to request for information and advice on particular issues relating to the protection of consumers. Although the decisions of the Councils are recommendatory but they may have a significant impact on the several authorities concerned with the matters of consumer protection.

### State Consumer Protection Councils

The State Governments are also empowered to establish Consumer Protection Councils for their respective States. The State Council shall consist of such members as may be notified by the State Government by notification from time to time. The objects of every State Council like Central Council shall be to promote and protect within the State the rights of the consumer as laid down in the clauses (a) to (f) of section 6. So far 22 States and Union Territories have set up the Consumer Protection Councils under the Act. But, how far these Councils have been successful in protecting the consumers interest, is not free from doubt.

## REDRESSAL OF CONSUMER DISPUTES

The Consumer Protection Act, 1986 provides for the establishment of a three-tier quasi-judicial machinery for redressing consumer grievances as under—

A. District Forum
B. State Commission
C. National Commission

### District Forum

A consumer Disputes Redressal Forum to be known as the "District Forum" is required to be established by the State Government with the prior approval of the Central Government in each district of the State.

### Composition of the District Forum

The Act provides that each District Forum shall consist of a president and two members, to be appointed by the State Government. The President of the Forum is required to be a person who is, or has been, or is qualified to be a District Judge. Out of the two members of the Forum one must be a person of eminence in the field of education, trade or commerce, and the other must be a lady social worker. The intention for having the members from other than the legal profession seems to be that the District Forum should be able to understand and appreciate the over-all technical and social impact, while deciding the issues under the Act. The inclusion of a lady social worker in District Forum is of considerable importance keeping in view the nature and functioning of the Forum.

Every member of the District Forum shall hold the office for a term of five years or upto the age of 65 years, whichever is earlier, and shall not be eligible for reappointment. However, a member may resign his office in writing under his hand addressed to the State Government and on such resignation being accepted, his office shall become vacant. The vacancy so caused may be filled by the appointment of a person possessing any of the qualifications mentioned above in relation to the category of the member who has resigned.

**Jurisdiction of the District Forum**

The District Forum shall have a jurisdiction to entertain complaints where the value of the goods or services and the compensation, if any, claimed is less than rupees one lakh. A complaint shall be instituted in a District Forum within the local limits of whose jurisdiction—

(i) the opposite party or each of the opposite parties, where there are more than one, at the time of the institution of the complaint, actually and voluntarily resides or carries on business, or personally works for gain, or

(ii) any of the opposite parties, where there are more than one at the time of the institution of the complaint, actually and voluntarily resides, or carries on business, or personally works for gain, provided that in such case either the permission of the District Forum is given, or the opposite parties who do not reside, or carry on business, or personally work for gain, as the case may be, acquiesce in such institution, or

(iii) the cause of action, wholly or in part, arises.

A complaint in relation to any goods sold or delivered or any service provided, may be filed with the Forum by—

(i) the consumer to whom such goods are sold or delivered or such services provided;

(ii) any recognised consumer association, whether the consumer to whom the goods sold or delivered or service provided is a member of such association or not; or

(iii) the Central or the State Government.

It is evident from the aforesaid provisions that the complaint may be filed by the affected consumer himself or by any recognised consumer association even if that consumer is not the member of such association. The recognised consumer association means any voluntary consumer association registered under the Companies Act, 1956, or any other law for the time being in force.

Further, the Central and State Governments have also been vested with wide powers to file complaint in relation to any goods sold or delivered or any services provided. The Governments may file the complaint of their own, whenever they find that the goods sold are defective, or services provided are deficient; or prices are over-charged.

## Complainant

Clause (b) of section 2(1) of the Consumer Protection Act defines the term complainant which means—

(i) a consumer; or

(ii) any voluntary consumer association registered under the Companies Act, 1956 (1 of 1956) or under any other law for the time being in force; or

(iii) the Central Government or any State Government, who or which makes a complaint.

For the first time, the registered consumers' associations have been recognised and have been assigned important role of protecting the consumers. According to the rules, every consumer association which is desirous of being recognised as a registered consumer's association, must have not less than ten consumers as its members and shall make an application on the prescribed form with a requisite fee of Rs. 500 to the Central Government in the Department of Company Affairs. The Department of Company Affairs may after scrutiny, issue a certificate of recognition or may refuse to issue such certificate. The applicant shall be informed of the reasons for such refusal. However, before issuing a certificate of recognition, the applicant may be required to furnish such additional information as may be called for. Every registered consumers' association is required to furnish a copy of the certificate of recognition to the concerned Consumer Disputes Redressal Commission established under the Consumer Protection Act.

## Consumer

The term 'consumer' has been defined in clause (d) of section 2(1) of the Consumer Protection Act, 1986. 'Consumer' means any person who,—

(i) buys any goods for a consideration which has been paid or promised or partly paid and partly promised or under any system of deferred payment and includes any user of such goods other than the person who buys such goods for consideration paid or promised or partly paid or partly promised or under any system of deferred payment when such use is made with the approval of such person, but does not include a person who obtains such goods for resale or for any commercial purpose, or

(ii) hires any services for a consideration which has been paid or promised or partly paid and partly promised, or under any system of deferred payment and includes any beneficiary of such services other than the person who hires the services for consideration paid or promised, or partly paid and partly promised, or under any system of deferred payment, when such services are availed of with the approval of the first mentioned person.

The aforesaid definition of 'consumer' is wide enough to include not only the person who buys any goods for consideration but also includes any user of such goods other than the buyer. Similarly, it covers any person who hires any services for consideration and also includes any beneficiary of such services other than the hirer.

However, it does not include a person who obtains any goods for resale or for any commercial purpose.

### Complaint

Clause (c) of section 2(1) of the Consumer Protection Act defines 'complaint' which means any allegation in writing made by a complaint that—

(i) as a result of any unfair trade practice adopted by any trader, the complainant has suffered loss or damage;
(ii) the goods mentioned in the complaint suffer from one or more defects;
(iii) the services mentioned in the complaint suffer from deficiency in any respect;
(iv) a trader has charged for the goods mentioned in the complaint a price in excess of the price fixed by or under any law for the time being in force or displayed on the goods or any package containing such goods, with a view to obtaining any relief provided by or under this Act.

### Complaint against Defective Goods

The complaint may be in respect of the goods which suffer from one or more defects. The term 'goods' has the same meaning as defined in the Sale of Goods Act, 1930. According to section 2(7) of the Sale of Goods Act, 'goods' means every kind of moveable property other than actionable claims and money; and includes stock and shares, growing crops, grass and things attached to or forming part of the land which are agreed to be served before sale or under the contract of sale. The definition is comprehensive one. It includes grass, crops and standing timber which are agreed to be cut before sale or under the contract of sale. It also includes stocks and shares.

The term 'defect' has been defined in clause (f) of section 2(1) of the Consumer Protection Act. 'Defect' means any fault, imperfection or shortcoming in the quality, quantity, potency, purity of standard which is required to be maintained by or under any law for time being in force or as is claimed by the trader in any manner whatsoever in relation to any goods. The definition is wide enough to cover all kinds of faults, or shortcomings in the quality, quantity, potency, purity or standard of goods. The 'trader' in relation to any goods means a person who sells or distributes any goods for sale and includes the manufacturer thereof, and where such goods are sold or distributed in package form, includes the packer thereof. Thus, the term 'trader' is not restricted to only seller or distributor of the goods but also extends to the manufacturer and packer of such goods. 'Manufacturer' means a person who—

(i) makes or manufactures any goods or parts thereof; or
(ii) does not make or manufacture any goods but assembles parts thereof, made or manufactured by others and claims the end-product to be goods manufactured by himself; or
(iii) puts or causes to be put his own mark on any goods made or manufactured by any other manufacturer and claims such goods to be goods made or manufactured by himself.

Where a manufacturer despatches any goods or part thereof to any branch office maintained by him, such branch office shall not be deemed to be the manufacturer even though the parts so despatched to it are assembled at such branch office and are sold or distributed from such branch office.

## Complaint against Deficient Service

The complaint may relate to any services which suffer from deficiency in any respect. The term 'service' has been defined in clause (o) of section 2(1) of the Consumer Protection Act as under:

'Service' means service of any description which is made available to potential users and includes the provision of facilities in connection with banking, financing, insurance, transport, processing, supply of electrical or other energy, board or lodging or both, entertainment, amusement or the purveying of news or other information, but does not include the rendering of any service free of charge or under a contract of personal service.

The aforesaid definition is similar to the definition of 'service' given in clause (r) of section 2 of the M.R.T.P. Act. The definition is very wide and inclusive. It includes amenities and facilities like provisions of finance, transport, energy, etc. which satisfy the various desire and needs of the society. The services rendered by Hotels, Cinemas, Laundries, etc. are also covered by the above definition.

However, the definition excludes two types of services, namely—(i) rendering of any service free of charge, or (ii) under a contract of personal service. It may be noted that the services like medicine, law, accountancy, engineering, etc. have not been specifically enumerated. But it seems that these services are also covered within the scope of the above definition since these are available to potential users.

The literal meaning of the word 'service' is work done to meet some general need, an act of helpful activity, the supplying of utilities as water, electricity, gas, required by the public; supplying of repair service; supplying of public communications or public transport. The use of the expression 'made available to potential users' in the above definition reveals that the service must be made available to potential users who are willing to pay for the service. Further, the expression, 'but does not include rendering of any service free of charge' indicates that the service must be rendered for remuneration.

The complaint can be made in respect of only those services which suffer from any deficiency. 'Deficiency' means any fault, imperfection, shortcoming or inadequacy in the quality, nature and manner of performance which is required to be maintained by or under any law for the time being in force or has been undertaken to be performed by a person in pursuance of a contract or otherwise in relation to any service. The definition is sufficiently wide to cover any fault, shortcoming, etc. in the quality, nature and manner of performance of any service.

### Complaint against Excess-Price

A complaint may be made against a trader who has charged for the goods a price in excess of the price fixed by or under any law for the time being in force or displayed on the goods or any package containing such goods. This is a very important provision under which a relief may be claimed against over-charging of prices. Nowadays, it is a common practice to display maximum price with local taxes extra on the package of containing goods. Many times it has been noticed that the retailers charge 15-20% more than maximum price on the pretext of local taxes and they do not issue any bill, cash-memo, etc. indicating such taxes. It is submitted that such cases should also be covered within the scope of the aforesaid provisions and the sellers and retailers should be held liable accordingly.

### Procedure to be followed by the District Forum

Section 13 of the Consumer Protection Act lays down the procedure to be followed for the settlement of consumer dispute by District Forum. According to these provisions the Forum shall on receipt of a complaint relating to any goods or services refer with a copy of the complaint to the opposite party directing him to give his version of the case within a period of thirty days. However, the period may be extended upto fifteen days by the District Forum. Thus, in no case the opposite party be allowed to give his version after the expiry of forty five days.

Where the opposite party denies or disputes the allegations contained in the complaint, or omits or fails to take any action to represent his case within the above stipulated time, the District Forum shall proceed to settle the consumer dispute on the basis of the evidence brought to its notice.

However, where the defects alleged in the goods are such that they cannot be determined without proper analysis or test of the goods, the District Forum is required to obtain a sample of the goods from the complainant. The District Forum must seal the sample so obtained and authenticate it and refer it to the appropriate laboratory. But, before sending any sample to any laboratory, the District Forum may require the complainant to deposit to the credit of the Forum such fees as may be specified, for payment to the laboratory for carrying out the necessary analysis or test in relation to the goods in question. The Forum shall remit' the amount so deposited to the laboratory to enable it to carry out the analysis or test.

The Forum shall direct the laboratory to make an analysis or test with a view to finding out whether such goods suffer from any defect alleged in the complaint or suffer from any other defect. The laboratory is required to submit its report to the Forum within a period of forty-five days of the receipt of reference or within such extended period as may be granted by the Forum.

The Forum shall forward a copy of the report along with such remarks as it may feel appropriate to the opposite party. If any of the parties disputes the correctness of the findings of the appropriate laboratory, or dispute the correctness of the methods of analysis or test adopted by the appropriate laboratory, the Forum shall require the opposite party or the complainant to submit in writing his objections in regard to the report made by the laboratory. The Forum thereafter give a reasonable opportunity to the complainant as well as the opposite party of being heard as to the correctness or otherwise of the report made by the laboratory and also as to the objection made in relation thereto and issue an appropriate order under section 14 of the Consumer Protection Act.

However, section 13(3) of the Act provides that no proceedings complying with the aforesaid procedure shall be called in question in any court on the ground that the principles of natural justice have not been complied with. It may be noted that the requirements of natural justice do not remain fixed nor they remain the same in every case and in all circumstances. The applicability of the principles of natural justice depends on—(i) the scheme and policy of the statute; (ii) nature of jurisdiction conferred on the authority; (iii) character of rights of the persons affected; and (iv) relevant circumstances disclosed in a particular case. Under the Consumer Protection Act, the procedure to be followed requires—referring of complaint to the opposite party; providing him an opportunity to give his version of the case; analysis or testing of the goods by appropriate laboratory; and considering the evidence produced by the complainant and the opposite party. This procedure seems to be on the lines of the principles of natural justice.

**Power of District Forum**

For the purpose of the settlement of the consumer dispute under the Act, the District Forum has been vested with the same powers as vested in a civil court under the Code of Civil Procedure, 1908, while trying a suit in respect of the following matters, namely—

(i) the summoning and enforcing attendance of any defendant or witness and examining the witness on oath;
(ii) the discovery and production of any document or other material object producible as evidence;
(iii) the reception of evidence on affidavits;
(iv) the requisitioning of the report of the concerned analysis or test from the appropriate laboratory or from any other relevant source;
(v) issuing any commission for the examination of any witness; and
(vi) any other matter which may be prescribed.

Further, section 13(5) of the Act expressly provides that every proceeding before the District Forum shall be deemed to be judicial proceeding within the meaning of sections 193 and 228 of the Indian Penal Code and the Forum shall be deemed to be a civil court for the purposes of section 195, and Chapter XXVI of the Code of Criminal Procedure, 1973. Thus, the proceedings before the Forum will be judicial proceedings for certain purposes like contempt of court, giving of false evidence, etc. and the Forum shall be treated as a civil court for these purposes.

**Production of Documents, etc.**

The District Forum has the power to require any person to furnish such books, accounts, documents, or commodities, the examination of which may be required for the purpose of the Act. The Forum may also require a person to furnish such information as may be required for the purpose of the Act. The expression 'required for the purpose of the Act' is quite significant to determine the relevancy of the document for the purpose of proceedings. Whether a person, when called upon to produce a document, etc. can raise an objection on the ground of irrelevancy of the document etc.? It appears that he has a right to object on the ground irrelevancy of the document, etc. at a proceeding, but such irrelevancy must be demonstrated.

**Powers of Entry, Search and Seizure**

Where during any proceedings under the Act, the District Forum has any ground to believe that book, paper, commodity or document which may be required to be produced in such proceeding are being, or may be destroyed, mutilated, altered, falsified or secreted, it may, by written order authorise any officer to exercise the power of entry and search of any premises. Such authorised officer may also seize such books, papers, documents or commodities as are required for the purpose of the Act. The seizure must be communicated to the Forum as soon as it is made or within a period not exceeding seventy-two hours of making such seizure, after specifying the reasons for making such seizure. The Forum on examination of such seized documents or commodities, may order the retention thereof or may return it to the party concerned.

It is yet to be seen how far the Forum will make use of this provision, but it is hoped that the effective use of the provision will certainly strengthen the hands of the Forum for the redressal of the consumer dispute.

**District Forum—whether a quasi-judicial body**

The provisions of the Act reveals that the District Forum is not a court and is not bound to follow the procedure prescribed for trial of action in courts nor by strict rule of evidence. For the settlement of the consumer dispute the Forum has to follow the procedure laid in section 13 of the Act which is quite parallel to the principles of natural justice. Thus, it seems to be a quasi-judicial body.

### Orders of the District Forum

Where the District Forum is satisfied that the goods complained against suffer from any of the defects specified in the complaint or that any of the allegations contained in the complaint about the services are proved, it shall issue an order to the opposite party directing him to take one or more of the following things, namely—

(i) to remove the defect pointed out by the appropriate laboratory from the goods in question;

(ii) to replace the goods with new goods of similar description which shall be free from any defect;

(iii) to return to the complainant the price, or, as the case may be, the charges paid by the complainant;

(iv) to pay such amount as may be awarded by it as compensation to the consumer for any loss or injury suffered by the consumer due to the negligence of the opposite party.

Every order made by the Forum shall be signed by all the members constituting it, and, if there is any difference of opinion, the order of the majority of the members constituting it shall be the order of the Forum.

### Appeal Against the Orders of the District Forum

Any person aggrieved by an order made by the District Forum may prefer an appeal against such order to the State Commission within a period of thirty days from the date of the order. However, the Commission may entertain an appeal even after the expiry of thirty days, if it is satisfied that there was sufficient cause for not filing it within that period. The expression 'sufficient cause' requires liberal construction so as to advance substantial justice where no negligence or any inaction or want of bonafide is imputable to the party. The determination of 'sufficient cause' will depend on facts and circumstances of each case. It is a discretion to be exercised by the Commission in a judicial manner and in the interest of justice.

### State Commission

A Consumer Disputes Redressal Commission to be known as the 'State Commission' is required to be established by the State Government with the prior approval of the Central Government in the State.

## Composition of the State Commission

Each State Commission shall consist of a President and two other members, to be appointed by the State Government. The President should be a person who is or has been a judge of a High Court, appointed by the State Government. The two other members should be persons of ability, integrity and standing and should have adequate knowledge or experience of, or have shown capacity in dealing with problems relating to economics, law, commerce, accountancy, industry, public affairs or administration, one of whom should be a woman. However, the appointment of a sitting judge of a High Court to the Commission can be made only after consultation with the Chief Justice of that High Court. The salary or honorarium and other allowances payable to, and other terms and conditions of service (including tenure of office) of, the members of the State Commission shall be such as may prescribed by the State Government.

## Jurisdiction of the State Commission

The State Commission shall have jurisdiction—

(i) to entertain complaints where the value of the goods or servicers and compensation, if any, claimed exceeds rupees one lakh but does not exceed rupees tel l lakhs; and

(ii) to entertain appeals against the orders of any District Forum within the State; and

(iii) to call for the records and pass appropriate orders in any consumer dispute which is pending before or has been decided by any District Forum within the State, where it appears to the State Commission that such District Forum has exercised a jurisdiction not vested in it by law, or has failed to exercise a jurisdiction so vested or has acted in exercise of its jurisdiction illegally or with material irregularity.

Thus, the jurisdiction of the State Commission is original as well as appellate. The original jurisdiction is vested in the Commission only in respect of complaints where the value of goods or services and compensation claimed exceeds rupees one lakh but not more than rupees ten lakhs. The appellate jurisdiction is confined to appeals from the orders of any District Forum within the State. Further, the State Commission may call for records and pass orders in any consumer dispute where it appears that a District Forum has acted illegally or with material irregularity, or has exceeded its jurisdiction or has failed to exercise its jurisdiction.

## Procedure Applicable to State Commission

The procedure for the disposal disputes to be adopted by the State Commission shall be the same as is to be followed by the District Forum. Thus, the procedure specified in sections 12, 13 and 14 and the rules made thereunder for the disposal of complaints by the District Forum shall, with such modifications as may be necessary, be applicable to the State Commission. Further, rule 10 of the Consumer Protection Rules confers the same additional powers to the Commission as are vested to the District Forum regarding the production of documents, search and seizure.

It may, however, be noted that the State Governments have yet to make their own rules in exercise of their powers under section 30(2) of the Act. It is submitted that the State Governments may adopt the similar rules as laid down by the Central Government, namely, the Consumer Protection Rules, 1987. It will help in maintaining the uniform law in all over the country.

## Appeal Against the Orders of the State Commission

Section 19 of the Act provides that person aggrieved by an order made by the State Commission on a complaint (where the value of goods or services and compensation claimed exceeds. rupees one lakh but not more than rupees ten lakhs) may prefer an appeal against such order to the National Commission within a period of thirty days from the date of the order. However, the National Commission may entertain an appeal after the expiry of the said period of thirty days if it is satisfied that there was sufficient cause for not filing it within that period.

It may be noted that an order made by the State Commission on an appeal against the orders of the District Forum, is not appealable to the National Commission. Thus, the provision exists only for a single appeal to the State Commission from the orders of the District Forum and no further appeal will lie from the orders of the State Commission to the National Commission.

An appeal under section 19 of the Act can be preferred only by a 'person aggrieved'. The expression 'person aggrieved' does not mean a person who is disappointed or annoyed at a decision. The word 'aggrieved' connotes some legal grievance, e.g., deprivation of something an adverse effect on the title of something and so on. He must show that the order affects his own right or is not in accordance with law or confers a right on a person to which he is not entitled. The expression 'aggrieved person' does not include a mere busybody who is interfering in things which does not concern him. Since the

Consumer Protection Act deals with the matters of great public importance, it is submitted that the word 'aggrieved person' should be given a wider meaning and not a narrow construction.

### National Commission

The highest authority to settle the consumer disputes under the Act is an independent statutory body—the National Commission.

### Composition of the National Commission

The Act provides that National Commission shall consist of a President and four other members to be appointed by the Central Government. The President should be a person who is or has been a Judge of the Supreme Court. The person to be appointed as a member should be a person of ability, integrity and standing with adequate knowledge or experience, or capacity in dealing with problems relating to economics, law, commerce, accountancy, industry, public affairs or administration. One of the member should be a woman. However, no sitting Judge of the Supreme Court shall be appointed under the aforesaid provisions except after consultation with the Chief Justice of India. Before appointment, the President and members are required to take an undertaking that they do not and will not have any such financial or other interests as is likely to effect prejudicially functions as such member.

It may be noted that no act or proceedings of the National Commission shall be invalid by reasons only of the existence of any vacancy among its President or members or any defect in the constitution thereof.

### Removal of the President and Members

The Central Government may remove the President or any member from office on any of the following grounds, namely—

(i) he has been adjudged an insolvent; or

(ii) he has been convicted of an offence which, in the opinion of the Central Government, involves moral turpitude; or

(iii) he has become physically or mentally incapable of acting as the President or the member; or

(iv) he has acquired such financial or other interest as is likely to affect prejudicially his functions as the President or a member; or

(v) he has so abused his position as to render his continuance in office prejudicial to the public interest.

The issue of control over the price of petroleum and petroleum products like diesel, kerosene and cooking gas deserves some attention, because more often than not. They become public issues and have vide political ramifications. Since 1973 when the opec countries started raising the international price of crude oil from time to time. The Indian government has been involved in controlling the selling price of petroleum and all petro products.

Government Levies substantial customs and excise duties on both imported crude and domestically produced crude. Then government owns nearly all oil companies like Indian Oil, Oil India, Hindustan petroleum and Bharat Petroleum. The price at which they sell their products in the market is often determined by the Central government under statutory price control. This price control was abolished in 2002, again reimposed in 2004 and once again removed in 2011, leaving it to the Oil Companies to charge the market price that reflects the high price of crude in the international market. But government still is the party responsible for oil price in the eyes of the public.

Another commodity where government very often controls imports and exports that influence the market price is sugar. When market price falls government allows exports and when the market price rises the government imports if necessary. There are also cases like onion where the price often rises or falls leading to political repercussions.

# CHAPTER 10
# Import Control

Import control has now lost some of its relevance after the massive liberalisation from 1991 onwards, but still continues to be an important tool in the government's armoury of economic controls. Import tariffs in some form or other constituted an essential feature of mercantilist economic policy during the greater part of the 16th and 17th centuries. From about 1860 this policy was discouraged with the spread of the free trade movement, sponsored largely by Britain which had an industrial monopoly in the world. However towards the end of the century, there was once again a growing move away from free trade spearheaded by Frederick List in Germany who sought to establish protected zones—Zollvereins—to shelter and stimulate nascent domestic industry. This took the form of a general movement in most countries towards protection of the country's own industrial and agricultural interests from foreign competition and this tendency has prevailed ever since, assisted by special circumstances from time to time, e.g. the two World Wars which interrupted international trade and led to new crops of restrictions. The great depressions of the 1930s also accelerated this movement, and many countries took to a policy of "export of unemployment" by obliging the citizens to buy home-produced goods instead of imported ones.

It has also been seen that development and rising national income always produce a strong tendency for imports to rise rapidly in the absence of special measures to the contrary. A higher income in any country calls for an increased supply of the goods and services which are traditionally imported. In India this rise has been more than proportional to the rise in national income on account of the consumer's preference for spending a bigger proportion of his income on manufactures of more advanced type (automobiles and electrical goods, etc.) and the higher proportion of imported machinery in the overall ratio of imports to income. The resultant strain on foreign exchange also makes import and exchange control a necessary tool for a country's economic development. The old controversy between free trade and protection has become largely unreal today. Protection and import control are everywhere regarded as essential parts of national economic management and national planning everywhere. While tariff constitutes the traditional method of import control, a reliance on quantitative restrictions on import has increasingly been found necessary in recent times specially by the developing countries.

To sum up, import control can be said to have the following general objectives:

(i) To apportion the available foreign exchange among the various users to meet the industrial input requirements of the capital goods and priority industries.

(ii) To achieve a policy of progressive import substitution so that the pressure built up by adverse balance of payments is reduced over a few years.

(iii) There is also an element of industrial protection, viz. enabling home industries to grow to the exclusion of competition from foreign industries.

In the Indian situation there are several special factors as well which have influenced the Government's import policy since independence. First, in the initial years after independence, an object behind Government control of import was to moderate price fluctuations on account of the shortages of the aggregate supply of certain commodities in the home market. This situation was further complicated by India's obligation to the Sterling Area which prevented the free conversion of her sterling reserves into hard currencies. Hence, for several years in the early 1950s, India allowed almost unrestricted import of consumers' goods through the introduction of an Open General Licence, and this had the effect of depleting her sterling reserves considerably. Secondly, import control in India has also assumed a new dimension because some of the imports are said to be vital to the very operation of industrial economy, e.g. raw materials for current operation in some important industries like non-ferrous metals, oil, raw jute, long-stapled cotton, machinery for replacement or new development. Some of these were in acute shortage, because the partition had taken away the traditional source of supply.

Thirdly, another new dimension was added by the recurrence of food crises from the mid-fifties increasing India's dependence on import. On an average food worth Rs 120 crores was imported every year from 1956 onwards till the end of the 1960s. This, coupled with the emphasis on industrialisation in the Second Plan and an unfortunate clamour among import licences both in the public and private sectors to complete their licensed import quota for the entire Plan period, immediately exhausted our sterling balance (over £ 124 crores) by 1957-58. This created a huge deficit in India's balance of payments which remained more or less a standing backdrop of India's economy until the year 1974-75. The failure of monsoon in 1966 and 1967 further aggravated the problem and import of food on a massive scale was unavoidable. Even after the food grains availability substantially improved in the 1970s Government still found it necessary to have massive imports in the interest of building a buffer stock. Fourthly, the need for importing defence equipment on a massive scale from 1962 onwards during the Third Plan Period made the balance of payments position further acute. Finally, the crude price hike by the petroleum exporting countries from 1973 onwards except the recent year decline in POL imports in 1997-98 put a severe strain on India's balance of payments. Overnight India's annual oil import bill was quadrupled from Rs 300 crores to Rs 1,200 crores and has since then been rising periodically in a galloping manner as in 1979-80 or in 1990 after the Kuwait crisis. This has made continuance of import control necessary despite the recent improvements brought about by an impressive rise in exports and remittances from abroad.

## LEGAL FRAMEWORK

Historically, import and export controls were first introduced in India in 1939 as a war-time measure under the Defence of India Act and Rules, 1939 primarily with a view to regulating available foreign exchange and the limited shipping facilities for the war and the limited civil purposes. After the war this control was continued by an ordinance, and thereafter by the Imports and Exports (Control) Act 1947 which was initially meant to be in force for only three years, but has been extended from time ever since. After independence import control did not undergo any structural change, but its objectives became quite different: no longer the regulation of war-time or post-war economy, but to help and guide planned economic development. Apart from this general legislation, there are some special legislations having their bearings on various aspects of the import or the export of specific commodities, e.g. the Foreign Exchange Regulation Act 1947, the Customs Act 1962, the Coffee Act 1942, the Tea Act 1953 and the Coir Industries Act 1953.

The Import and Export (Control) Act is a short enactment of eight sections. The key section is Section 3 which empowers the Central Government to make provisions by order published in the Government Gazette "for prohibiting, restricting or otherwise controlling the import into, and export of goods out of India." This gives the Government the absolute power not only over the export and import of any commodity, but also over the ordinary trade in any imported commodity. Again, under Section 3, the Central Government promulgated the Import (Control) Order 1955 and also the Exports (Control) Order 1962. The Import Control Order gave rise to the system of import licensing. The goods indicated in this order could not be imported without a licence from the appropriate licensing authority unless the Government had granted an exemption to any commodity from licensing. Until recently, the list of goods mentioned in the order was very long and nothing worthwhile was left out of it. The order prescribed some very general factors for guiding the issue of licence, e.g. non-availability of foreign exchange, the interests of the state etc. The detailed guidelines were, however, given through annual announcements made by the Central Government (Ministry of Commerce) in the Import Trade Control Policy Book, popularly known until recently as the Red Book, which was published on or shortly after the 1st of April every year. There was another accompanying publication titled Import Trade Control—Hand Book of Rules and Procedures, popularly known as the Hand Book containing procedural and related matters concerning import licensing. For at least three decades the Red Book and the and Book symbolised India's administration-ridden import control regime. In the wake of the sea changes in trade policy in recent years there is now a much smaller five year Export and Import Policy and a shorter Hand Book of Procedures. The procedure has been considerably simplified.

The basic instrument of control ever since the exchange crisis of 1956-57 was quantitative restriction or blanket ban. For some unexplained reasons the use of tariffs to mop up import premia, or the use of price mechanism to regulate imports did not find much favour in India. There was complete reliance on administrative decisions for the allocation of foreign exchange for practically all uses in the economy.

Imports had to be categorised between the import of raw materials, spares and components on the one hand and the import of capital goods and equipment on the other. There was to be an elaborate administrative rationing of different permissible imports by these categories among industries, and further still, by firms and plants. For every half year, April to

September and October to March, the Foreign Exchange Budget branch of the Department of Economic Affairs in the Ministry of Finance prepared an estimate of the Foreign Exchange available for the half-year period. After meeting the first charge expenditures such as debt repayments and Embassy expenditures the residual amount of available foreign exchange was allocated among different users. Hereafter food, fertilisers, petroleum, and its products and defence pre-empted first. At the next stage the administrative allocation proceeded on the basis of (i) allocation for both raw materials and equipment for the different public sector undertakings under different ministries, and (ii) a bulk allocation for the private sector's imports of raw materials, spares and components. There is considerable proliferation of agencies in the matter of industry and unit-wise allocation under each of these heads. Thus a single unit may receive its iron and steel through the Iron and Steel Controller, nonferrous metals from the Department of Mines and other imports from the bulk quota of DCTD.

Prior to the phenomenal import liberalisation during the 7th Plan (1985-90) there was a strict import procedure. For each category of licence there were two overriding principles to be considered; "essentiality" of the import, and "indigenous availability" of the article.

Thus in addition to the licensing authority there was a sponsoring agency certifying essentially and a clearing agency for indigenous clearance.

The Red Book along with the Handbook prescribed the following three broad categories of importers: (a) established importers, (b) actual users, and (c) registered exporters. The intense importance of these categories has varied from time to time depending on the needs of the country and the availability of foreign exchange. In the beginning the established importers constituted the major category and the category of registered exporters was not there. At present this category of established importers' has dwindled into insignificance, while the categories of 'registered exporters' and 'actual users' have gained prominence. There were two simple criteria for determining entitlement of individual importers, viz., "historical shares" and "registered capacity." In the case of established importers the licence were usually given on the basis of fixed percentage of the past import. Similarly a registered exporter was entitled to an import licence for a specified commodity to be used in the licensee's factory for the manufacture of an exportable commodity. While other factors like anticipated changes in production were usually taken into account, the prime consideration was to regulate the current allocation of import to that made in the past years. In the case of 'actual users' the import authorities enjoyed a wide discretion.

The actual users were divided into three broad sub-categories, viz. small scale industries; scheduled industries registered with the Director General Technical Development (DGTD); and scheduled industries like textiles and jute not registered with the DGTD and also non-scheduled industries. Depending on the broad subcategory the DGTD, the Textile Commissioner, Jute Commissioner etc. had a key role in the sense that without their recommendation the licensing authority could not issue the licences. In this situation the discretion of individuals more often than played the decisive role. There was little of announced guidelines or identified machinery for redressal of grievances. This increased the scope for arbitrariness and whimsicality.

It may be mentioned that one striking feature in the administration of import control is the separation as a rule between the statutory authority for issuing import licences and the actual authority on whose recommendations the licences are issued. For instance, in the case of the import of capital equipment for scheduled industries registered with the DGTD the licensing authorities in actual practice were more or less bound by the recommendations made by the Capital Goods Committee, an inter-ministerial body for scrutinising applications for importing capital goods. This separation between the statutory and the real authority, apart from it doubtful legality, must be considered a lacunae in the administration of the import control. It could cause endless confusion to the applicants who would go on troubling the office of the Chief Controller which is the nominal statutory authority but is in actual practice only a signing agency following mechanically the recommendations made by the Capital Goods Committee or other sponsoring authorities.

Clearly, one major test of the success or failure of import control is the degree of import substitution which has been achieved. It is difficult to make a value judgment as to whether import substitution in a given field was desirable. Import substitution in respect of consumer goods was particularly rapid during the Second Plan period and after on account of increased domestic production as a result of tight import control and accelerated investment. The share of capital goods in the total import substitution has continued to rise all along, although import substitution has been more pronounced since the Second Plan reflecting the emphasis on the production of capital goods from the Second Plan onwards.

During the 1950s and 1960s the contribution of import substitution to the demand for domestic production was most important for capital goods, and least important for consumer goods. It was only for a short period i.e.

1965-66 to 1970-71 that, in response to the country's economic situation following devaluation of the rupee in 1966 and two bad harvests, the share of non-food consumer items and of basic goods in total non-food imports rose at the expense of capital goods. During the period 1971-72 to 1975-76 the share of basic imports in total non-food imports in terms of value has continued to rise at the expense of capital goods. However the price escalation from the oil crisis of 1973 onwards distorted these trends completely. Imports were considerably liberalised during the 1990s. Under section 5 of the Foreign Trade (Development. and Regulation Act), 1992 Central Government formulates and notifies the EXIM Policy.

### Administrative and Economic Cost of Import Control

The common points of criticism against the import control system in India are not with reference to its philosophical base or its rationale, but with reference to the cumbrous and time consuming administrative procedure, the absence of a well-defined set of principles and criteria based on a correct system of priorities, and therefore, the arbitrariness and adhocism which appear to characterise it.

The following adverse economic effects may be identified: 1. procedural delays, 2. multiplicity of authorities and lack of co ordination, 3. discrimination against small men, 4. corruption, 5. administrative and other expenses, 6. inflexibility, 7. absence of competition, 8. an inherent bias in favour of industries based on imported rather than domestic inputs. 9. anticipatory and automatic protection given to some industries regardless of costs, 10. a discrimination against exports vis-a-vis domestic sales. 11. government's loss of revenue, 12. distributional effects of administrative allocation, 13. encouragement of indiscriminate growth of non-essential industries on the basis of import substitution. Administrative delays are inherent in the working of India's secretariat system with its multiplicity of authorities, the long vertical movement of files from the bottom to the top and the general methods of work. The import or the exchange control system or for that matter any administrative control system inevitably becomes time-consuming in this process.

A large number of authorities are involved in the licensing procedure: sponsoring bodies, indigenous clearance authorities, and actual licensing authorities. Very often these authorities do not appear to follow any common set of priorities. Besides the quality of information on which their decisions are presumably based leaves very much to be desired. The Directorate of Industries of State Governments which are supposed to process the import applications for the small scale sector in the first instance and to attach the essentiality certificate do not have adequate information. Similarly in respect of units which must seek indigenous clearance from the DGTD, the DGTD Directorate concerned does not usually maintain adequate information on indigenous suppliers, their capacity, capacity utilisation and the quality of their products and general plant conditions. To be called upon to give indigenous clearance prior to permitting imports and even to determine the quantitative mix of permissible imports in many cases on the basis of inadequate or doubtful information is naturally fraught with the possibility of wrong decisions or miscalculations by the DGTD. There is always some kind of communication gap between the administrative authority and the business community, and amongst Government agencies themselves such as the Chief Controller and the Customs authorities. Common people do not understand the administrative language of policy documents such as the Red Book or the complex procedure. They also get confused as a result of the separation between the statutory authority and the actual effective authority lying somewhere in the sprawling Government structural. Quick changes in the import policy from time to time also confuse them.

As regards inflexibility, it is easy to see how the rigid enforcement of the principles of essentiality and indigenous non-availability coupled with the virtually non-transferability of import licences bring about considerable inflexibility to the pattern of utilisation of imports. The rigid pattern of permissible imports, their strict itemization often by specified value for different items and the considerable uncertainty about getting modifications approved or even the timely availability of foreign exchange inevitably create inflexibility leading to economic inefficiency. This may sometime lead to an excessive holding of inventories by Indian firms in the absence of flexibility in the matter of inputs-mix and the transfer of inputs from one set of users to another.

As regards absence of competition, it is very obvious that the import allocation system virtually eliminates the possibility of competition, either foreign or domestic. Foreign competition is ruled out because of the principle of indigenous availability. The combination of capital goods licensing and actual users' licensing on a fair share basis among rival firms in any industry and industrial licensing also eliminate the possibility of entry by new firms as well as efficiently managed expansion by the existing firms. The fact that each firm is entitled to its share of actual users' licences, and no more, ensures that the efficient firms cannot even legally increase their productions from the existing capacity by competing away the scarce imports from less efficient firms. The absence of effective competition results in the absence of incentive to reduce cost per unit of output and in preventing the growth of competitive efficiency in the most efficient units and industries. It is easy to see how a bias is created in favour of the industries using imported inputs; they can get relatively greater allocations for imports under actual users' licences and hence obtain these inputs at import-premium-exclusive prices whereas the other industries would have to buy import-substitute, indigenous items at premium-inclusive prices (because these items fetch a price equal to c.i.f. price plus the import premia). The former industries using relatively more imported inputs automatically operate under a bias in their favour.

Another significant impact of the import control policy in India was that as people were forced to buy domestic import substitutes, protection was automatically extended to industries producing these substitutes regardless of costs, efficiency and comparative advantage. So long as they made their capacity and product known to the relevant agencies e.g. the DGTD, in charge of indigenous clearance this protection was assured. This policy of automatic and anticipatory protection served to divorce market-oriented investment decisions from any guidelines that international opportunity costs might have otherwise provided. As regard discrimination against exports, it is quite obvious that as the average effective export exchange rate is generally less than the effective import rate and as domestic prices of many finished goods tend to be higher than the export prices, industries which depended on export found themselves handicapped in the absence of significant export subsidization schemes. Thus from the beginning of the Second Plan until the late 1970s the industrial licensing policy and import policy were unfavourable towards export-based manufactures, largely because they had to contend with a substantial inward-looking bias. Another noteworthy effect of the import control system was the loss of Government revenue that it involved in passing the profits on scarce imports to the private sector. Wherever the import of such scarcity items was through traders e.g. established imports' licences, Government lost revenue. If the Government had channelled these through its own agencies or auctioned them off or levied suitable tariffs, the scarcity premium would have accrued to it as revenue.

Finally, since the fifties the import of manufactured consumers' goods of a non-essential nature was banned or severely restricted. Paradoxically the same principle of non-essentiality has not been extended to the domestic production of the same or similar goods. On the other hand domestic production of such goods was often encouraged at considerable foreign exchange cost although sacificing considerations of scale. Thus the question of comparative advantage was ignored. The question has to be considered whether from a long-range point of view the country does not stand to gain br allowing very limited quantities of such consumers' durables to be imported with heavy duties rather than committing substantial resources including foreign exchange to be used for allowing inefficient domestic production for meeting limited demands. Another long-term consideration is whether the object of prohibiting non-essential consumers' goods is not better achieved by prohibitive tariffs rather than by an administrative control system with its detrimental effects.

In 1976-77 following unprecedented improvements in India's foreign exchange reserves which reached Rs 3,200 crores at the beginning of 1977-78, Government announced a number of significant policy relaxations in the import of capital goods benefiting a wide range of industries. This policy continued for several years.

But instead of utilising the position to forge a long-term import policy the government succumbed to the temptation of resorting to indiscriminate import of non-essential consumers' goods and frittering away the valuable exchange resources. This process was helped by the devastating effect of the second oil price hike (1979-80) over India's oil import bills and led to adverse balance of payments. India's trade deficit went up from Rs. 2,725 crores in 1979-80 to Rs 5,838 crores in 1980-81. This sharp deterioration in the external payments situation made India seek a massive borrowing from the International Monetary Fund (Rs 5 billion) under the Extended Fund Facility of the I.M.F. Under the terms of this credit India had to enter into a liberalised imports regime. This had both positive and negative effects. On the one hand, it shook Indian industry from its complacence caused by over protection. On the other hand by imports of raw materials, machinery and other products for which sufficient capacity had already been established in the country, this policy served to hurt Indian industry in a manner which could have been avoided.

The massive I.M.F, loan of 1981 provided India a cushion to carry into effect certain necessary structural adjustment measures in her economy which showed their import in several years. These measures which formed part of the Sixth Plan included massive investment in key import-saving sectors such as petroleum, vigorous export efforts, strengthening the industrial base through import of technology and capital goods, and efforts to mobilise inward remittance by non-resident Indians. These measures bore fruit. As a result of increase in the domestic production of crude oil (11.8 million tonnes in 1977-80 to 27 million tonnes in 1984-85), import of oil as per cent of consumption declined from over 70 per cent in 1980-81 to about 34 per cent in 1984-85. (Rs 5,239 crores in 1980-81 to Rs 3,237 crores in 1983-84). During the early 1981, there was a declining trend in trade deficit despite the continued imports of foodgrains, iron and steel and edible oil. On the whole, there was also a favourable balance of trends and increase in foreign exchange reserves. The rate of growth of imports which had touched 37.3 per cent in 1980-81 slowed down to 8.4 per cent in 1981-82, 5.5 per cent in 1982-83 and 9.8 per cent in 1983-84. In fact a comfortable balance of payments position enabled India to decide not to draw the last tranche of the IMF loan. But by 1985-86 with exports growth slowing down and imports showing a sign of coming down (an increase of 25 per cent in imports against a 0.7 per cent decline in exports). Indian trade deficit has once again become a matter of serious concern. The balance of payment difficulty reached a crisis by 1990-91 forcing India to once again approach the IMF for massive loan. This once, again necessitated a liberal import regime. The new government (June, 1991) announced substantial dismantling of the strict import control regime on 4th July, 1991 and a comprehensive statement on Trade Policy was announced on August 13, 1991. The process was further carried over in the EXIM Policy, 1997-2001 and subsequent amendments.

In the wake of massive liberalisation from 1991 onwards imports have been deregulated on a large scale. There is no import ban on major group items now. Also the prohibitive customs tariff of yesteryears have been substantially reduced from the level of 200-300 per cent on to 45 per cent or so and are being lowered further. India joined the WTO in 1994, and accepted a liberal import regime as an obligation under this treaty. This also led to removal of import restrictions and sharp lowering of customs duties causing much suffering to domestic industry hitherto thriving in a protected sellers market. But there is a general feeling that in 1997 and 1998 the Indian government bent over backwards in meeting WTO's requirements and in many instanced reduced customer duties to lower levels than what the WTO envisaged and ahead of WTO's time limit. Some other countries taking advantage of this situation are dumping commodities on the Indian market. The anti-dumping authority of the Commerce Ministry has not been particularly effective in preventing such indiscriminate dumping which has adversely effected a cross section of Indian industry.

India has also taken significant policy initiatives at the multilateral level for nationalisation of the non-tariff measures. The country made commitment to the WTO for phased removal of all balance of payments related quantitative restrictions by 1 April, 2001. The country also made binding tariff commitment to the WTO for all agricultural products and 67 per cent of the manufactured product. QRs in respect of 714 items have already been withdrawn w.e.f. April 1, 2000, and remaining 1429 tariff lines. are to be removed by April 1, 2001. But India has to be more alert and an institutional mechanism will have to be evolved to study, analyze and recommend appropriate tariff structure to maintain balance between the interests of producers and users/consumers. In this regard Tariff Commission, like the Anti-dumping Directorate should be made effective, and strengthened to play the role of an independent, expert body to advise on these matters.

Other key liberalisations such as the full convertibility of rupee on trade accounts and the recent liberal Export and Import Policies have also changed the perspective. Import policies are no longer annual, despite the quick political changes of recent years, and despite the clamour of protectionists from time to time, The protectionists argue that Indian industry was never prepared to face competition from overseas business with its inherent superiority in terms of freedom from import and scale restrictions and other quantitative restraints. This line of argument cannot be easily brushed aside. Indian industry has been treated like an infant all these years. If that infant is now all of a sudden, thrown into the mid stream and told to swim along with the creatures of water, there is strong likely hood of its getting drowned. It should have been given a notice period to put its acts together. Industries—especially small-scale like that of electronic items, bicycle, milk, edible oils, garments, tea, food processing.

The growth of imports and exports, down at -5 p.c and -3.5 p.c. in 2009-10 on account of the 2008 U.S. meltdown, rebounded to 28.2 p.c and 40.5 p.c respectively in 2010-11. India's share in global exports and imports rose from 0.7 p.c and 0.8 p.c. in 2000 to 1.5 p.c and 2.2 p.c in 2010. However since then there has been a deceleration as a result of the continuing crises in the U.S. and the new crises in the Euro countries. But India's success in diversifying her export and import markets from Europe and America to Asia. ASEAN countries and U.A.E is remarkable. In fact on account of increase in net capital inflows foreign exchange reserves increased by U.S. $25.7 million 279.1 billion in March 2010 to 304.8 billion in March 2011. India's external debt stood at U.S $ 326.6 billion in September 2011. But there are signs of deceleration.

There are many who have already started crying against removed of quantitative restrictions. Much of the industrial capacity our nation has built in four decades could be in danger. Already, a country like China is taking advantage of the liberalized import regime to dump their bulk products at throwaway prices on the Indian market. The Commerce ministry has set up an anti Dumping Authority to receive specific complaints from Indian parties about dumping of goods in India by foreign competitors. India has also started using the WTO forum for this purpose. A topic of considerable public interest is permitting foreign retail chains in India. There is much interest abroad. There is one view that this will eliminate unscrupulous middlemen and help both common men and primary producers. But there is also the issue of a large number of small retailers being thrown out of business. The experience of the few Indian chains such as Reliance Fresh and Pantaloon should be taken into account before a major policy shift is attempted.

The coming into being of the World Trade Organisation (WTO) during the first decade of the present century was an event of major importance. India was among the first countries to join the WTO and to that extent become subject to the restrictions imposed by this world today. It also became beneficiary in respect of a number of things such as being given automatically the status of the most favoured nation by all the member countries. There is no doubt that membership of the WTO has brought about a massive expansion of India's role in world trading both in imports and exports. There are also provisions for antidumping measures in cases where some countries are dumping certain goods on other countries. There has been some criticism on the part of ideologues about India joining this world trade body on grounds such as loss of sovereignty which are not really maintainable in the present day contest.

## REFERENCES

1. For a good discussion on the economic impact of quantitative import controls in India see Bhagawati and Srinivassan, *Foreign Trade Regimes and Economic Development in India,* Macmillan, Chapters 12, 13, 15, 16 and Part V.
2. Also see J. Bhagawati, "Indian Balance of Payment Policy and Exchange Auctions." Oxford Economic Papers, February, 162.

# CHAPTER 11

# Exports and Government Policy

The legal frame of export control is provided the Exports (control) Order, 1962. The executive authority in respect of export control is vested in the Chief Controller of Imports and Exports now renamed as Director General of Import and Export. He is also charged with responsibility of taking all follow-up actions in respect of all categories of export obligation cases, i.e. cases where industrial licence, capital goods import licence and foreign investment/collaboration have been allowed subject to an obligation to export a specified percentage of the product. The export obligation is enforced through a legal agreement between the Chief controller and the undertaking supported either by bank guarantees for an amount equivalent in value to the value of the goods to be exported, or in lieu of a bank guarantee (option with the exporters), with alternative penalties and charges including handing over twice the shortfall in export to any agency nominated by the Government (usually the State Trading Corporation). The CCI&E also initiates penal action in case of violation the terms of the agreement. Apart from the authority given by this law, Government also uses fiscal measures for controlling exports as and when necessary, either to discourage export do any particular product or for other reasons, e.g., the export duty on jute after 1966 devaluation, the recent export duty on tea, etc.

But while export control has always been an accepted tool in country's economic policy, what has been much more important in the Indian context in the last four decades is export promotion rather than export control. India's exports constitute only about 9 per cent of her GNP. This makes her a country with very modest export growth record. The chronic foreign exchange shortage from the mid-fifties onwards and the needs for importing large quantities of foodgrains, defence equipment and other capital goods imports have made vigorous export promotion a plain necessity. The aim of export growth is essentially to increase the real capacity to import. The periodical crude price hike from 1973 onwards had made it all the more necessary to launch a vigorous export drive symbolized in the slogan being preached among industrial circles—'export or perish.' The EXIM policy,1992-97, made a concious effort to boost exports. The policy coincided with 8th Plan and yielded impressive growth in exports.

The growth of India's exports in spite of the spectacular increases in recent years has been slow over a period of three decades. Our exports constitute only about 9 per cent of our GNP. A comparison of the volume indices of world's and India's exports as shown in the following table reveals the stagant India's share, i.e. less than one percent from 1970 to 1996, in the world trade.

**Table 1: India's Share in World Trade**

| | 1950 | 1960 | 1970 | 1980 | 1990 | 1992 | 1994 | 1996 | 1998 | 1999 |
|---|---|---|---|---|---|---|---|---|---|---|
| India's Exports | 1.1 | 1.3 | 2.0 | 8.6 | 18.0 | 19.6 | 25.0 | 33.1 | 33.6 | 26.6 |
| Exports | 61.9 | 129.9 | 314.6 | 2022.4 | 3486.1 | 3735.0 | 4265.3 | 5309.3 | 5405.1 | 4027.8 |
| % of 1 to 2 | 1.8 | 1.0 | 0.6 | 0.4 | 0.5 | 0.5 | 0.6 | 0.6 | 0.6 | 0.7 |

Source: UNCTAD Handbook of International Trade and Development Statistics, 1995; and Government of India, Economic Survey 1999-2000.

It may also be highlighted that India's exports grew at the rate of only 2 per cent per annum between 1950-51 and 1968-69 and 6 per cent per annum between 1968-69 and 1971-72. The galloping. increases thereafter (22.3 per cent in 1972-73, 28 per cent in 1973-74, 32 per cent in 1974-75, 18.4 per cent in 1975-76) to a large extent reflects inflation or special windfall opportunities such as sugar and silver[2] During the period 1980-89 India's exports rose by only 4.7%. It rose at the rate of 14.2 per cent per annum (16 per cent if low increase of 7.4 percent if 1996 is excluded) during 1993-96. However, in dollar terms exports registered an average growth of 20 per cent (during 1993-94 to 199596). During 1996-99 this rate declined to about 4 per cent the world trade has undergone significant changes since 1996 due to a host of developments including a sharp fall in international prices for manufactured products and the emergence of economic crises in certain parts of the world. In addition, protectionist policies and practices adopted by various industrialised countries during the recent years in the form of non-tariffs seriously affected the export efforts of developing countries including India. India's Exports' dismal performance as compared to the export growth of the other countries especially China. Both China and India were exporting at roughly the same level around 1971-72 (worth $2.2

billion and $2.2 billion respectively). In 1998 India's exports rose barely to the level of $33.6 billion while China's exports shot up to the staggering level of $183.6 billion of major traditional exports, viz., jute manufacturers, tea, coffee, cotton piece goods and semi-processed leather in India's total exports declined from 53.5 per cent in 1955-56 to 28 per cent in 1974-75[5] The combined share of seven products (jute goods, tea, cotton textiles, leather and leather products, iron ore, oil cakes and cashew kernels) which accounted for 60 per cent of the earnings from foreign trade in 1965-66 fell down to 38 per cent in 1975-76 and to18.7 per cent in 1998-99. However, some of the products like coffee, tea, leather and spices have maintained their command in world trade in recent years too. In 1997 India accounted for 12.6 per cent, 11.9 per cent, 1.8 per cent and 11.0 per cent of world trade in rice coffee and coffee substitutes, tea and mate, leather and spices respectively. True that in the seventies there were significant spurts in the export of some of the newer items, e.g. engineering goods (from Rs 23 crores in 1966-67 to over Rs. 408 crores in 1975-76 and to Rs.16,483 crores in 1998-99), garments (from Rs 2 erores in 1966-67 to over Rs 100 erores in 1976-77 and to Rs. 14,405 crores in 1998-99) and handicrafts (from Rs 39 crores in 1966-67 to over Rs 182 crores in 1974-75 and to over Rs.23347 crores in 1998-99).

To round up, we should note that despite the improvements from time to time in the overall export growth rates, and the fast growth of a number of new items, India's overall long-term performance has been modest, that the earlier dominant categories of exports have stagnated while even in the newer fast growing categories she has fallen behind major competitors, and that growth has not been as impressive as it could have been except when the base is markedly lower than that of those competitors. Thus there is no ground for complacency, and we should seriously examine the policy system, the variables which are within India's control as distinct from those which are not, and the effectiveness of the incentives and promotional structure.

Expanding exports depend both on factors which are within India's control (e.g. volume of exports) and those which are outside (e.g. market access, export prices, import prices). We are only concerned with the former. The volume of export is the most important factor which India can influence with least difficulty. A 1 per cent per annum rate of growth of the volume of export can have the same effect on the actual capacity to import as an equivalent rate of improvement in the term of trade which is much more difficult to achieve. The volume of exports is determined by several key factors, viz. demand, price, quality and availability. These will vary from product to product.

## BASIC CONSTRAINTS

Despite export promotion having always been on the agenda of the government, exports could not grow as at a desired rate and level because of may constraints. hi a globalised environment these constraints, if not removed, may disturb not only the balance of payments but whole of the economy.

Apart from the basic economic inefficiency of India's industrial structure and the high cost of inputs, there are also many other problems created by the policy environment, e.g., restrictions on multiple shift specially affecting industries like electronic and garment; price control on some industries; canalizing of imports through state trading agencies creating delay and raising cost; the uncertainty, delay and adhocism characterizing the system, etc. Other important factors for India's lacklustre export performance are: (1) undue dependence on traditional exports (2) the absence of international competitive efficiency in terms of price, quality and available quantity (3) a more attractive domestic market (4) infrastructural inadequacies e.g. power supply, telecommunication, transport, port capacity (5) unsatisfactory labour relations, productivity and aggressive trade unionism (6) inadequate and more costly export credit (7) external constraints such as recessionary conditions in several regions, the strict quota system followed by some countries and groupings and the collapse of the former USSR and rupee trade agreement with East European countries (8) the recent import compression which affected the import intensive export units.

Chronic shortfall on infrastructure front and procedural hurdles are hunting the exporters. Because of these shortfalls, the Transaction Costs of exports becoming abnormally high, thereby, making our exports uncompetitive in the fierce global market. According to a study by Exim Bank, Transaction Cost as a percentage of export revenue is very high in the case of textile (15 per cent), chemicals (14 per cent), engineering, pharmaceuticals and software (10 per cent); fish and marine products (8.5 per cent) and tea exports 3 per cent). Had the transaction cost been brought down by 1-2 per cent, exports could have been on an average increased by 5-6 per cent. So for a sustained and steady growth of exports in real terms, and maintain competitiveness, it is most essential that takes appropriate measures to cut the Transaction Costs. For this, concerted efforts are called for on several fronts such as improvement of port infrastructure and developing satellite ports to decongest major ports, improve availability of power, transport services, communication, warehouse facilities, roads and bridges etc. and major investments need to be made in these areas. Procedural complexities, have had negative impact so far on growth of exports. To ease out the hardships being faced by the exporters, policy and procedures need to be further simplified in real sense, and facilitate exports to grow. Availability and cost of finance are found to be very expensive in India. Faster and more efficient credit delivery system, definitely reduce cost of exports. Incentives in one form or the other, to push up exports, may not found to be fruitful and may even face anti-subsidy or countervailing duties in the importing countries and proves to be counter productive. Instead, it is wiser to employ resources in productive means, which will ensure sustained growth of exports on a long run by investing in infrastructure and such promotional activities, which create demand for Indian products abroad.

India's export strategy is necessarily conditioned by her general policy of industrial growth and the basic inadequacies and inefficiency of the industrial policy system. Her industrial policy has traditionally been characterized by an excessive reliance on quantitative restrictions on increase of production by firms and on the import of essential inputs, an emphasis on across-the-board import substitution as an overriding aim, a non-recognition of the value of the economies of scale and the resultant low scale production and inadequate emphasis on the cost aspect. These policies are administered by a highly bureaucratized economic administration which is more often than not remote from the scene of action and which is not known for quick or timely decisions. The pathetic fact remains that Indian industry is not organised efficiently enough to respond to needs and demands of international business.

By any recognised international standard India's industries are fragmented into a large number of small firms. Just to take a few examples, seven firms shared a total production of 32,000 tractors in 1972-73, and ten manufacturers shared a total installed capacity of 81,000 units of commercial vehicles. Such fragmentation, apart from making high price inevitable, also. creates problems in marketing, services, product development, research and development, and obsolescence, the last two factors preventing Indian firms from keeping up with world developments. The quality of production in a rather uncompetitive environment is often poor. Many industries established under a policy of import substitution with the sole object of meeting the limited domestic market find it difficult to thrive in the competitive international environment. In the prevailing sellers' market they are not accustomed to product development, product improvement, cost control or cost benefit studies based on the economies of scale and good marketing including prompt delivery and after sales service—qualities which are preconditions for successful international marketing. Also there are rigid curbs on collaboration agreement, import of technology and capital equipment, and import of cheaper raw materials and components. These not only make India's exportable products costly and unsatisfactory, but also saddle the economy with high cost industry. This is further compounded in many cases by high levels of excise and import duties which tend to push up the cost of both raw materials and finished goods above their world prices and thus make our exports non-competitive. Experience has shown that it is not always possible to combine import-substitution with export promotion. The strong bias in favour of import substitution encourage firms to produce a large number of products rather than concentrating on a few which can compete in the international market. Here again, formal or informal restrictions on the expansion of the large business houses and foreign companies sometimes stand in the way of building up an exportable surplus. The rising domestic market, combined with the. uncertainty and lower profitability of export discourages these firms from the export market and encourages them to concentrate rather on the sheltered domestic market where high prices and near-monopolistic conditions prevail. There is no incentive for either efficient production or modernization, both of which are essential conditions for good export performance. These constraints tend to impair production even when it is planned for export.

The domestic prices of many commodities are generally well above international prices. Hence exports on a full cost basis do not become profitable without the export incentives. Even with the incentives export profitability appears to be roughly of the same level as that of domestic sale. As the export prices are well below the domestic prices, there is no particular compulsion from the angle of business profitability to concentrate on export. Naturally the highest ratio of exports to sale is observed in those industries where exports appear to be most profitable, e.g., textile machinery. A long-term export policy for India must therefore depend on the elimination of some of the clearly identified constraints, viz., (1) discouragement of the economies of scale, quality production and product development, (2) severe restrictions on imports of inputs and capital goods required for export, (3) an exchange rate and export duty subsidies which do not make export really attractive. The immediate and main thrust in policy should be to create an environment where exports are made profitable in comparison with domestic sales and where Indian industry can easily create exportable surplus production without being hampered by policy or physical constraints or by shortage of the required imports. A policy for continuous long-term growth will also require a very significant reorientation of the business strategy of India's major firms with a lot of attention to better marketing and after sales service, better quality control and improved delivery, and also corresponding changes in Government's industrial and trade policies.

FDI (Foreign Direct Investment) led export growth as demonstrated by China is an eye opener for India. Over one third of exports from China are contributed by Foreign Investment Enterprises (FIE's). Constraints of funds in core sectors as well as in growth oriented industrial activities can be overcome by right strategic Policy approaching FDI. State Governments too have to involve and participate actively in the promotion of exports from the respective State. This will ensure more employment generation as well as more revenue, directly or indirectly to the State Governments. Strategy also need to make changes in export policy to make them compatible with the norms of the World Trade Organization (WTO) and take Proactive measures to combat, threats in the form of Non-Tariff barriers. In certain aspects both the Government and the Industry in collaboration has to fight it out in the WTO.

## INCENTIVES SYSTEM

This brings us to the incentives given by the Government till recently for encouraging export. The export incentives which were adopted in the past took three broad forms: (1) fiscal measures such as outright cash subsidy, exemption from sales tax on final sales, refund of indirect taxes, direct tax concessions through duty drawbacks, rail freight concessions for offsetting the transport disadvantage; (2) import entitlement schemes; and (3) concessional credit. These also include other miscellaneous things such as assistance in market research, award for outstanding export performance, release of foreign exchange for export promotion, blanket permits for export promotion tours abroad, and priority treatment in the allotment of scarcity raw materials used in export production at concessional prices. special incentives have been extended to units set up in Export Processing Zones (EPZs), Electronic Hardware Parks, Software Technology Parks, (EHTP /STP), etc. Export Oriented Units (EOUs) have also been extended such special benefits merchant exporters have been made eligible for special facilities. But the system of incentives and subsidies apart from being very costly tended to be administration-ridden and introduced much distortions and for exemption.

## EXPORT CREDIT

In the field of export finance on which export promotion depends considerably, the Reserve Bank of India played a crucial role. It controls and co-ordinates the banking facilities to make export finance available at the right time and in right quantum. It maintained concessional interest rate that varied from time to time. For several years the RBI's functions were mostly taken over by IDBI which established its own export credit division. This continued till 1982 when the newly set up Export Import Bank took over from the IDBI the export financing and refinancing schemes which the latter was discharging till then.

The Central Government has also set up the Export Credit and Guarantee Corporation for providing investment risk insurance to exporters. It has extended its operation to cover joint ventures and turnkey projects in third countries and to blanket credit coverage to banks in respect of all pre-shipment advances. In the monetary and credit policy announced by the RBI in October, 1999 has tried to reduce financing cost and to provide credit at reasonable terms to the exporters.

Setting up of export oriented units or processing zone (EOU /EPZ) with 100 per cent exporting manufacturing units has also received considerable attention in recent years. There are several such zones, e.g., the Kandla Free-Trade Zone, the Santa Cruz Electronics Export-processing Zone; Cohin Export Processing Zone; Madras Export Processing Zone, Falta Export Processing Zone; Chennai Export Processing Zone; Noida Export Processing Zone; and Visakhapatnam Export Processing Zone. Software Technology Parks (STP) Scheme is also a 100 per cent Export Oriented Scheme for undertaking Software Development for export using data communication link or in the form of physical exports including export of professional services. Electronic Hardware Technology Park (EHTP) Scheme intends to boost the hardware exports. Units set up under EOU/EIZ/EHTP or STP Scheme are also given special incentives.

### Special Economic Zones

A major step in the Annual EXIM Policy, 2000-2001 was taken to establish Special Economic Zone (SEZs) in different parts of the country. In China such zones have demonstrated an eye opening performance in the exports growth. The idea basically is that in their areas zones export production can take place free from the plethora of rules, and regulations governing import and export. The units operating in these zones will have full flexibility of operations. They would be able to import capital goods and raw materials duty free and would also be able to access the same from the Domestic Tariff Area (DTA) without payment of Terminal Excise Duty. No permission would be necessary for inter unit sales or transfer of goods. There would be no wastage norms or input-output norms. They would be able to undertake job work for the DTA units and would also be able to get their good processed in the DTA. The only condition would be that the units in the zone would have to export the entire production and that DTA sales would be permitted only on payment of full applicable customs duties and additional duties without any concession.

### Export Obligations

In the 60s and 70s, in order to offset the comparative attractiveness of the domestic market the Government imposed general and specific export obligations in many cases. General obligations were imposed on MRTP or FERA companies whenever they are granted industrial licences in areas not open to them under the licensing policy. Special obligations are imposed at various stages of the licensing process in response to specific situations. Sometimes Government policy encourages setting up 100 per cent export-oriented units. Such a policy is all right when an overseas firm with a captive market takes advantage of India's cheap labour and infrastructure facilities wherever they exist. It simply does not work if a domestic firm launches without any export experience an export-oriented business just to take advantage of tax concession. For such a firm some sort of back-up of domestic market becomes an essential condition for long-term export growth.

### Export Servicing

Servicing by export promotion bodies is recognised by the Government of India as one of the important inputs for the growth of exports. Various export promotion institutions like the Indian Trade Promotion Organization (resulted from a merger of the erstwhile Trade Fair Authority of India and Trade Development Authority), Export Promotion Councils, Commodity Boards (e.g. Tea Board, Coffee Board, Tobacco Board), Federation of Indian Export Organization and a few other organizations are actively engaged in providing export services. The roles played in recent years by the Confederation of Indian Industries (formerly Confederation of Engineering Industries) and the Engineering Exports Promotion Council in spectacularly stepping up the export of Indian engineering goods have been commendable.

The following is a list of organisations to meet the information needs of exports:

(i) Department of Commercial Intelligence and Statistics ( CI&S)
(ii) Directorate of Exhibitions and Commercial Publicity (DECP), Ministry of Commerce
(iii) Small Industries Development Corporation (SIDC)
(iv) Export Promotion Councils for various industries
(v) Indian Institute of Foreign Trade (lIFT)
(vi) Federation of Indian Export Organization (FIEO)
(vii) Indian Investment Centre (lIC)
(viii) Association of Indian Engineering Industries
(ix) Export Credit and Guarantee Corporation (ECGC)
(x) Five Commodity Boards, e.g. Tea Board, Coffee Board, Tobacco Board, Rubber Board and Spices Board
(xi) Marine Products Development Authority
(xii) India Trade promotion Organisation ( ITPO)
(xiii) Export Inspection Council
(xiv) The Indian Institute of Packaging, Mumbai (lIP) (xv) National Centre for Trade Information (NCTI)
(xvi) Directorate General of Anti-dumping and Allied Duties (DGAAD)

The Indian commercial representatives abroad, and the export wings of the various Chambers of Commerce, and Trade and Industry Associations also playa useful role in this area.

## Role of States in Export Promotion

A scheme is being started to involve the state governments in the export promotion particularly for encouraging agro exports. Assistance for infrastructure development for exports would be broadly linked to export performance of each state.

## Role of the Public Sector

Despite some improvements in recent times, the public sector's role in exports has been a mixed bug. This is despite the public sector trading companies, such as the State Trading Corporation (STC) and The Projects and Equipment Corporation of India (PEC) the Minerals and Metals

Trading Corporation (MMTC) acting as canalizing agencies in respect of export of specified goods. Thus the STC was responsible for all export of sugar, tanned hides and silver, while the MMTC exports all iron ore except from Goa. The Steel Authority of India is responsible for all exports of steel. Several other bodies like the Projects and Equipment Corporation. the Handicrafts and Handloom Export Corporation and Tea Trading Corporation are becoming important promoters of exports. Many State Governments have also launched their own Export Corporations. But the pathetic fact remains that the biggest five among Public Sector Undertakings export goods equivalent of just around 4 per cent of their turn-over after several decades of their creation. Indeed exports do not appear to be a priority on the agenda of the PSUs. Even enterprises operating in high-tech and new frontiers like Indian Telephone Industries. HMT and Bharat Electronics have poor track records. True. that most of them are just now suffering from savage budgetary support cuts and other constraints like redundancy, obsolescence and cost overruns. But they should see themselves as important partners in the nation's efforts for export drive and earning of foreign exchange to cover their own import bills and to remove the strain on the balance of payments. They must put export of goods and services on the forefront of their agenda, and take full advantage of the devaluation and globalisation processes.

We should also note two other areas, somewhat inter-related in nature, which offer exciting potentiality in relation to India's total export efforts in coming years:

(i) consultancy services and
(ii) joint ventures, abroad.

**Consultancy Services**

During the 70s Indian consultancy organizations, both in the public and private sectors, have established themselves in the developing countries because of the comparative attractiveness for them of the intermediate technologies developed in India and also because of their lower costs compared to the cost of Western consultants.

There were a number of Indian consultancy organizations. which have been able to give efficient technical services to developing countries. These services have resulted not only in direct earnings of foreign exchange, but in a number of cases in increased exports of Indian manufacturers.

Following are some of the consultancy organizations established in the public sector;

Broadcast Engg. Consultants India Ltd;
Central Mine Planning and Design Institute;
Educational Consultants (India) Ltd;
Engineering Projects (India) Ltd;
Engineers India Limited;
Hospital Services Consultancy Corp. (India) Ltd.;
Metallurgical and Engineering Consultants (India) Limited;
National Industrial Development Corporation Ltd.;
National Small Industries Corp. Ltd.;
Power Grid Corporation of India Ltd.;
Rail India Technical and Economic Services;
Telecommunications Consultants (India) Ltd;
Water and Power Consultancy Services (India) Limited.

But as the decade of the 80s wore on, the overall performance declined. Most of them gave way to superior competitors from countries such as South Korea. Clearly the prevailing work ethos the productivity norms, infrastructural inadequacies for drawal of inputs from home trade and lack of concern for timely completion and cost and time overruns do not help the growth of international competitiveness.

### Joint Ventures Abroad

Joint ventures abroad by Indian firms have become significant in recent years. Sometimes they take the form of joint enterprises with firms from the major trading partners of India in third countries. The changing pattern of India's trade has also brought out the need for investment abroad by Indian exporters of capital goods and turnkey projects. Recent trade agreements between India and several countries have emphasized such joint projects. The Ministry of Commerce is the focal agency which approves joint ventures abroad, on the basis of scrutiny by an inter-Ministerial Committee. Initially, the contribution by the Indian party could only be in the form of capital goods. But later on the Government also decided to permit cash participation in equity in special cases. The Indian joint ventures numbering around 300 by 1985. But as a result of the transparent and liberal framework more than 200 approvals are issued annually in the recent years. Today Indian joint ventures have become significant in a number of countries in Asia, Africa and Europe. There are some leading success stories.

Unfortunately the mortality rate of these joint ventures has been very high and about 50 per cent of them till now seem to have fallen by the way side. Then again, their impact by way of net inflow of resources has been insignificant. There is prima facie suspicion that industrialists often use these joint ventures abroad as a device to spend money or build up hidden reserves abroad. There is therefore considerable room for introducing correct project appraisal, cost benefit analysis and better administrative supervision along with required commercial flexibility. Joint ventures abroad are important not because of what they have achieved, but because of what they are capable of achieving.

### Export-Import Bank of India

In 1982 the Central Government established a specialized institution viz., the Export-Import Bank of India, on the lines of the Japanese or the US Export-Import Banks; to meet the special needs of export· financing. Initially the Export-Import Bank took over from the Industrial Development Bank of India its functions of direct participation credit scheme, refinancing eligible banks in respect of term loans granted by them to exporters for financing exports on deferred payment terms. The Bank has also successfully floated several bonds in the overseas capital market.

## SOME RECENT POLICY LIBERALIZATIONS

During the 90s there have been some significant shifts in emphasis in the export promotion policy of the Government in tune with the new trends towards pragmatism seen in the overall industrial licensing policy and procedure. These are important because they are likely to have a favourable impact on the export performance. The EXIM policy of 1992-97 was the important step in this direction. Another step was the EXIM policy of 1997-2002, formulated in April, 1997. A subsequent revision was made in it on April 13, 1998. A package of incentives were announced in Ausut 1998. These two export policies were the right steps in direction to achieve the targeted growth rate of exports i.e. 20 per cent. Thrust of the revisions and amendments carried on time to time is to enhance export competitiveness by simplifying procedures, minimising transaction costs and delays and improving the attractiveness of various schemes besides increasing the incentives to the exporters. Some of the measures are:

(i) Threshold limit for EPC zero duty scheme has been brought down to Rs. 1 crore uniformly for Agriculture and Allied Sector (from Rs. 5 crore) and for Electronics, Textiles, Leather, Gems and Jewellery. Sports goods and Food Processing sectors (from Rs 20 crore) and to Rs 10 lakh in the case of the software sector;

(ii) DEPB scheme will neutralise not only the basic customs duty but also the special customs duty; setting up of private bonded warehouses has been permitted for exports and imports;

(iii) exports of all oil seeds, when exported for consumption purposes, and of vegetable oils have been made free without any quantitative and licensing requirements; and

(iv) in addition, changes have been announced in depreciation limit, value addition norms, threshold limit, threshold limit for export houses, SIL entitlement, for providing inputs to exports

The comprehensive package of stabilisation measures were followed by the new 5-year Exim Policy announced on 31st March, 1992 which has brought about massive deregulation of government's functions and has made trade free subject to a small negative list. A summary of this short document is given in the Annexure to this chapter. The remaining of the office of Chief Controller of Imports and Exports as Development Commission of Exports symbolises the change.

## Prospects

For long-term export growth the removal of the known constraints on efficient production in India's industrial system must form an important part of the export strategy. Some of the basic points that need emphasis in the overall policy system are:

(i) Incentives are required over a longer time-horizon given the general penalisation of exports implicit in the trade policy system. The incentive system should be simple, easily understood and applied on everyone equally with an automacity rather than on discretionary judgement by individuals.

(ii) The cash incentive system being prone to abuses, incentives through tax reliefs and concessions as an alternative system should be considered. The possibility and comparative merits of differential rates of taxation on profits earned on exports should be seriously examined. Also export incentives shall be linked to the performance of individual firms or on the ratio of exports to sales.

(iii) Exporters must have easy access to whatever imported inputs are required without having to pay customs duties which make their products costlier than those of overseas competitors.

(iv) The creation of exportable surpluses in an environment of rising demands will have to be given some attention. Some of the recent improvements have been partly due to conscious deprivation of the home market. We have to avoid comic situations such as the unloading of export cargo of cotton from ships that took place in 1994 just because the Textile Ministry had imposed a ban on export of cotton. Such highhanded action not only meant reneging on contracts which have been entered into, but the loss of export market after it has been created with much effort. A balance has to be struck between home consumption and exports. It is necessary to emphasize the need to link exports with specially sponsored export-oriented projects designed to produce exportable surplus.

(v) Emphasis should be on the most efficient use of India's own resources on the basis of better utilization of the unit value rather than the export of any and all goods manufactured in India. To take one example, the present system offers parallel incentive to all export commodities irrespective of their relative competitive ability and economic strength. But we should also consider having a more discriminatory approach where some commodities may need greater incentive than others. Similarly, since export prices differ according to destination the destinational aspects of exports must also receive special consideration.

(vi) India has a natural advantage of proximity in relation to the expanding West Asian and East and South-East Asian Markets. A vigorous marketing strategy should enable her to gain their markets and also the market of developing countries for those goods in which she has an export potential, all the more so when a world-wide inflation has made her goods relatively competitive. Traditionally, India has relied .heavily on the western world for her exports. In 1983-84, 44.2 per cent of her exports went to the industrialised countries including Japan. Eastern Europe and OPEC accounted for 16.3 per cent and 8.9 per cent respectively. Developing countries excluding OPEC form the destination for 15.8 per cent of India's exports in 1983-84. Thus, it will be seen that although the percentage of OECD countries as destinations of India's exports has come down substantially from the level of about 70 per cent in the 70s, it is still overwhelmingly the largest. India's share in the imports of the oil-rich West Asian countries is only 1.5 per cent in spite of her, geographical closeness and cultural ties. Nearly, all the developed countries, and even a developing country like South Korea have made more significant head ways in these regions. Her share in the fast expanding imports of South-East Asia is only 0.9 per cent. A vigorous concerted export drive in these two regions is a welcome move. India's rain fall, soil conditions round the year and cropping pattern make her ideally suited to build up an exportable surplus for a large number of agriculture produces and food articles, including, processed fruits and vegetables, flowers and horticultural products. What is needed is production drive, aggressive marketing, quality control, proper packaging and speed of delivery.

(vii) The collapse of the former USSR and with it the rupee trade arrangements with USSR and other East European countries should be viewed not as a misfortune, but as a long-term opportunity. India should be a cheaper source of supplies for them of agricultural products, consumers, durables, light machinery and a host of services. Conversely, India will continue to need considerable volume of petroleum products, hardware, industrial machinery and equipment from Russia. These will make it advantageous for India to enter into long-term trade relations with Russia, the other former Soviet republics and selectively some of the East European countries on the basis of countertrade or even payment in hard currency. The advantage of doing away with the present artificially valued high rouble vis-a-vis Indian rupee and designatory transactions in dollar-terms is not to be lost sight of.

(viii) We have been spending much time, energy and resources on some traditional export items, and on restrictive barriers imposed by a few countries on few items (e.g. quota on textiles). This engrossment has overlooked important shifts in export products, patterns of trade and the emergence of new markets. To take one example, Hong Kong, Korea and lately China are exporting toys worth billions of dollars to North America. There are no quotas in these products. What has prevented India with her tradition of craftsman from taking advantage of these growing markets?

(ix) Export efforts in India are considerably handicapped by the inadequate infrastructure, particularly in the fields of telecommunication, roads, air services, port and shipping facilities, railways and power supply. Inadequate and irregular power supply, uncertain telex on telephone facilities and difficulties communication pattern make it uncompetitive for Indian exporters vis-a-vis exporters in export-oriented economies. India's ports are serious bottlenecks. Their performance needs to be improved in an accelerated manner or an every any fair.

(x) We have to make a determined effort to involve the State governments in the export efforts. While in China the provinces can export on their own, in our country the state authorities have an indifferent and at times even hostile attitude to exports which, in their perception, benefit only the Central Government. This attitudinal barrier needs to be broken by devising ways and means through which State governments can be given some incentives in all incremental export gains e.g. a share in the use of the foreign exchange earned through additional export efforts.

(xi) Export credit must be delinked from the general credit and monetary policies, and made cheaper. Otherwise, our exporters borrowings funds at 11 per cent or so, just cannot compete with exporters elsewhere with access to funds at 4 per cent or 5 per cent.

(xii) A direct nexus can be established between the open foreign direct investment being followed by some countries in recent decades and their impressive export performance e.g. China, Malaysia. Singapore, Thailand, Indonesia. India's notorious negative policy since the late 1960s in relation to foreign direct investment has also been a contributory factor to the unimpressive export performance.

(xiii) The controversy that erupts from time to time as to whether India should follow export-led growth or growth-led export is academic and fruitless. A Committee on Trade Policy (1985) after weighing the pros and cons of both approaches came to the conclusion that our accent should be on growth-led exports rather than on export- led growth. For India both growth and exports are important and there should never be 'either-or' approach. The most recent example of the turmoil and slide-down in some of the East Asian and South East Asian countries which followed export-led growth do not invalidate this thesis. These countries have suffered for other unwise economic sins they committed and not because they have pursued export-led growth. There are countries in the region such as Taiwan and China which have not fallen sick of this Asiatic flu, because they did not succumb to these sins even while exporting feverishily. While, for India growth at a fast pace is important that need not be at the cost of fast export growth which can in fact contribute much to economic growth.

If these constraints are eliminated and if the trends in the recent past are any indication, around 13 to 15 per cent growth of exports per annum seems maintainable. Even the 8th Plan target of 13.6 per cent in value terms was actually achieved over the five years period. In 1993-94 exports grew at a rate of over 21 per cent in dollar terms and over 33 per cent in rupees. The least that India can do is to try to continue this rate or atleast keep pace with the average rate of increase in world exports which had grown at an annual compound rate of 15 to 20 per cent during the last two decades.

In the long run India's export growth will depend both on continued vigil with regard to traditional exports and determined stride forward in certain non-traditional items. We have to recognise the downward trends of our traditional items like jute, cotton textiles and oil cakes and try to reverse them by taking special steps such as investments in increased production of high potential textile items like denim, canvas etc., and in finding newer uses of jute. On the other hand, continued emphasis is necessary on some non-traditional items like engineering goods, machine products, apparels, handicrafts, electronic goods, and finished leather and leather goods, all of which have the potential to grow at 15 per cent per annum. A leading example is software export which had grown in the last five years at a fantastic pace from 0 to over Rs 1,000 crores. It should not be difficult to increase the export ratio of leading companies to say; 20 per cent of the production and that alone should boost up the total export figures very appreciably. But for achieving that, along with Governmental help and incentive, simplification of policies and procedure and a reorientation of export marketing is essential. Marketing has all along been a weak point with Indian industry. Indian exporters must diversify in respect of both newer commodities and newer countries in West Asia, Africa, and South-East Asia which offer vast opportunities. They must draw up long-range marketing plans based on actual market surveys and implement them with sincerity, dive and imagination. Other deficiencies which must be remedied are poor and uncertain quality, delayed delivery, absence of after-sales services and lack of team spirit or consortium approach among Indian manufacturer-exporters. Indeed, pragmatism should be the guiding motive at a time when despite the increase in her exports India is facing a yawning adverse trade balance. Her technological capability, larger and diversified industrial base and skill make a high export growth rate possible. A comparison of the export performance of India with those of China and South Korea during the last two decades is revealing. China by pursuing a bold export vision and highly pragmatic and non-doctrinnaire fiscal and industrial promotional policies, have dramatically pushed up the value of her exports from around US$ 2.3 billion to US$ 150 billion, while the value of India's exports during the same period has grown from US$ 2.2 billion to US$ 31 billion. China's real break-through came only from 1980 when she started her determined pursuit of modernisation, efficiency and productivity. South Korea, with a size of some of India's smaller states exports much more than India in value terms, although she imports nearly all the inputs, including crude and iron ore. From this point of view the recent de-regulatory steps are in the right direction. If these are followed without slackening and are backed up by good overseas promotional efforts to change India's image as a difficult, highly bureaucratic country, it may not be difficult to repeat China's export performance. But there has to be a government-industry partnership backed by political will and determined efforts. The ongoing globalisation efforts provide more opportunity than constraints for India's export scenario. India has had striking export growth during the 8th Plan period. In the aggregate it surpassed the 8th Plan target of annual growth rate of 13.6 per cent. But thereafter with the clubbing of exports profits, with a company's overall profits under Minimum Additional Taxation (MAT) in 1996, the process of declining exports set in. There has been negative growth in a number of quarters recently and overall growth has fallen. This situation has been aggravated by slowdown in world trade and the currency turmoil in East Asian and South East Asian countries which has lowered the value of the currency of these countries as compared to India and has reduced the demand for goods and services from India and by making their products and services more competitive.

Export promotion efforts will have to be upgraded with the current needs and requirement as the onset of globalisation has made these efforts more difficult. Era of unilateral and bilateral trade seems to have lost its significance in the face of multilateral trade and multilateral organizations, like WTO. Resources, goods and services of competitive quality can be sourced now from anywhere in the globe at the competitive price. Thus Indian exports have to be internationally competitive if these are to find a place in the globe. Moreover, India has to represent her case effectively at WTO and all other international bodies which also requires skills at the negations over various trade/investment/technical/social related and other matters. In this connection, India being the one of largest economics in the third world has to playa leader's role to put developing countries case effectively so that these countries can take benefit equally (as developed countries) from the process of globalization.

## Globalization of the World Economy

Gradually sweeping aside national frontiers imposed by tariff walls and control over flow of information from the 1980s the process of globalization has swept over the world like a giant tidal wave. The new information technology—the world of e-mails, telefaxes and web-sites and other aspects of the all powerful computer technology was both the cause and effect of globalization. It does not admit of national frontiers as no nation can control it. It was also aided by the vast improvements in aviation technology making it possible for airplanes to carry hordes of travelers to long distances across the globe within a few hours. Globalization has made it possible for business enterprises to draw their raw materials and intermediaries from any other country where they get it at the cheapest price. Also they can sell their products anywhere they get the best prices. They need not be tied down in both activities by the various limits of national fractions. The world trade has grown several times in recent years. Competition has increased enormously and with its competitiveness. Those who can take advantage of the enormous opportunities provided by globalization can look forward to exciting prospects of growth. Those who still cry for protection and restrictions on competition as in yester-years only stagnate and languish. They have to learn to accept globalization as in unstoppable and universal process.

## World Trade Organisation

The coming into being of the World Trade Organization (WTO) during the first decade of the present century was an event of major importance. India was among the first countries to join the WTO and to that extent become subject to the restrictions imposed by this world body. It also became beneficiary in respect of a number of things such as being given automatically the status of the most favored nation by all the member countries. There is no doubt that membership of the WTO has brought about a massive expansion of India's role in world trading both in imports and exports. There are also provisions for antidumping measures in cases where some countries are dumping certain goods on other countries. There has been some criticism on the part of ideologues about India joining this world trade body on grounds such as loss of sovereignty which are not really maintainable in the present day contest.

## REFERENCES

1. Ministry of Commerce, *Annual Report,* 1975-76.
2. Manmohan Singh, *India's Export Trends,* Oxford 1964.
3. Bhagawati and Desai, *India, Planning for Industrialisation,* Oxfore University Press.
4. See Annual Report of the Ministry of International Trade, Government of India, 1963-64, p.14.
5. *Op, cit.,* pp. 73-74.
6. S.N. Panigrahi, Export—Challenges in the New Millennium, Ex-Imp. *Times,* Feb. 7, 2000.

# CHAPTER 12

# Public Sector Development Banking

Before Independence one major constraint for the development of industries was the absence of institutional arrangements for providing industrial finance on any significant scale. It was, therefore, very natural that after independence Government took steps to fill this vacuum and create a number of national and State level financial institutions one after another. These financial institutions are not banking institutions in the conventional sense, but development banks which serve as development agencies not only carrying on lending operation, but also developmental activities including promoting projects and guiding and advising the clients in their problems and difficulties.

## Scope and Significance of Development Banking

The institution of "Development Banking" is largely a post-war creation, first introduced in Europe and Japan, and has now come to be accepted by most developing countries. The principal function of a development bank is to provide medium and long-term capital for investments. Capital markets in most developing countries are comparatively underdeveloped. Underwriting facilities are generally absent; there is rarely an environment of confidence amongst investors. In many cases there is a marked absence of entrepreneurs, and existing business displays a disinclination to venture into new areas and lacks the incentive to do so. To overcome these obstacles development banks in additional to providing finance are expected to have a promotional role in "enterprise creation."

In the recent past, an increasing number of developing countries have promoted development banks. These banks have been created in response to the particular needs of the country they were to serve and to the political, economic and social environment in which they were to function. In consequence there is considerable variety among these institutions both in organisational structure and in the scope of activity, although all such institutions have been sponsored by Governments, which exert a varying degree of influence on their policies and operations. Some are owned exclusively by Government, others by private interests, and still others by combination of the two. Some are devoted to the promotion and financing of Government enterprises, some others exclusively to private investment, and still others to both fields. Some have broad planning functions. Some can only lend while some others can lend and take equities. Some can set up and manage enterprises on their own account. Some are concerned with the entire economy, others with but a single sector. Some are regional, others national. Ownership, sources of finance, degree of dependence on Government, objectives and methods of operation, differ over a broad range of possibilities.

The development banks in underdeveloped countries in earlier years were often primary agents for executing Government investment projects. Among them were institutions such as the *Etibank* of Turkey, created to exploit mineral resources on behalf of the Government. The *Corporation de Fomento de la Production* of Chile was intended to draw up a general plan to promote production in all sectors of the economy, and to obtain credit from abroad. The *Sumerbank* of Turkey concentrated on establishing, financing and managing industrial enterprises on behalf of the Government; the *Corporation Bolivara de Fomento* devoted itself largely to financing highway construction and a Government-owned petroleum production authority.

The Germin Bank of Bangladesh set up by the Dr. Mohd. Yunus to emphasize the collective repayments responsibilities of woman is also a case in point.

The basic task of a development bank then is to mobilise resources and to deploy them for industrial growth judiciously as the manner of deployment has significant implications for the economy. The kind of entrepreneur assisted determines the pattern of ownership of the means of production and the technology employed in the projects has relevance for generation of employment opportunities. Besides ensuring as wider a dispersal of industries as possible, care has also to be taken to strike a balance between the supply and demand of the industrial products. The foreign exchange resources being scarce, implications of assisted projects in terms of net foreign exchange saved or earned and the cost at which such saving or earning is affected, are also important from the point of view of international competitiveness of the assisted units. And, finally, investment activity should help to trigger off further self-sustaining-growth. Thus financial institutions play an important role in promoting industrial growth providing direction to the orderly growth of industry and enforcing discipline on the corporate sector and in safeguarding the public interest.

A development bank has now come to be increasingly accepted as a financial institution designed to mobilize resources and skills, and to channel them into approved sectors of industry consistent with the overall industrial policy of the country. Closely linked to its major role as a financing institution, a development bank has two essential functions: to mobilize savings and to allocate them. A dynamic approach is required of a development banker to induce and attract savings, and to search for new and better and productive investments. The hard core of the activities of a development bank is financing. This involves evaluation of investment projects in the light of the declared objectives of the industrial policy of the Government. Sound appraisal also requires that the development bank goes through the same viability appraisal in the project that the entrepreneur himself goes through, asking much the same questions about product-mix, the scale of operations, the technology, the plant facilities, the financial structure, the marketing arrangements, the managerial arrangements, the financial results, etc. The commercial banker finds himself in the posture of moulding, modifying, and advising on the proposals before him, so as to minimize the risks of failure of the business. He brings to the entrepreneur his background of experience in projects, and forces his clients to re-examine their plans, to understand their implications more clearly, and particularly the available options. A development bank because of its deep immersion in the daily operations of firms has an intimate knowledge of the market place. This aspect of the vast potential of development banks to improve the financial attractiveness of an investment proposal is beginning to be realised. What specific application a development bank makes of its experience is the upshot of several factors; the condition of the business community of the country, the institutional framework that serves the community, the attitudes and policies of the Government, and the management of the development bank itself. Once the concept of directing efforts towards specific development objectives is accepted it follows that the efforts should change from time to time. It should be reviewed periodically, and should be reoriented in the *light of the development bank's own experience, and of the changing public view of the country's needs.* Two examples are—the increasing emphasis given in policy of regional aspects of economic development, and a more equitable distribution of income. In the former the development bank can take an active part in encouraging loans in backward areas. To take one example the total assistance given by the I.F.C. since inception has gone to such areas. The Korean Development Bank is a good example of how a development bank can contribute to more equitable income distribution. In regions where the influence of the unorganised money market was strong, it advanced finance to companies with attractive projects even though these companies did not satisfy the usual bank requirements.

## ESTABLISHMENT OF DEVELOPMENT BANKS IN INDIA

The Industrial Finance Corporation was the first all-India term lending institution set up under the Industrial Finance Corporation Act, 1948. This was followed by the establishment of complementary State level institutions known as State Financial Corporations under the State Financial Corporation Act, 1951. These two laws provide for the Central Government and the concerned State Government respectively guaranteeing: (i) the share capital, (ii) dividend at minimum rates on it, and (iii) loans and debentures raised by these respective corporations. Though the State Financial Corporations were placed under the administrative jurisdiction of the concerned State Governments, the Reserve Bank of India's Industrial Finance Department has been performing the coordinating function, and, as an expert body, has been advising them practically in all their operations.

In 1955, in order to handle large foreign exchange loans expected from the World Bank, the Government of India agreed to the promotion of another all-India term lending institution, namely the Industrial Credit and Investment Corporation of India Limited, incorporated as a joint stock company. At about the same time, the National Small Industries Corporation Ltd. (NSIC) was established to assist small-scale industries through marketing, financing and other supporting activities.

In 1956 life insurance was nationalised and the Life Insurance Corporation of India was formed. The share capital of the Life Insurance Corporation of India is wholly held by the Central Government.

In 1958, in order to utilize the American counterpart funds for helping industry, the Refinance Corporation for Industry was incorporated as a limited company under the Companies Act. Its share capital was subscribed by the Reserve Bank of India, the Life Insurance Corporation of India and a few commercial banks. Its main function was refinancing Commercial Banks which gave term loans to industry.

In 1963, the Unit Trust of India was formed by an Act of Parliament with the help of development finance provided by the financial institutions. Its object was to attract small investors who want a regular return and yet do not want to take the risk of buying equity shares readily. It would raise resources by selling units to the public, investing its funds in, the corporate sector through shares and bonds, and paying dividend to their unit holders out of its earnings.

In 1964, the need for a coordinating agency was felt. It was also thought that such a coordinating agency should preferably be kept under the Central Banking authority of the country on the model of the Canadian Development Bank. Accordingly, the Industrial Development Bank of India was established under the Industrial Development Bank of India Act, 1964 as a wholly owned subsidiary of the Reserve Bank of India. The shares held by the Central Government and the Reserve Bank of India in the Industrial Finance Corporation were transferred to the Industrial Development Bank of India, and further shares were issued by the Industrial Finance Corporation to be wholly subscribed by the IDBI so that IDBI became a 40 per cent shareholder in the IFC. The IDBI has been conceived not merely as one more direct financing agency, but also as a refinancing and rediscounting as well as promotional agency. In view of its refinancing functions, it was no longer felt necessary to retain the Refinance Corporation for industry as a separate body; it was merged with the IDBI.

In 1971, a new institution known as the Industrial Reconstruction Corporation of India Limited, was established as a limited company in order to look after the sick and closed industrial units and make efforts to revive them by providing finance and restructure their management. This was converted into a full-fledged financial institution in 1985 and renamed as Industrial Reconstruction Bank of India. Again this was converted into Industrial Investment Bank of India from March 27,1997.

Another investment institution, more analogous to the LIC and the UTI than to the normal term-lending institutions came into being in 1973; the General Insurance Corporation of India after the Central Government had nationalised general insurance. The GIC operates through four subsidiaries.

## INDUSTRIAL FINANCE CORPORATION OF INDIA (IFCI)

Prior to the public issue of share capital in 1993, the share capital of IFCI established in 1948 (wholly guaranteed by the Central Government with guarantee for payment of dividend at minimum rates) as follows:

| | | |
|---|---|---|
| (i) | IOBI | 50 per cent |
| (ii) | Life Insurance Corporation and General Insurance Companies | 20 per cent |
| (iii) | Scheduled Commercial Banks | 20 per cent |

(iv) Cooperative Banks 7.71 per cent
(v) Others (Trusts and Charitable Institutions) 0.29 per cent

Its main function is to provide medium and long-term credit to industry, especially when accommodation from normal financial sources is inappropriate, or recourse to the capital market is impracticable. The IFCI Act specifies that the Corporation would confine its operations to public limited companies and cooperative societies. The functions of the IFCI listed in the Act are as follows:

(i) Guaranteeing loans floated in the public market which are repayable within a period of 25 years.
(ii) Underwriting the issue of stocks, share and debentures, but to be disposed of within 7 years.
(iii) Granting loans or advances repayaple within a period of 25 years.
(iv) Extending guarantees in respect of deferred payments by importers who are able to make such arrangements with foreign manufacturers. Such guaranteeing facilities were subsequently extended to cover loans raised from scheduled or cooperative banks and deferred payments for purchase of capital goods within the country.

The IFCI operations are confined to public limited companies and cooperatives. It has therefore a built-in bias in favour of the larger industrial sector. But it is required to pay attention to circumstances where normal banking accommodation is inappropriate. The IFCI has frequently not paid much attention to this requirement. The Estimates Committee (3rd LS), 1962-63, observed, "The committee formed the impression that there were concerns (visited by IFCI) which could have perhaps raised their funds from the market."

It was only in 1965 that a deliberate system of priorities was applied in the matter of choice of enterprises. The priorities accepted were that the project should make a contribution to (a) defence, (b) agriculture, (c) exports, (d) import substitutions. But these guidelines are sufficiently broad to accommodate practically any pattern of distribution, and a review of the industry-wise distribution of assistance does not show any major changes.

The share of cooperatives increased from 20 per cent in 1968 to 31.5 per cent in 1972-73. Sugar received over 90 per cent of the assistance to cooperatives. Other cooperative units were cotton spinning and vegetable oil. During 1988-99, IFCI's assistance to projects in notified less developed districts/areas was about 43 per cent of the total assistance sanctioned covering 103 projects out of 242 total projects. Cumulatively, till end of March, 1999 IFCI sanctioned total amount of Rs. 4,72,452 crore for 4877 projects out of which 47 per cent, was sanctioned to 2169 projects located in notified less developed districts/areas.

A significant change in 1993 was the decision to end the statutory status of the IFCI, and to incorporate it as a company under the Companies Act like the ICICI. This was followed up by partial privatisation of the share capital leading to the gradual introduction of private sector norms of efficiency. IFCI was till recently for all practical purposes a non-government company with government holding less than 50 per cent shares. But just now the Central Government has converted its loans into equity thereby once again turning it into a government company. Also it has promoted a number of special purposes subsidiaries such as the Tourism Finance Corporation, the Indian Credit Rating Agency (ICRA) and a corporation for promotion of venture capital and technology development.

## INDUSTRIAL DEVELOPMENT BANK OF INDIA (IDBI)

This was set up in 1964 under the IOBI Act as a wholly owned subsidiary of the Reserve Bank of India with the following functions:

(i) to coordinate the activities of other financial institutions,

(ii) supplement their resources,

(iii) plan and promote industries of key significance, and

(iv) adopt priorities to promote industrial growth.

In 1976 under the Public Finance Institutions Laws (Amendment) Act, 1976, the ownership of IOBI was transferred from RBI to the Government of India, and it was turned into the apex development bank with all other India development banks as its subsidiaries and having a coordinating function in respect of all financial institutions. The amended charter describes it as "the principle financial institution for coordination in conforming with national priorities, the working of institution engaged in financing, promoting or developing industry, for assisting the development of such institution, and in providing credit and other facilities for the development of industry and for matters connected therewith."

Till 1970 its attention was concentrated on strengthening its own organisational framework towards achieving the above-stated objectives tasks which are basic for the evolution of an all-India apex development bank. Since then it has entered a new phase of innovative activity "enterprise creation"—related to promoting industrialization over a wide front.

Unlike other financial institutions, IDBI is not hampered by any statutory limitations. The Act provides for substantial operational flexibility. The Bank has been empowered to finance all types of industrial concerns engaged in the manufacture and processing of goods, mining, transport, generation and distribution of power, in both public and private sectors, irrespective of the forms of organisation. There are no restrictions as regards the nature and type of security that may be accepted from industrial concerns. Nor are there any maximum or minimum limits prescribed either for assistance to a concern or for the size of the concern itself. In consequence the IDBI has assumed a leading role in assisting directly large industrial projects in the following industries: fertilisers, petrochemicals, aluminium, alloy steel, paper, tyres and cement. Also, for smaller projects in electronics and light engineering industries, which have been promoted by technician entrepreneurs, the IDBI has also taken a similar leading role. For a number of small and medium projects the IDBI performs its two role—purveyor of supplementary resources, and coordinator through its scheme of refinance assistance and bills rediscounting assistance to the commercial banks and the SFC's. These schemes have enabled the IDBI to facilitate industrialization in a number of States and backward areas. Similarly, in the field of medium and long-term export financing, through its refinancing assistance to banks as well as direct participation with the banks, the IDBI has also assumed a leadership role, and brought banks and export houses into close liaison with each other.

IDBI has been instrumental in financial structure of the SFC's as well as the other term lending institutions through its subscriptions to their bonds and shares. To meet the special assistance requirements of sick enterprises, the IDBI took the initiative in setting up in 1971 the Industrial Reconstruction Corporation of India (IRCI). However, IRCI has been turned into Industrial Investment Bank of India (IIBA).

In order to playa promotional role it was essential for the IDBI to develop live and intimate contact with the economic situation, and potential in the different regions and States of the country. As a first step the IDBI opened regional zonal offices in the North, East and South. It has opened branch offices in each State. The second major step related to the identification of projects in backward areas. Accordingly the IDBI with the assistance of other term lending institutions initiated surveys of backward States in 1970, for the purpose of identifying specific projects in the light of natural and other resources, demand conditions and infrastructural facilities likely to emerge over a period of the next 5 to 10 years. So far 18 such surveys have been completed. It was not possible for the IDBI to undertake on its own all the different tasks related to project work. Under the leadership of the IDBI an Inter-Institutional Group was formed representing financial institutions like

SFC, SIDC, SHC, the "lead" banks in the States, State Government Industries Departments and other term lending institutions, such as the IFCI, the ICICI and the ARC. This Group is expected to take decisions with regard to the following functions:

(i) identification and discussion of project,
(ii) preparation of preliminary feasibility studies,
(iii) search for entrepreneurial talent and provision of appropriate training to potential entrepreneurs and managers,
(iv) preparation of detailed project report,
(v) provision of technical and financial assistance on a consortium basis to projects ready for implementation. Such inter-institutional groups have been formed in 17 states.

## INDUSTRIAL CREDIT AND INVESTMENT CORPORATION OF INDIA (ICICI)

The ICICI was set up in 1955 with the following share capital structure:

| | | |
|---|---|---|
| (i) | Foreign shareholding | 30 per cent |
| (ii) | Public sector banks | about 48 per cent |
| (Hi) | Public shareholders | about 22 per cent |

The World Bank played an important role in its establishment because it was interested in providing assistance to the private sector for the imports of capital goods. But since the number of applicants involved would be considerable the Bank recognised that it would not be feasible for it to appraise each project individually. It was therefore interested in channelizing its funds through a development bank which would undertake this task on its behalf.

The central objective of the ICICI was to encourage and assist industrial investment in the private sector. This was to be accomplished by providing long-term and medium-term loans in rupees and foreign currencies by equity participation, by underwriting new issues of securities and by guaranteeing loans from other private investment sources. In recent years the scope of its operations has been extended to include joint sector enterprises.

The ICICI primarily provides funds for the purchase of capital assets in the form of land, building and machinery. There are no fixed limits for the size of assistance granted, but ordinarily Rs 5 lakhs is the lower limit. Although in the past the ICICI provided assistance only to public limited companies, since 1969 it started providing foreign currency loans to proprietary and partnership concerns either directly or in association with State Financial Corporation and banks.

In assessing its performance, the following points may be stressed:

(i) The major contributions of the ICICI has been that it is virtually the only lending institution that provides foreign currency loans. For this task, it was initially given an advance of $ 10 million by the World Bank and since then further instalments have also been advanced. In addition its foreign currency resources have been enlarged by credit from the USA, Germany and UK. The ICICI also entered the foreign capital market for the first time in 1973 by issuing bonds of Swiss Frances 8 million in the European Market.

(ii) From the beginning a special emphasis has been given to underwriting in view of the underdeveloped nature of the Indian capital market. The ICICI has been buying shares of companies with long-term promise, but which failed to get sufficient response from the market, and selling these in later years.

(iii) Since the ICICI provides a major share of its assistance in foreign currency there is a built-in preference for industries which require greater foreign credit.

(iv) The ICICI accounts for around one-sixth of institutional finance, 5 per cent of capital goods imports, and about 3 per cent of private fixed industrial investment. It has accounted for over 70 per cent of finance for private industry in foreign exchange (recently, over 80 per cent) and between one-third and one-half of the import content of private industrial investment.

(v) As a result of the overall slow industrial growth ICICI's gross disbursements in the seven years up to 1971-72 increased in real terms at only 1.3 per cent annually.

(vi) There are several other institutional factors that help explain ICICI's undramatic performance, which become evident if one takes a long, historical view of industrial and institutional developments. ICICI has, for example, tied the bulk of its activities to its foreign exchange loans, in which the foreign exchange is tied to the loan—i.e. one cannot get foreign exchange without a loan. The Government since the 1957-58 foreign exchange crisis followed an absolute policy of banning the import of all goods, capital or intermediate, which can be manufactured locally. This policy has successfully cut down the import of capital goods, so much so that they are now less in absolute volume than they were in 1960-61, and relatively to industrial investment, only about half as important in the early 70s as in the early 60s. This means that ICICI has tied the largest element in its business to a declining element in the economy, although it is a critical element with enormous and rising investment leverage.

(vii) During its initial years, ICICI also possessed some unique functions, such as underwriting. It played a pioneering role in this area, as well as in equity financing during the first five years. Gradually, however, other institutions have sprung up or existing institutions have enlarged their role to include new activities, and activities that overlap with ICICI's activities. New functions were added to the existing ones by several institutions, e.g. export financing or guarantees, hire-purchase finance for machinery, refinance of other institutions, industrial rehabilitation, project promotion surveys, technical assistance and industrial research, cooperation of institutional lending policies, assistance for small industry and backward areas. ICICI's participation in some of these activities has been modest. There is still, to a degree, a specialisation of lending to industries by institutions. IFCI still specialises in textiles, cooperatives etc. but this specialisation is breaking down. The result is that today, the large free foreign exchange loans apart, ICICI does not have any unique function that cannot also be undertaken by one, or usually more, of the other financial situtions.

(viii) It is amongst the financial institutions not inhibited by its original objectives from assisting only public sector enterprises. Public enterprises have accounted for a third of industrial investment over the past decade, and a great proportion of the modern sector, but ICICI has a strong private sector orientation. The early history of ICICI reveals dearly that, as a result of a coincidence of views between the World Bank/IFC and the group of Bombay-oriented financial statesmen who steered ICICI into existence, it emerged with a strong private sector orientation. Its objective is to carry on the business of assisting the creation, expansion and modernisation of industrial enterprises within the private sector in India, in general by encouraging and promoting the participation of private capital, internal and external, and encouraging and promoting private ownership and the expansion of investment markets. It has not yet taken serious notice of the vast and fast expanding public sector and joint sector. It specialises in providing term finance in free foreign exchange to the private sector, and in this field is, for all practical purposes, in a monopoly position. But the ICICI could play a much larger developmental role. The time has come to explore the possibility of making ICICI's financial and technical resources available to public sector enterprises, whether Central or State, and to joint sector enterprises in which the Government is in a majority position. Such enterprises suffer disproportionately from teh problems facing new investments in India, problems that ICICI, with its extensive experience in appraisal, marketing and company re-organisation could help tackle. Joint enterprises with the Government in an ostensibly minority position are already being financed by ICICI. It would be necessary to examine the safeguards against pressures to make unwise investments. It would also be necessary to consider in some depth the kind of problems likely to be encountered in public enterprises, that would in turn warrant additions to the range of skills in ICICI's staff. ICICI took a major innovative role when, through two fresh public issues, it brought down government holding below 50 per cent. Thus it is no longer a government company, and is a full-fledged private sector company. It has also set up subsidiaries for venture capital technology development, credit rating and assets management. It also promoted Shipping Credit and Investment Corporation (SCICI) which became a financial institution by its own right. However, the SCICI was merged with the ICICI in April, 1998 to effectively face the emerging challenges. It also promoted the Housing Development and Finance Corporation which has also become for all practical purposes an independent housing finance company, and an independent nucleus which has promoted its own cluster of finance related enterprises such as the Infrastructure Leasing Finance Corporation (ILFS). Carporation (ILFS), the ICICI Bank Ltd, the Over the Counter Exchange of India (OTCEI), and the CRICIL a debt rating agency. The ICICI Bank was merged with the ICICI creating one of the top banks in India.

## STATE FINANCIAL CORPORATIONS (SFCS)

From 1952 onwards the State Financial Corporations were established in various States in order to provide loans to small and medium industries. Under the stature a State Financial Corporation cannot grant assistance to any party exceeding Rs 30 lakhs. Nor can it assist any industrial concern with its paid up capital and reserves exceeding Rs 1 crore in the aggregate. For all loans over Rs 30 lakhs up to a limit of Rs 2 crores, medium or large industrial units generally approach the IFC.

The share capital of an SFC is wholly guaranteed by the concerned State Government with a guarantee for payment of dividend at minimum rate. It has the following break-up:

(i) State Government 20 per cent

| | | |
|---|---|---|
| (ii) | IDBI | 20 per cent |
| (iii) | LIC and scheduled commercial banks | 40 per cent |
| (iv) | Others (Trusts and charitable institutions etc.) | 20 per cent |

The activities, coverage and overall performance of State Financial Corporations (SFCs) have expanded considerably over the years. However, with the passage of time, their operations have thrown up several problems connected with the organisations, management, resource mobilisation, operational efficiency and overall financial health. Some of the SFCs have eroded their networth and their operations have become moribund. With the introduction of financial sector reforms, the business environment of SFCs along with other financial institutions is becoming increasingly competitive.

The role of the State Financial Corporations like that of the State Industrial Development Corporations has become somewhat uncertain in the changed economic policy environment since 1991. They no longer enjoy the special facilities like IDBI refinancing that they did in the past. Their role in the present context should be redefined enabling them to concentrate on entrepreneurship and small business development, venture capital etc. Also, they should be partially privatised.

## LIFE INSURANCE CORPORATION (LIC), GENERAL INSURANCE CORPORATION (GIC)

While IDBI, IFCI, ICICI, SFCs and IRCI are developmental term-lending financial institutions, the Life Insurance Corporation, the General Insurance Corporation and the Unit Trust of India are not development banks in the conventional sense, but are considered as investment institutions. As they hold very substantial share in the equity structure of the private corporate sector, their operations are of crucial importance, They work in close collaboration with the public sector development banks in so far as they also assist in financing industry. The entire share capital of the LIC which was set up in 1956 after the nationalisation of life insurance is held by the Central Government. The GIC was set up in 1973 after the nationalisation of general insurance. It is wholly owned by the Central Government, and has four subsidiaries Viz., National Insurance Company, The New India Assurance Company, The Oriental Insurance Company and the United India Insurance Company. The LIC and GIC in partnership with other financial institutions also participates as a minor partner in direct financing of industries including industrial co-operatives. In the field of development finances both LIC and GIC as well as UTI sanction assistance in the shape of giving underwriting support to the issue of capital by companies in participation with other institutions.

## UNIT TRUST OF INDIA (UTI)

UTI was set up in 1964 by an Act of Parliament, i.e. UTI Act, 1963. UTI presently occupies a special position in Indian capital market. With a servicing and distribution network of 53 branch offices, 320 chief representatives and about 87,000 agents, UTI provides the complete range of services to its investors, It is India's largest mutual fund. It has set up associate companies in the fields of banking, securities trading, investor servicing, investment advice and training, towards creating a diversified financial conglomerate and meeting investors' varying needs under a common umbrella. The most notable development pertaining to contractual savings in the recent years has been enactment of Insurance Regulator and Development Authority (IRDA) Act, 1999. The IRDA Act marks the end of monopoly of the government in the insurance sector because it seeks to promote the private sector (including 26 per cent foreign equity) in the insurance sector. The Act provides for establishment of statutory Insurance Regulatory and Development Authority to protect the interest of holders of insurance policies and to regulate, promote and ensure orderly growth of the insurance industry. It also seeks to amend Life Insurance Corporation Act, 1956, General Insurance Business (Nationalisation) Act, 1972 and consequential provisions in Insurance Act, 1938 with a view to cease the exclusive privilege of LIC and GIC in life and non-life business respectively. Steps have also been taken to strengthen and improve the competitiveness of the nationalised insurance companies. These companies are being given further autonomy to meet the competition. The management of these companies have been given adequate powers of investment and now they are much more board run companies, autonomous and will be able to meet competition effectively and improve their quality of services.

It is important to note that the UTI does not sanction term loans like the LIC which does so in partnership with other institutions. Principally it holds shares and debentures in public limited companies and at times offers short-term deposits to companies. The UTI has made phenomenal progress since 1980 in the wake of the upsurge in the capital market, its investible funds having crossed Rs 10,000 crores. By virtue of its substantial portfolio holding and the ability to buy or sell shares in the market it also plays a significant role in sustaining the share market. It has now emerged as one of the biggest mutual funds in the world. In the 1980s it set up two off-shore funds viz the

India Growth Fund in the U.K. and the India Fund U.S.A. with the object of mopping up funds from non-resident Indians and foreign investors for portfolio investment in Indian companies. Recently, following other institutions, UTI has also set up its own private sector bank and an asset management company. UTI is the largest mutual fund in the country, one of the largest in the world and has a leading role in financing industry.

## INDUSTRIAL INVESTMENT BANK OF INDIA (IIBI)

IIBI, formerly Industrial Reconstruction Bank of India (IRBI), was an all India Development Financial Institution fully owned by Government of India. IIBI started functioning as a full-fledged development financial institution from March 27, 1997. Originally set up as industrial Reconstruction Corporation of India in 1971 with the object of reviving and rehabilitating sick industrial units in the country, the organisation was later converted to IRBI in 1985 by an Act of Parliament. There exits a provision for dilution of Government share holding upto 51 per cent. IIBI's resources comprises; share capital, reserves, internal generation, borrowing from the government of India, long-term credit from reserve bank of India, and market borrowing by way of bonds.

Against the backdrop of the financial sector reforms initiated in the country and the emerging competitive environment, the organisation was restructured and converted into a company in 1997.

But it became a sick outfit under the burden of non-performing assets (NPAs) which was later turned into the IIBI. For all practical purposes it has ceased to exist.

## EXPORT-IMPORT BANK OF INDIA

Export Import Bank of India was set up by an Act of Parliament in September 1981, and commenced operation in 1982 as a specialised development bank to deal with export and import credit and took over the functions of the international divisions of the IDBI. This bank promotes Indian exports by providing finance and a variety of advisory and information services, research and analysis. These programmes are tailored to meet the needs of various customer groups, namely, Indian exporters, overseas contacts and commercial banks. Exporters from India can take advantage of investment lines, export product development lines and lines for export marketing, pre-shipment credit, suppliers credit, venture development finance, bulk import finance, overseas investment finance and also under-writing facilities. Foreign companies and agencies are offered buyers' credit and lines of credit. Remittances to commercial banks are extended through suppliers' credit and also term loans to export oriented units. The bank also participates in guarantees issued by commercial banks on behalf of Indian exporters. Encouragement is given to two-way technology terms for ventures, resulting in higher financial investment in India and setting up more joint ventures abroad. EXIM Bank, therefore, offers a diversified range of programmes at various stages in the export cycle, viz. export product development, export 'production, export marketing, pre-shipment and post-shipment finance covering a variety of customers. The bank has extended these activities to a variety of export contracts abroad secured by Indian companies, including turn-key projects. The volume of its business and the funds at its disposal have steadily increased. During April to December, 1999 the bank sanctioned loans worth Rs 1953 crores under various loan programmes. Disbursements during the same period were Rs 832 crores. The largest share of the loans sanctioned was for exports to Asia (85 per cent) followed by Europe (9 per cent) and sub-saharan Africa (5 per cent). Disbursements were mainly for exports to West Asia (54 per cent), North Africa (19 per cent) and South Asia (16 per cent). The bank also provided a number of innovative export marketing finance projects such as market entry support to 27 companies in 1993-94 to position their products in competitive markets, as well as for obtaining ISO 9000 certification for their units.

There can be no doubt that with the on-going structural reforms in the Indian economy and the growing trends towards globalisation, this specialised institution is poised to play much greater role in the future. It has established good linkages with multilateral financial bodies like the World Bank and the Asian and African Development Banks and has set up offices at overseas centres like Washington, Singapore, Rome, Johannesburg, and Budapest. It has also seven regional centres in India But there is considerable need for de-regulation in its procedure and avoiding delay m sanctions and disbursements. The bank's declared object is to accelerate the process of change and globalisation and to help Indian companies build up their sustainable global competitiveness and integration with the world economy.

## RECONSTITUTION OF THE IDBI AS AN INDEPENDENT APEX HOLDING COMPANY, 1976

From its very inception the IDBI was a wholly-owned subsidiary of the Reserve Bank of India. On the one hand it was being realised that it was not possible for the Reserve Bank of India to combine its heavy and complex task as the central bank of the country with the additional duty of coordinating the activities of financial institutions. On the other hand, as an appendage of the Reserve Bank the IDBI found itself hamstrung by conventional banking norms in discharging it developmental and promotional duties and also its coordinating role among all financial institutions. By 1973 the Government decided to delink the IDBI from the Reserve Bank of India and to make it an independent apex body which would also serve as the holding company for all the public financial institutions operating in the field of development banking. A Bill known as Public Financial Institution (Amendment) Bill was, therefore, introduced in December 1973 and it became a law by 1975 as a result of which the IDBI was restructured as an independent apex public financial institution with supervisory control over others.

The principal object of these changes was to make IDBI an umbrella or apex body to coordinate the functioning of the other financial institutions including the State level ones.

As apex financial institution, IDBI coordinated directed and monitored operations of the all-India financial institutions, viz. IFCI, ICICI and IRCI, all India Investment Institutions LIC, UTI and GIC and the 18 SFCs and 24 SIDCs/ SIICSs set up in various States. The institutions that come under the purview of the supervisory role of IDBI under Section 9(1) of the IDBI Act were the 18 SFCs and 24 SIDCs.

IDBI was assigned the key role of coordinating the working of institutions engaged in assisting, financing, promoting or developing industry.

In 1990 IDBI set up another all-India subsidiary viz. Small Industries Development Bank of India (SIDBI) with the specific responsibility of assisting small scale industrial enterprises.

IDBI also provided significant support in the development of the capital market through setting up of Securities and Exchange Board of India, National Stock Exchange of India Ltd., Credit Analysis and Research Ltd., Stock Holding Corporation of India Ltd., Investor Services of India Ltd., National Securities Depository Ltd.

In 1992, for the first time, IDBI accessed the domestic retail marked with its Deep Discount Bond and also, it registered path-breaking. success. IDBI got linked to the Society for Worldwide Interbank Financial Telecommunication (SWIFT network that processes and exchanges messages relating to overseas banking can foreign exchange business. In March 2000, it set up IDBI Intech Limited as a subsidiary to undertake IT related activities.

In 1994, IDBI Act, was amended to permit public ownership. Initial Public Offering of Equity was initiated in July 1995 and nearly Rs. 20 billion was raised. Government stake was reduced to 72.14 per cent and can be further reduced upto 51 per cent in 1999 IDBI entered into a JV agreement with the Principal Financial Group, USA for participation in equity and management of IDBI Investment Management Company Ltd., erstwhile a 100 per cent subsidiary of IDBI. Government converted 247 million equity shares to preference shares in July 2000 reducing Government equity stake to 56 per cent.

In the new economic policy environment since 1991, the apex character of the IDBI has been eroded. It does enjoy an element of primacy. But in reality all the institutions were competing among themselves in project financing. Some of them have also set up their own commercial bank e.g. IDBI Bank, ICICI Bank, UTI Bank, in order to move towards universal banking as providing both working capital and project lending and catering to both small depositors and large depositors. In 2003 IDBI was converted into a regular commercial bank viz. the IDBI Bank.

The development banks have, over the years, made a phenomenal contribution to the growth of industry by evolving different schemes of assistance and by encouragement to socially and economically desirable objectives. Their sanctions and disbursements of assistance have shown a continuous upward trend and there has been a phenomenal increase in their operations during the last decades, especially since initiation of the economic reforms. But after 1991 their earlier overbearing role declined. Commercial banks could now lend to industry. The capital market could also mop up huge funds through public issues. Also a liberal foreign direct investment policy and permission to foreign institutional investors to operate in India was yet another favorable factor. In such situation the public financial institutes gradually turned into commercial bank e.g. IDBI Bank and ICICI Bank.

Recent years have therefore witnessed a blurring of the barriers between banks and development financial institutions (DFI). DFIs have entered the area of working capital financing and banks have entered into project financing. Also DFIs are setting up their own commercial banks thereby moving towards universal banking.

With these sea changes there was inevitably a fundamental change in the role of the IDBI. As the 21st century opened IDBI gave up its apex and coordinating role and became just a leading bank. The commercial bank that had been set up as a subsidiary was merged with the IDBI.

New areas of concern for the institutions in recent times have been replacement and modernization in a few industries assisting venture capital, assets management for individual and institutional investors, mutual funds, promoting commercial banks and preventing sickness in industrial units and taking over of management of certain sick or closed industrial undertakings. While the IRCI was the primary institution for taking over sick units and helping them to return to industrial viability, the other institutions also are concerned in a limited way with problems of industrial sickness.

The problem of reviving sick units in a large number of industries requires a special type of expertise and skill and financial institutions as development bankers must devote some attention to it. Industrial sickness has become widespread in a number of industries like textile, jute, sugar and engineering. A large number of the units in these industries have become the responsibility of the financial institutions. While it is possible to nurse many of them back to health by ensuring proper management there may be some which are beyond redemption and may, therefore have to be scrapped. In dealing with the sick units it is of utmost importance that credit dispensation is speed and timely. Successful rehabilitation and modernization of weak units can bring into use considerable idle capacity.

It can also maintain considerable volume of employment with much smaller investment than what will be necessary for creating identical capacity by establishing new units.

In 1992, for the first time, IDBI accessed the domestic retail market with its Deep Discount Bond and also, it registered path-breaking success. IDBI got linked to the Society for Worldwide Interbank Financial Telecommunication (SWIFT) network that processes and exchanges messages relating to overseas banking and foreign exchange business. In March 2000, it set up IDBI Intech Limited as a subsidiary to undertake IT related activities.

In 1994, IDBI Act was amended to permit public ownership. Initial Public Offering of Equity was initiated in July 1995 and nearly Rs. 20 billion were raised. Government stake was reduced to 72.14 per cent and can be further reduced upto 51 per cent. IDBI, in 1999, entered into a JV agreement with the Principal Financial Group, USA for participation in equity and management of IDBI Investment Management Company Ltd., erstwhile a 100 per cent subsidiary of IDBI. Government converted 247 million equity shares to preference shares in July 2000 reducing Government equity stake to 56 per cent.

In the new economic policy environment since 1991, the apex character of the IDBI has been eroded. It does enjoy an element of primacy. But in reality all the institutions were competing among themselves in project financing. Some of them have also set up their own commercial banks e.g. IDBI Bank, ICICI Bank, UTI Bank, in order to move towards universal banking as varying both working and project landing both small depositors and large depositors. In 2003 IDBI was converted into a regular commercial bank—the IDBI Bank.

The development banks have, over the years. made a phenomenal contribution to the growth of industry by evolving different schemes of assistance and by encouragement to socially and economically desirable objectives. Their sanctions and disbursements of assistance have shown a continuous upward trend and there has been a phenomenal increase in their operations during the last decades, especially since initation of the economic reforms.

But after 1991 their earlier overbearing role declined. Commercial banks could now lend to industry. The capital market could also mop up huge funds through public issues. Also a liberal foreign direct investment policy and permission to foreign institutional investors to operate in India was yet another favorable factor. In such situation the public financial institutions gradually turned into commercial banking e.g. IDBI Bank and ICICI Bank.

CHAPTER 13

# Interface between the Public Sector and Government

The Central Public Sector Enterprises which numbered only 5 in 1951 (assets Rs.29 crores), number about 248 now excluding 7 insurance companies. (assets Rs. 666848 as on 31.3.2011). Independent India inherited from colonial regime the railways, the post and telegraphs, the ordinance factories, all India Radio and the few enterprises like the Government Salt factories which were departmentally managed. India's visionary leaders drew up a road map for developing the public sector as an instrument for self reliant, economic growth for self sufficiency in the production of required goods and services and for ensuring moderate and stable prices. These visions led to the Industrial Policy Resolution of 1948 and the Industrial Policy Resolution of 1956. The 1956 Resolution gave primacy to the role of the State in industrial development and the public sector was accepted as the major instrument. It grew phenomenally in the years that followed until following the phenomenal economic policy changes from 1991 onwards, it started losing its preeminent position. Private sector initiative once again became an important instrument of Government policy. The public sector also lost most of its earlier privileges such as purchase preference by Government agencies and price preference. Many of them also lost their monopolistic position and had no to compete with both domestic and foreign competitors. But despite these changes the CPSEs acquitted themselves well and have gone from strength to strength. Thanks to the administrative system and procedures in India, the CPSEs also operate like their private sector counterparts under much strain and constraint. They also become victims of a cumbersome and time consuming procedures and policy system. Thus the issue of inter-facing with the Government agencies become of great importance.

Many eminent economists argued that Government should not venture into those areas were the private sector could undertake job efficiently. Lot of emphasis was laid on market driven economies, rather than State controlled administered economies. The collapse of socialist economy of the Soviet block convinced the policy planners, around the world, that the role of the State should be that of a facilitator and regulator rather than the producer and manager. It may be worth mentioning that, in various countries, the turn towards liberalism including deregulation and decontrol also led to discontent amongst some sections of population as its benefit did not flow down to the weaker and disadvantaged sections of society. This reached a climax in a concerted move in the Western countries towards massive privatization during the 1980s and 1990s spearheaded by Margaret Thatcher's privatization programme in Britain.

This gathered strength following the collapse of the Soviet Union in the early 1990s and the fall the Communism in Eastern Europe and the adoption of market oriented programmes in Communist China, Cuba and Vietnam. However, the Wall Street collapse from 2008 onwards and spectacular failure of the banking system in the Western Europe, Japan and several other countries served as an antidote once again strengthening the forces for State intervention.

According to the annual Public Enterprises survey (2009-10) the turnover of both the manufacturing and mining sector declined. over the previous years. But this was only a reflection of the difficult economic environment the nation was facing. The public sector employment has expanded from approx 56,000 in 1991-92 to approx 15 lakh employees in 2009-10. They have amongst them the Indian Company with the largest turn-over viz. IOC, the most profitable company viz. the ONGC, the largest public utility company, the NTPC and the company with the highest market capitalization viz. the Coal India. The aggregate turnover of the CPSEs from Rs, 118,000 in 1991-92 to Rs. 1,250,000 in 19 2009-10 and their combined profit from Rs. 2,272 crores to Rs. 9,300 crores during this period.

Government has in recent years taken many significant steps for improvement and modernization of the CPSE's. The system of entering into MOU agreements every year with individuals CPSE's has bought about a lot of discipline in the performance of these companies. The practice of appointing to their Boards independent Directors and officers from amongst professional and private sector managers has also brought about noticeable improvement in their performance. Another significant step is the practice of designating top performers as Maharatna, Navaratna and Miniratna. The CPSE's so designated enjoy varying degree of autonomy and flexibility which enable them to perform better.

The report of the second Public Sector Pay Revision committee (2008) was a land mark. It enabled salaries higher than the salaries in the Govt. to be paid to Board Directors so long as these come out of the profits of the company. It also made the Board of Directors, the key decision making authority.

A number of CPSE's have been referred to the BIFR, set under the Sick Industries Corporation Act. But the BIFR and its appellate body the AIFR became much too judicialized causing much delay and prolonging much uncertainties in the working of some of the CPSE's referred to this body. To this day not a single CPSE has seen revived or turned around through the BIFR. In 2003 Government decided to abolish the BIFR and to transfer all the pending cases to the Companies Tribunal. But these changes have not yet been brought to effect on account of the Companies Tribunal not coming into existance under the amended companies Act.

India escaped the global age of massive privatization following Margaret Thatcher's lead in Britain. Spells of political uncertainty during the 1990's combined with the lack of political will accounted for this, although there was a vocal public opinion favouring selective privatization. The NDA government (1999-2004) attempted privatization on a significant scale. Examples were the sale of VSNL to the Tata's that of IPCl of Baroda to Reliance Industries and the sale of hotels like Centeur and ITDC' hotels, Modern Food Industries to Hindustan Unilever and the privatization of Hindustan Zinc, Bharat Alum Industries and Maruti Udyog. This policy was abandoned by the UPA Govt. which came to power in 2004. A new policy was now adopted of making serious efforts to revive every sick public sector enterprise and deciding on closure only as a last resort after all turn-around efforts have failed. This task was assigned to a newly created organization called the Board for Reconstruction of Public Sector Enterprises (BRPSE) in 2005. Ministries are to refer case of sick enterprises to this Board for its recommendation. The Board has also the power to suomotu take up any public sector undertaking for study. Since the BRPSE's inception 59 cases have been referred to it. The Board had submitted reports on all these cases and the Cabinet has approved 43. 15 among them have already turned around making profit for three years or more and altogether 24 of them have posted profit. The Board has recommended closure in only 3 cases. Thus the BRPSE has very significantly contributed to the task of turnaround of sick CPSEs. The number of sick CPSEs is steadily going down just as the number of profit-making CPSE's is steadily going up.

The introduction of the MOU system has ensured satisfactory performance by the CPSE's. The DPE and the SCOPE have together introduced the annual MOU Excellence Award for the best turn around company and a SCOPE Gold Trophy in The Turnaround Category. The BRPSE also gives prizes for all turn-around companies.

Along with other public sector majors such as State Bank of India in the banking sector, Life Insurance Corporation in the insurance sector and Indian Railways in transportation, the CPSEs are leading companies of India with significant market-shares in sectors such as petroleum (e.g. ONGC, GAIL and Indian Oil Corporation), mining (e.g. Coal India Ltd. and NMDC), power generation (e.g. NTPC and NHPC), power transmission (e.g. Power Grid corporation Ltd., nuclear energy (e.g. Nuclear Power Corporation of India Ltd.). heavy engineering (e.g. BHEL), aviation industry (e.g. Hindustan Aeronautics Ltd. And Air India Ltd.), storage and public distribution system (e.g. Food Corporation of India and Central Warehousing Corporation), shipping and trading (e.g. Shipping Corporation of India Ltd., and State Trading Corporation Ltd. and telecommunication (e.g. BSNL and MTNL).

## BOARD STRUCTURE OF CPSEs

The CPSEs are categorized into four Schedules namely 'A', 'B', 'C' and 'D' based on various quantitative, qualitative and other factors. The pay scales of Chief Executives and of full time Functional directors in CPSEs are determined as per the Schedule of the concerned CPSE. Proposals from various administrative Ministries/Departments for initial categorization/up-gradation of CPSEs in appropriate schedule, personal up-gradation, creation of posts in CPSEs, etc. are considered in DPE in consultation with the Public Enterprises Selection Board (PESB).

There are 60 Schedule 'A', 71 Schedule 'B', 46 Schedule 'C', 4 Schedule 'D' and 67 uncategorized CPSEs as on 31.3.2011. One CPSE (THDC India Ltd.) has been upgraded from Schedule 'B' to Schedule 'A', one CPSE (Hindustan Prefab Ltd. has been upgraded from Schedule 'D' to 'C', one CPSE (Orissa Mineral Development Corporation) has been categorized as a Schedule 'B' CPSE and one CPSE (Bisra Stone Lime Company Ltd.) has been categorized as a Schedule 'C' CPSE.

In pursuance of the policy on public sector enterprises being followed since 1991, several measures have been taken by the Department of Public Enterprises to professionalize the Boards of public enterprises. The guidelines issued by DPE in 1992 provide for induction of outside professionals on the Boards of CPSEs as part-time non-official directors. The revised guidelines issued by DPE in 1992 provide for induction of outside professionals on the Boards of CPSEs as part-time non-official directors. The revised guidelines provide that the number of functional directors should not exceed 50 per cent of the actual strength of the Board of Directors (BOD) and the number of Government nominee Directors on the BOD should not exceed two. In the case of listed CPSEs with an Executive Chairman, the guidelines provide that the number of non-official Directors shall be at least 50 per cent of the Board Members. In the case of CPSEs with a Non-executive Chairman, at least one-third of the Board Members will have to be non-official Directors. The Functional Directors including the Chief Executive of the CPSEs are appointed by the concerned administrative Ministries on the recommendation of the Public Enterprises Selection Board (PESB). It has been decided that the candidates from State Level Public Enterprises (SLPSEs) and the private sector will also be considered as non-internal candidates besides the candidates from CPSEs for selection to the post of Functional directors in CPSEs subject to the eligibility criteria. There is a special selection board in the Department of Public Enterprises headed by the Chairman PESB for selecting independent directions in CPSE's from a panel of suitable candidates.

The strength of India's Public Sector was especially visible during the recent global slowdown. During the global recession, India's Public Sector showed tremendous amount of resilience. Our public Sector in fact became India's shining white night during this period of crisis. The process of listing them on the Stock Exchanges has also added to their strength and already they are leaders among listed companies. Six CPSEs account for among the first fifteen companies listed on the Bombay Stock Exchange in term of market capitalization. It is not out of turn to mention that the huge success of IPO of Coal India Ltd., the world's largest coal producer, shows the reposed confidence and faith by the investor community in the public sector enterprise. We need not feel apologetic about them any longer. The future is surely bright and bold. The nation should be proud of our public Sector.

There is no doubt that the public sector has come to occupy a very important role in the economic portfolios of India. Public sector in India has grown very impressively over the last half a century. Their aggregate, turnover increased from Rs. 118,000 crores in 1991-92 to Rs, 1,250,000 crores in 2009-10, and their combined profit increased from Rs. 2272 crores in 1991-92 Rs. 9300 crores in 2009-10.

Indeed the public sector occupies an important place in the nation's economy and is a key determinator of the nation's economic progress. However, the situation established by Industrial Policy, 1956 has been changed because of Industrial Policy, 1991 with regard to Public Sector. Since then Government's strategy towards this sector has continued to encompass a judicious mix of strengthening strategic units, privatising non-strategic ones through gradual disinvestment of strategic sale and devising viable rehabilitation strategies for weak units. The Industrial Policy Resolution, 1956 reserved 17 industries (Appendix 'A') exclusively for the public sector, and 12 more (Appendix 'B') for all future projects in general. It was expected to provide a countervailing power to the growth of large houses, and further charged with the responsibility of developing a wide range of ancillary industries and promoting decentralized production by making available to small-scale and cottage industry its expertise in technology and management.

The Industrial Policy, 1991 places only three industries under reservation for this sector and the rest are opened up for the private sector. Although in dereserved areas public sector units can exist, as it is also the case in reality, but compulsions of economic environment will see them either to compete or to die.

The public sector's role in creating employment is considerable. It employs over 15 lakh people. It has also built up a vast reservoir of technology and managerial expertise. The contribution of Public Sector companies to the country's total industrial production is indicated in Table 17.4. The nation's economic performance therefore depends substantially on the public sector's capacity utilization, profitability and exports.

Resources needed by the public enterprises are met from external sources in the form of share capital, long-term and medium-term loans and cash credit from banks besides internal resources generated by the enterprises from their retained profits and provisions like depreciation and write off of deferred revenue expenditure. Harnessing of resources and their utilization as on 31.3.1997 in respect of 240 enterprises covered in the public Enterprises Survey (1998-99).

Several aspects of the Public Sector have been the themes of intense debates and discussion in our country in recent years,. We shall restrict ourselves to the interrelationship or interfacing between the Ministries and the enterprises. However, before we proceed to this theme, a few general observations may not be out of place:

Broadly, the Central public sector units fall into the following three general organisational categories:

(i) Departmental undertakings, e.g. Railways, Post and Telegraphs.

(ii) Joint Stock Companies registered under the Companies Act, e.g., State Trading Corporation, Minerals and Metals Trading Corporation Steel Authority of India, Hindustan Machine Tools.

(iii) Statutory Corporations, e.g., O.N.G.C, Damodar Valley Corporation.

The undertakings in categories (2) and (3) are separate legal entities with separate commercial accounts. Their employees are not civil servants in the normal sense. Nor are they required to obtain parliamentary approval for spending money every year as a Government department is required to do.

Public sector in India has originated in the following ways:

(i) There is historical legacy of giant enterprises like Railways, Post and Telegraphs, and Ordinance factories which have been inherited from the pre-independence colonial regime. These arose in response to specific needs at different periods. Sometimes enterprises which had been started initially by private investors were taken under Government ownership after the initial contractual period had expired as in the case of the railways.

(ii) There are new ventures in such fields as steel, aluminium, export trading, cement, fertilizer and electronics which have been promoted in pursuance of Government policy.

(iii) Sometimes units established in the private sector have been nationalised or just brought over under Government management in pursuance of national policy, e.g., coal mines, Indian Copper Corporation.

(iv) Sometimes units established in the private sector have been acquired by Government not by any nationalisation measure or ordinance, but by market operation or accident or sometimes even by conscious . design. Examples are Indo-Burma Petroleum, Hindustan Petroleum (formerly Esso), Balmer Lawrie, Bharat Refineries (formerly Burma Shell), Andrew Yule.

For our present purposes those in the first group viz. the departmental undertakings are excluded from the scope of public sector as it is known today in normal understanding. Today when we talk about the Central public sector we loosely mean about 249 commercial enterprises run in very diverse fields by various ministries of the Central Government, not as departmental undertakings in the conventional sense, but as corporate bodies taking the form either of Joint Stock Company registered under Companies Act or of statutory corporations. These are all subject to some loose supervision by the Department of Public Enterprises.

Serious discussion on whether the state should own or control the bulk of the means of production and distribution began after Independence. There is the all-pervasive political argument of those who profess socialism that public ownership of the means of production and distribution should be an essential object of the national policy and should be viewed as a means of radical change in the structure of society and its economy. But in addition to this there are a number of strong pragmatic and non-political arguments which had from time to time provided impetus for state ownership or take-over of various production activities. These can be summarised as follows:

(i) Public ownership of monopoly power in essential services is an essential condition for controlling monopoly power.

(ii) Preventing wasteful and unnecessary competition in some essential services.

(iii) Effective economic planning can be achieved only when the planners can control the resources of the community. The best control is through ownership, and public ownership of these resources is therefore essential for the success of planning.

(iv) It is necessary to control the economic power which arises from control over large enterprises and over the vast resources and in the influence which goes along with this. Nationalisation or public ownership in these sectors are therefore extremely important.

(v) The national interest, in particular defence needs, demand that some basic and key industries must remain under state ownership.

(vi) There are some very important industries, e.g., coal, steel railways where efficiency can only be improved by considerable rationalization of the entire structure and where there is a need for such massive injection of capital which the State alone is in a position to give.

There are also several oft-repeated arguments against indiscriminate and thoughtless extension of public ownership. The following are important:

(i) Government monopoly can turn into the worst form of monopoly, as it combines in itself the economic power of a monopoly with the administrative and political authority, prestige and power of a Government body.

(ii) In a public enterprise the entire degree of remote control inevitably leads to loss of sensitivity to consumers' requirements.

(iii) There is a basic incompatibility between Governmental procedure and efficient commercial operation. The results are higher charges to the consumers or losses which the tax-payer has to make good.

(iv) The lack of profit motive not only effects motivation but also brings down over-all efficiency of the organization.

... Poor profitability in the early years not only vitiated the performance of the economy, but imposed severe budgetary strains on the Government. It is in this context that we have to view the recent policy pronouncements viz. the duty of public enterprises not to rely for ever on budgetary support from the government, but to generate surpluses both for future growth and for ensuring a return on government's investment, to reduce their cost of production per unit rather than making up the losses by hiking up the prices, or by non-Plan budgetary support. The 8th and 9th Plan documents repeatedly enjoined upon them to build up a culture of productivity, to generate surplus and declare dividends, and in general to stop relying on budgetary support and depend on their own internally generated resources and on the capital market.

The public sector in India has not fulfilled all the bright hopes of its more dogmatic advocates. Nor has it been exactly an unmitigated failure as its enemies have all along predicted. Apart from the broader considerations of national policy, under which the development of public sector was undertaken, not only for economic growth, but also for promoting social justice, there can be no doubt that it has played an extremely valuable role in the growth of national economy in the last three decades. In many areas industries would not have developed had not Government stepped into them. The private sector has itself been a great beneficiary of Government entrepreneurship. It has been provided machinery, industrial raw materials and intermediate products at prices lower than international prices and has been selling the finished goods at higher prices to squeeze out maximum profits. The fact that some of the public sector units have been running at a loss should not blind us to the fact that so many other units have been steadily making profits over the years, or that many more private sector units also run at a loss and turn sick. Many well-established units in the private sector have at times taken years before they could reach a stage of profitability. The framers of our industrial policy did not consider public sector and private sector as competitors or rivals, but envisaged their roles as essentially complementary to each other. It is very unfair to always compare profitability of the public sector units in general with that of some of the best-run private sector units. It should also be understood that public sector units jointly make substantial contribution to the exchequer in the form of various taxes.

Secondly, the long gestation associated with these industries where public sector has by and large gone should not be forgotten. In fact very often private sector units dealing with consumer articles have been allowed to make handsome profits only because the public sector has patronised them or has produced basic raw materials required by the former which have been made available at a reasonable price. In fact an obsession in some circles to compare them with well-run private enterprises only from the angle of financial profits has given rise in recent years to a strong move for the entry of public sector units into the more profitable areas of consumer goods which had traditionally been the preserve of the private sector.

Lastly, it is often overlooked that when we embarked on the process of industrial development it was realised that the required massive investment was beyond the ability and initiative of the private sector which was unlikely to go into the areas where the gestation period was long, profitability was uncertain and low, and massive investment was needed.

In recent years the public sector in India has played a crucial role in meeting global economic challenges. From the Wall Street Crash of 2008 onwards the public sector stood solidly behind the Indian government in meeting the global crisis. It did not cut down on employment or production unlike European or American enterprises. In fact it produced more and recruited more.

For a long time there has been a basic confusion about the criteria by which the performance of public sector enterprise should be assessed. This again is due to political disagreement about the role of these enterprises. There are those who start from the assumption that public sector enterprises should be judged strictly on "business or commercial principles" in the same way as private enterprises are judged. Others have emphasised the social and economic objects to the exclusion of the market forces. In their view the financial results of a public undertaking should have no significance except as a part of the Government's social and economic policies. In today's context there can be no disagreement that both these sets of criteria should be applied. Both the Industrial Policy Resolution, 1956, and the Industrial Policy Statements stress the importance of operating public sector enterprises on profitable and efficient lines in order to ensure that investment in those industries pays an adequate return to society. If the social obligations were alone all-important and if the public sector undertakings were not expected to achieve some positive financial results in terms of indicators such as profitability or financial usability, then it would have been more appropriate to include them in the social welfare budget of the Government, and not to incorporate them as commercial bodies.

Public sector has a multitude of objectives set for them such as to help in the industrialization and rapid economic growth of the country to establish the necessary infrastructure for industrial development which private sector is not willing to do for want of profitability, to earn adequate return on investment so as to generate resources for development to create employment opportunities, to promote development of backward areas, to assist the growth of small-scale and ancillary industries, to promote import substitution and to strengthen indigenous capability, and to act as a countervailing force to concentration of economic power. The performance of the public sector has often suffered on account of being saddled with so many objectives which at times conflict with one another.

It is now well-established both in India and abroad that the public sector must be both economically efficient and socially accountable and responsive. While maintaining the academic convention of keeping out of the political controversy over public sector versus private sector, or Government control versus free enterprise we should rather emphasise that basically there is no disagreement between the objectives of generating a surplus and being socially responsible. In today's context in India, many private sector units often find themselves in a position of accountability to the Government, Parliament, and the public. The need for profitability as distinct from profiteering on the other hand is being increasingly stressed in relation to public enterprises. We should, therefore, emphasise that many problems of the public sector are really problems common to all large-scale industries in the modern economy irrespective of their ownership.

## PROBLEMS OF RELATIONSHIP BETWEEN MINISTRIES AND ENTERPRISES

The question of an ideal relationship between the Government and the public enterprises attracted considerable attention in the 1950s when the public sector was still in its infancy. The Krishna Menon Committee in the early sixties dwelt at great length on this and made concrete recommendations on how to reduce dependence of public sector enterprises on the Central Secretariat. But surprisingly this aspect has received very little academic attention in recent years. One reason can be that after the report of the Administrative Reforms Commission (1968) which also devoted much attention to this question of autonomy, there has been maximum possible delegation on paper to the enterprises. But the question of a correct relationship between the two, or in other words, the question of how autonomous and sovereign a unit should be in relation to the Ministry has still remained a central issue. The Industrial Policy Resolution 1956 declared that the management of the Government enterprises should be on "business lines" and also that they should augment the revenues of the State and provide resources for further development in fresh fields. The Third Plan declared that the efficient conduct of industrial and business enterprises requires that operational decision should be prompt and that if an enterprise does not have real autonomy it is not likely to be effective. In fact it is the desire to ensure autonomy of the enterprise which has been responsible for incorporating most of these enterprises in the form of joint stock companies.

If we were to go by the declared policies today the public sector enterprises have been delegated the maximum possible autonomy. This is also supported by the pronouncements made by the Government (vide Bureau of Public Enterprises Government Policy for the Management of Public Enterprises, Vol. I, General Management and Financial Management) to realise this. If the real life situation is sometimes contrary to these pronouncements one has to blame the human factor. Delegation to be successful depends on the attitude of mind on the part of both the delegator and those to whom authority is delegated. In some cases, contrary to declared policy, Ministers and Secretaries, etc., show a tendency to oversee in the name of coordination or supervision even the day-to-day operation of an enterprise. On the other hand, some chairmen or chief executives also fall victims to the temptation of currying favours with the Ministers and ministry officials by keeping them "informed" of the important decisions and developments which in actual practice becomes an euphemism for obtaining orders of approval. Thus what we are up against is not just the question of formal delegation, but an inherited and pervasive organization culture which makes effective delegation very difficult.

The 'secretariat culture' brought by the initial band of civil service managers who manned the top and middle posts in the early years- got enshrined in the public sector. Its effects were compounded by political interference often at ministerial level. At times both these elements came in conflict with elements representing industrial culture or professional management. Unfortunately the true issue was somewhat blurred by an exaggerated emphasis on the conflict between private sector profit motivation and the social cost-benefit concept in public enterprises, or between private sector non-accountability and public sector accountability. These contradictions had their inevitable impact on the controversy over the autonomy of the enterprise management in relationship to Government control.

An enterprise has interface with several Ministries and agencies in the Central Government and also with the Parliament. The following are the major Ministries and agencies:

(i) Administrative Ministry.
(ii) Department of Expenditure (Ministry of Finance).
iii) Department of Public Enterprises (Ministry of Heavy Industry and Public Enterprises.
(iv) Planning Commission.
(v) Secretariat for Industrial approvals (Ministry of Industry).
(vi) Department of Corporate Affairs (for those enterprises which are registered as Joint Stock Companies under the companies Act).
(vii) Director General of Imports and Exports (Ministry of Commerce).

**Administrative Ministry**

This is the primary point of contact between the enterprise and the Government. Public enterprises are not only controlled by the government through the Administrative Ministry, but also generally conduct their dialogue with parliamentary committees, Comptroller and Auditor General and other government agencies through the Administrative Ministry. Some examples of an Administrative Ministry are the Ministry of Industry (for undertakings like Bharat Heavy Electricals Ltd., Hindustan Machine Tools and Hindustan Paper), Ministry of Steel and Mines (for undertakings like Steel Authority of India Ltd., National Mineral Development Corporation), Ministry of Commerce (for undertakings like State Trading Corporation and Minerals and Metals Trading Corporation); Ministry of Chemicals and Fertilizers (for undertakings like Fertilizers Corporation, Indian Drugs and Pharmaceuticals Ltd., Indian Petro-Chemicals Ltd.), Department of Electronics (Electronic Corporation of India); Ministry of Agriculture (Food Corporation), Ministry of Shipping and Transport (Shipping Corporation).

The Administrative Ministry is supposed to represent the President of India who owns almost the total shareholding in the undertaking. Usually the Secretary of the Ministry holds a small number of shares to meet the requirements of registration as a private limited company. The President's authority as shareholder is exercised by the Administrative Ministry. It stands at the top of the three-tier top management structure that has developed in the Indian public sector with its deep-rooted colonial type concepts.... Below it is the Board of Directors on which the Government is represented by at least one officer from the Administrative Ministry, and one from Finance Ministry. Below the Board of Directors are the Managing Director and functional Directors.

It is this general pattern which has raised the very important question of Government control versus the autonomy of the undertaking, an issue that is still not satisfactorily solved. Autonomy has been accepted in principle. Indeed from the latest circulars and pronouncements on this subject it is apparent that today very considerable authority has been delegated by the Ministry to the enterprises under it. But in practice, thanks to the persistence of the "secretariat culture," the Minister takes the final decision in a large number of cases on the advice of the Secretary. The prevailing hierarchical pattern of the Secretariat, the lack of clear conception of the scope of Government control, and the multiplicity of instruments case further managerial problems.

In theory, the Ministry exercises three general powers and three special powers. The general powers are:

(i) Appointment of Chairman, Managing Director, Executive Directors, and other members of the Board. In the initial years it was inevitable that in general Government officials were sent on deputation to fill these posts, and recruitment policies followed Government practices till the mid-sixties. There has also been the practice of appointing politicians as part-time Chairmen. An experiment was made with an Industrial Management Pool for recruiting a cadre of senior and middle-level managers with commercial or industrial experience, but this was not followed up after the initial recruitment. After the Administrative Commission's Report the power of making all appointments below the Board level has been delegated to the enterprise itself. As regards higher level appointments, in 1974, the Public Enterprises Selection Board (PESB) was set up. It selects the Chairmen, the Managing Directors and the members of the Board after examining the records of applicants and interviewing them, and forwards these names to the Administrative Ministry which appoints them after approval by the Appointments Committee of the Central Cabinet. The whole process tends to be long and time-consuming, and often vacancies in key posts continue for very long stretches causing dislocation of work in the enterprises and inviting public criticism. Apart from selecting members of the Board, the PESB is also associated ... appraisal, training and personnel development programmes, the selection of first-line managers and with the setting up of a data bank of suitable managerial candidates.

(ii) Approving the company's capital budget, long-term borrowings and investment proposals. In this area of financial management the transplantation of the procedures and practices prevailing in the Government organization has very adverse consequences. The founding fathers treated these enterprises largely as extensions of Government departments, a tradition that dies hard. Apart from too many accounts men serving as financial advisers or chief accounts officers, there is also the external financial control by the Ministry, in concert with the Ministry of Finance, and through the statutory audit and the audit board of the Comptroller and Auditor-General. It is only very recently that performance audit has been introduced.

(iii) Issuing general directions on the enterprise from time to time in national interest. The Articles of Association of nearly all the public sector companies contain an article to this effect. Apart from these three general powers, the Ministry also exercises three other functions in relation to the Parliament.

The special powers are:

(i) Laying down before the two Houses of the Parliament an annual report on the working of the enterprise, and piloting the discussion that may follow.

(ii) Dealing with the Parliamentary Committee on Public Undertakings (COPU) which has now emerged as the Parliament's major agency for overseeing the performance of the public sector enterprises. Every year the Committee takes up 7 to 8 enterprises for examination. Its recommendations are considered by the Administrative Ministry, and suitable instructions are issued for the guidance of the enterprise concerned. It also conducts functional studies in areas such as materials management, financial management, personnel management, industrial relations, etc. The Ministry has to act as the via media or buffer between the undertaking on the one hand and the COPU on the other. The other Parliamentary bodies which also get involved with public enterprises from time to time are the Public Accounts Committee and the Estimates Committee.

(iii) Answering questions relating to the enterprise in Parliament. In the past MPs were sometimes known to ask questions which imposed unnecessary burden on the enterprise management and the Ministry, or impinged on the internal autonomy of the enterprise. After careful consideration Government has now issued guidelines under which the following types of questions should be disallowed:

(a) Questions relating to day-to-day administration of the Public Enterprise.

(b) Questions which tend to throw work on the Ministries and the Public Enterprises incommensurate with the result to be obtained therefrom.

(c) Questions which seek to obtain information which the Members may obtain directly by addressing the managements of the Enterprises.

Questions identical to those which have already been answered and questions seeking statistical information which is normally available in the published documents, or annual reports etc. are also to be normally disallowed.[3]

In some industries the Administrative Ministry also exercise some measure of price and distribution control. This depends on the nature of the industry and its products. Such control, wherever it exists, operates for both public sector and private sector undertakings in the relevant industry.

The Administrative Ministry is also expected to maintain an over-view of the undertaking's overall performance through periodical performance review meetings, briefing by Government directors, an effective method of reports and returns, and periodic appraisals with the Department of Public Enterprises. How effective this system is varies from Ministry to Ministry depending largely on the personality of the Minister, the Secretary and the Chief Executive of the enterprise. Often we see that the principle of delegation, although near complete in theory, from the Government to the enterprise has not percolated through the enterprise, and all power is concentrated in the Board, or the Chief Executive; Government as the sole shareholder cannot naturally give up the Board's accountability to it. From the guidelines contained the Bureau of Public Enterprises publication, Government Policy for the Management of Public Enterprises, it appears that the accountability that is enjoined covers such diverse fields as policy formulation, management control and coordination, management objectives, integrating long-range and annual plans, production and materials management.

There is a general belief and complaint that although on paper there has been maximum possible delegation to the enterprise, nonetheless the ministers and civil servants make nearly all vital decisions affecting the main aspects of management. In the past civil servants working in public enterprises looked upon their superior civil servants in the Secretariat for guidance and order as they were accustomed to. Similarly the latter, in exercise of their divine right of overlordship, have sometimes imposed decisions on the public enterprises. Ministers have sometimes looked upon them as areas of patronage where they can usually get the things done which cannot be done within the rules and procedure of normal Governmental machinery. Moreover, the industries have become much more liable to Government control of their financial policies than was intended because of their insolvency and financial dependence.

To find a dividing line between public accountability and freedom of day-to-day administration in the heart of the problem of interfacing. Surely, the Ministries should have broad strategic control over areas like price fixation, control of investment, personnel policy and programmes of expansion. The Minister should be a kind of shock absorber between the corporation and Parliament protecting the former from Parliamentary invasion of its day-to-day freedom, and at the same time reporting to Parliament on those matters which are essential for public accountability. The distinction drawn by Herbert Morrison in Britain long ago between 'general policy' and 'day-to-day administration' is still the crux of the problem. The problem of how to reconcile commercial freedom with public control should not be an insoluble one. There should be room for carrying on the day-to-day operation with due regard to matters of national interest such as pricing. One of the main objects of public sector was to ensure that these very important and key industries were mindful of public interest and responsible to national needs without being subjected to the kind of control in their daily activities that would arise through the ordinary machinery of Government department.

Until recently, there was little clear idea either in the Parliament or in the Government about the objects or the criteria of performance of an enterprise. A kind of circular relationship with Government developed in the earlier years. It is only in the recent years that the Ministries have started producing clear and articulate policy statements. While there is paramount need for ensuring autonomy, the Ministry being accountable to Parliament can never divest itself of some degree of supervision. Efficiency cannot be improved simply by absolving the Ministries of their task. Even after the Ministry had laid down the corporate goals or objectives and also other policy frame like the pricing and return on investment, it remains the duty of the Ministry to ensure that the enterprise operates most efficiently within the parameters that have been laid down. The basic idea of reconciling freedom of day-to-day operation with public accountability seems to be too simplistic. There are some aspects of day-to-day operation which cannot be kept out of the area of public control. This has been amply demonstrated by regular Governmental intervention in such areas as prices or labour relations. Even the day-to-day operations must be carried on with due regard to the national interest. It would be wrong to put the duties of the enterprise management into a commercial box and give it to the management, and, on the other hand, put everything else into a box labelled 'public responsibility' and give it to the Ministry. These are not strictly speaking separate spheres in the modern concept. Some functions of each sphere have to be shared by both.

## BOARD OF DIRECTORS

The normal pattern of a Board is that it includes the Chairman the Managing Director (nowadays they are usually the same person), one or more full-time functional directors, officials representing the Administrative Ministry, Ministry of Finance, sometimes one or two other related Ministries and lastly one or two non-officials selected on account of their expertise or business experience. The question remains whether the Government should not go increasingly for functional boards by promoting key officials from the enterprise to the Board level so that the Board becomes a more cohesive and effective committee of management of the undertaking subject to whatever policy guidelines the Ministry may issue. Whether it is necessary to have representative from Ministries on the public sector company's board as a general routine is open to question. This might have been necessary in the early formative years of the public sector, or still now in exceptional cases where the work of the enterprise is of such nature that close daily contact with the Ministry is essential. But as a general pattern this does not seem to serve much useful purposes. Some of the Government officials sit on too many boards doing justice neither to the boards nor to their own functions in the Secretariat. Quite often they do not have time to do the basic homework needed for effective participation in the board-room deliberations. Thus their membership tends to be superfluous and non-functional. On the other hand their presence inhibits the management of the enterprise and adds to the normal duties of the senior functionaries which even otherwise are quite heavy. This practice does not facilitate the emergence of an autonomous enterprise management with initiative and operating effectiveness and yet at the same time responsible and responsive to Government guidelines and policies. From time to time there have been announcements about strengthening the P.S.E. boards by giving them true autonomy and appointing non-official directors with professional expertise or business experience. But these have by an large remained pious hopes. Recommendations of various committees on this subject have not been implemented except in a few cases. The basic problem is that no recommendations of the Cadbury Commission in the U.K on corporate governance are of considerable significance for our corporate sector. In particular the proposals for appointing larger number of outside directors as against insiders, and for appointing larger number of outside directors as against insiders, and for appointing several committees of the board such as an Audit Committee for exercising better supervision are worth implementation. The appointment of equal number independent directors on every board has been a good step.

## CONFUSION ABOUT THE OBJECTIVES

The Boards of public sector enterprises often do not appear to have a clear idea about the objects. The statutes concerned do not offer any guidance about the principle on which these enterprises should be run or the objects they should seek to achieve. As a result it becomes impossible sometimes to carryon a meaningful discussion about whether a particular enterprise is successful or not. As far back as 1968 the Estimates Committee of Parliament in its 32nd Report on the National Coal Development Corporation recommended that broad principles regarding financial and economic obligations of public sector enterprises should be laid down by Government. The same recommendation was reiterated by the 40th Report of the Committee on Public Undertakings (73-74) which regretted that Government should have taken so long to implement a recommendation of such far-reaching importance. The result has been that the performance of public undertakings continues to be judged by a variety of vague objects and considerations, and this affords scope for uninformed criticism which makes for dilution of managerial accountability. The Committee recommended that Government should present a white paper stating out inter alia the following:

(i) The frame-work of principles and the Government's general economic, financial and social strategy for public sector undertakings.
(ii) Micro-objects both financial and economic, of each public undertaking and providing for review from time to time.
(iii) Quantification of social objectives and obligations and the issue of Government directives in appropriate cases.

But no such white paper has come out so far. Before deciding the role and performance of the public sector it is essential to know the relationship between public sector and public interest. Public interest in India in the last analysis is determined by the Government and is expressed in the way the Government passes legislation, interprets it, announces its aims and the way it answers criticism of its performance in and outside Parliament. There is general feeling that public sector units are bound to feel more conscious about public interest than any private firm.

## COMPLICATED PROCEDURE OF PROJECT APPROVAL

We have already seen that in all matters involving major financial decisions it is necessary to consult through the Administrative Ministry, the Ministry of Finance, Department of Expenditure specially for the approval of the annual budget and the all matters of major expenditure. But here we concern ourselves with the long-drawn procedure and proliferation of authorities involved in project sanctioning an area which shows the worst form of interfacing. When a company has an investment proposal, it is required first of all to be approval by the Administrative Ministry, thereafter the Ministry of Finance, Department of Expenditure, and eventually by the Planning Commission (its Project Appraisal Division). Interestingly, the Department of Expenditure also has a Project Appraisal cell apart from the Planning Commission's own Projects Appraisal Division. Finally, it is placed before an interministerial Public Investment Board (PIB) which was set up in 1972 to scrutinise every project from the stage of feasibility study of final detailed project report. All investment proposals exceeding Rs 10 crores require approval of the government at the highest level even after PIB clearance. Investment proposals ranging between Rs 2 crores to Rs 10 crores are approved by an inter-Ministerial expenditure finance Committee chaired by Secretary, Ministry of Finance. Thus we already see how the multiplicity of organisation is at work.

There is one view that the Government should fix a minimum return on investment, and also the pricing system in advance, and thereafter keep itself completely aloof. This would leave the management of the enterprise to discharge its commercial role while leaving the task of determining overall public interests to the Government. It would also leave for decisions by the management a lot of areas such as costing, cost reduction, the quantity to be produced, productivity improvement, the improvement of industrial relations, technical innovations and development of new markets. But such a view is somewhat simplistic. No Government in today's context can afford to leave an undertaking completely autonomous in all these areas. But there is much sense in the argument that the Government should lay down the financial objects of every undertaking which can serve as a yardstick of performance and can be used both as a control and as an incentive for the workers and il l anagers.

Some serious thoughts should be given to the way the different clearance agencies of the Government operate in an uncoordinated fashion. Since many of the agencies do not know how their own work affects the totality of the inter-connected system, they defeat the overall objective. One comes across wide-spread complaints among public sector managers that private sector companies manage to get clearance from the Government quicker when the same principles apply to private sector and public sector. Public sector managements stress the need' of evolving a special mode of expeditious clearance of their proposals in the matter of importing critical items and detailed engineering items.

## COMPANY LAW

Another area where this problem of interfacing is illustrated in its undesirable manifestation is in relation to the Companies Act under which a joint stock company has to comply with a whole lot of restrictions.

For many years, the Government companies and non-Government companies were for all practical purposes treated at par in so far as the regulatory provisions of the Companies Act were concerned. The matters reached absurd proportions after 1974. Following the 1974 Companies Amendment Act when Section 43 of the Act was amended to say that all private limited companies with an annual average turnover of not less than Rs 1 crore will become "deemed" public companies, the great majority of the Government companies over-night became "deemed" public companies and to that extent subject to a whole lot of new restrictions. Thus even after the appointment of a Chairman, Managing Director and Directors of a Government company by the Appointments Committee of the Cabinet the approval of Department of Company Affairs became necessary thereby causing unnecessary duplication. It was only very recently that the need for distinction between Government companies and non-Government companies having regard to their structural differences particularly in the shareholding pattern and management control came to be appreciated. Relevant notifications have now been issued under Section 620 of the Companies Act exempting Government Companies from many of the provisions of the Act such as Section 269 dealing with the appointment of Managing Directors and whole time Director and fixing up of their remunerations. While some of the exemptions have been accorded to all

Government companies, i.e. (i) whenever government shareholding is more than 50 per cent, there are certain other sections namely Sections 225, 256, 257, 295, 297, 370, and 372 in respect of which exemption has been allowed only to wholely owned Government companies. Here again it is difficult to understand why distinction in this matter has been drawn between wholely owned Government companies and companies where Government holds more than 50 per cent shareholdings. The abolition of this artificial distinction will surely facilitate the smooth working of a very large number of Government companies where certain amount of minority private participation for shareholding exists.

Section 617 defines a Government company asa company where more than 50 per cent of the share capital is held by the Central Government or State Government or the Central and the State Governments taken together. One of the special measures applicable to the Government company is Section 619 under which the statutory auditor in a Government company is to be appointed or re-appointed by the Central Government (Department of Company Affairs) on the advice of the Comptroller and Auditor-General. The Comptroller and Auditor-General also has power to issue direction on the auditors to conduct test audit pending statutory audit. The audit report along with C and AG's comments has to be placed before the annual general meeting. Now the process of appointment of auditors usually takes unconscionably long time. The company applies to the Department of Company Affairs which in its turn forwards it to the C and AG. After the C and AG recommends an Auditor, the name is conveyed to the company by the Department of Company Affairs. This process usually takes a long time, and the annual general meetings cannot be held within the time schedule and are delayed from time to time on account of the non-appointment of the statutory auditor. The question is whether the Department of Company Affairs and C and AG may be divested of their authorities under Section 619 and whether the Government companies themselves cannot be given this power subject to whatever guidelines and policies are considered necessary. This strict control might have been necessary in 195-6 when the number of Government companies, a new species, was not large. But the number of such enterprises has increased enormously since 1956:

Under Section 619A, the Central Government is required to prepare within three months of the annual general meeting of the Government company an annual report on the working and affairs of the Government company and have it laid before both Houses of Parliament as early as possible. We have already hinted that Government should consider exempting the public sector companies from complying with many of the requirements which were considered necessary for private sector companies which were not under a certain degree of social discipline and responsibility, but which becomes unnecessary for a public sector company which in any case is subjected to very rigorous control by the Government and the Parliament.

Section 620 gives the Government the authority to exempt any Government company from complying with some of the provisions. It is understood why more advantage has not been taken of the provision.

## DEPARTMENT OF PUBLIC ENTERPRISES

Bureau of Public Enterprises has now become Department of Public Enterprise which is the focal point for CPSEs. In order to ensure coordination among public Sector enterprises which e are administratively controlled by a number of separate Ministries and evolve a uniform approach to the common problems faced by them. This was until recently located in the Ministry of Finance Department of expenditure. It was transferred to the Department of Public Undertakings created in September, 1985 in the Ministry of Industry. Now, the Department comes under the purview of Ministry of Heavy Industries and Public Enterprises. The department was set up following a recommendation made by the Estimates Committee of Parliament (Fifty-second Report—Third Lok Sabha) for a central coordinating organization to provide policy and overall guidance and also to make continuous appraisal of the performance of the various enterprises. It was assigned at that time the following functions:

(i) To provide a central point of reference, consultation and advice on important aspects of management of Public Enterprises;

(ii) to explore all avenues of economy in the Capital Costs of the Enterprises;

(iii) to devise steps to improve the productivity and profitability of Enterprise;

(iv) to review periodically the working of individual units as also examination of selected areas in their performance; and

(v) to present to Parliament or Government Agencies reports and review of their working.

The functions of the Department were enlarged consequent on Government decisions on the Report of the Administrative .Reforms

Commission on Public Sector Undertakings. The enlarged functions of the Department are indicated below:

(i) to maintain panels of suitable persons with a view to assisting the Administrative Ministries in making appointments to the Boards of Public Undertakings and providing consultation for such senior posts under the Corporations as may be prescribed; (The panels maintained by the Bureau are to be revised from time to time and kept up to date. The Bureau may also assist in the matter of deployment of persons from one Undertaking to another.)

(ii) to furnish periodical reports to Parliament and Government on the working of Public Undertakings;

(iii) to act as a data bank and as a clearing house of information in respect of important matters of common interest including information about organizational structure and pricing policies in Public Sector Undertakings in other countries of the world;

(iv) to coordinate the work relating to the examination of Public Undertakings by Parliamentary Committees;

(v) to compile information on the terms and conditions of service of employees and to advise Public Undertakings with a view to ensuring desirable uniformities in these matters;

(vi) to maintain liaison with the Department of Administrative Reforms in respect of matters like work-study, operations research and improved reporting systems to study incentive scheme in India and abroad for purposes of grant of production bonus to personnel at Manager's level;

(vii) to assist the concerned Ministries and Finance Ministry in making a more expert scrutiny and evaluation of feasibility studies/DPRs, to the extent practicable;

(viii) to assist the Ministries in controlling expenditure on residential and administrative buildings, residence of senior executives, townships and ancillary facilities with a view to securing a measure of uniformity in the matter of provision of amenities to labour; and

(ix) to advise Public Undertakings on matters on which advise is sought.

But it should be emphasised that this department is essentially a service evaluation and coordinating agency without any administrative control over the enterprises. It issues instructions and guidelines from time to time on various aspects of management for observance by the enterprises. But its authority is to a large extent recommendatory and is of little consequence unless it is backed and enforced by the Administrative Ministry. Thus it somewhat impaired its effectiveness. In fact for a number of years after inception it was little more than a statistics-gathering and academic agency. In recent years, however, with backing from the Government, it has become an effective body whose directives in various areas such as corporate social responsibility are being taken seriously and observed by the enterprises. In the context of the on-goining economic reforms and structural adjustment programme, and the need for deregulation and freeing of PSUs from as many centralized bureaucratic controls many people have doubted the justification of such centralized regulatory bodies as the DPE (forming BPE) and the Public Enterprises Selection Board. There are strong views that all these agencies should be abolished. The DPE also supervises the process of finalizing M.O.U's for all CPSEs and also select Maharatna, Navaratna and Miniratna CPSEs.

**Planning Commission**

All CPSEs are required to get their annual plans vetted by the Planning Commission. They have to appear before the commission and make representation.

## COORDINATION AND HOLDING COMPANY CONCEPT

The problem of coordination among public sector enterprises has assumed considerable importance. Increasingly the output of one enterprise is the input of another. Similarly the efficient performance of an enterprise is often not in its own hands, but depends a lot on the operation of sister enterprises. For instance, production in steel plants and power plants depends or coal supplies, just as coal production depends on supplies of heavy equipment machinery and power from other public enterprises. The performance of Coal India is overwhelmingly conditioned by the timely and adequate availability of railway wagons. There are also complex issues of pricing and payments on time. An inter-public sector price equilibrium is still to be reached. The case of Durgapur Steel Plant, virtually a captive plant for the railways, being forced to sell its products to the railways at a price below the cost of production is a typical case in point.

A major experiment in ensuring coordination between the Ministry and the enterprises, and between functionally related enterprises was the experiment of holding companies for enterprises in given sectors. The Administrative Reforms Commission in the report presented in 1967 had suggested sectoral corporation to avoid fragmentation and duplication of industrial efforts in the public sector and also to give public sector certain autonomy which it did not have under conditions of day to day bureaucratic control from the Ministries. It was not accepted by Government. But a major departure was attempted in 1973 with the introduction of the system of sectoral holding companies in the steel and coal industries. Under one corporate umbrella, the Steel Authority of India brought together as subsidiaries the undertakings operating in steel, cooking coal and iron ore, and further combined the Secretaryship of the Ministry with the Chairmanship of the holding company. A similar experiment was also launched in the mines sector. But possibly too much was being attempted through this single institutional device. Contrary to the original intention, both the Ministry and the holding company remained separate empires, and there was duplication rather than elimination of levels. The SAIL took many decisions over the heads of Chief Executives and constituent enterprises and interfered in such details a purchase proposals, contracts, recruitment and training and executive posts, fixation of pay scales, and allowances of executives and transfer of personnel. The constituent units were reduced to ineffectiveness. In this context the wisdom of shifting the headquarters of the apex steel body from Ranahi, which is at the centre of India's steel territory to distant Delhi has also to be doubted. The proximity with the Ministry did not surely compensate for the cost of remote control of the major steel mills, and the physical distance not only from the iron ore mines, but also the coal mines and the railways with which steel industry is so closely connected. In this context the experiment of putting a trade unionist in charge of an enterprise misfired, and Tulpule, the General Manager, Durgapur Steel had to resign. On the other hand there were complaints of the interests of other subsidiaries and of newer projects being overlooked in the interests of the Steel Authority. Thus an experiment which was introduced in steel with a bang in 1973 ended in a hamper in 1978. In 1978 the Government introduced a bill in Parliament for transforming the SAIL from a holding company with subsidiaries into a company with a number of units. With its passage, for all practical purposes the former Hindustan Steel at as revived under a different name.

The holding company still survives in coal where the complexities are somewhat less. The lesson to be learnt is that too much was attempted and too much was expected of the experiment. Further the SAIL did not confine itself to planning and coordination as the IRI or ENI do in Italy and turned itself into an implementing and executive agency. Lastly, while sectoral corporation for steel was a good concept it was a mistake to combine its Chairmanship with the Secretaryship of the Ministry. This seemed to have created more problems of interfacing than those which it was intended to solve.

## RECENT MEASURES AND MOUs

The issue of increasing the productive efficiency of the PSUs has engaged much attention since 1991 when government's economic reforms programme was launched. Budgetary support has been- eliminated or reduced to a minimum. There are serious proposals about reducing redundancy of labour, reference of sick enterprises to the B.I.F.R. and even closing down unviable PSUs and dealing with the unemployed labour force through the National Renewal Fund with schemes for compensation package, training and redeployment. Added to this controversy is the on-going process of partial privatisation of the PSUs. As a response to complains of adhocism; lack of consistency and professionalism; and excessive bureaucratization and politicization the government set up at official level several years ago a Disinvestment Commission as an advisory body to advise on the modalities of disinvestment from specific PSUs referred to the Commission. The Commission submitted nine reports upto March, 1999 on large number of PSUs whose cases had been referred to it. But there has been little action on the part of the government to follow up and implement these recommendations.

The only concrete, in many respects a model case of concrete action, has been dilution of government holding in Container Corporation of India (CONCOR) in 1998. Here government very rightly decided to follow the advice of designated merchant bankers and investment bankers and have successfully sold sizeable chunk of government holding collecting about Rs.256 crores. VSNL could raise money through GDR-cum-domestic offering successfully in 1999. GAIL could offload some of the shares in domestic market in 1999. Recently, the Government could manage to divest Modern Foods (which was sold to Hindustan Lever Ltd.). A number of PSUs which are chronically sick and unviable or lying closed for years will continue to face problems. These will not be getting good response in capital market. In all such cases the only solution would seem to be outfight sale of PSUs. Clearly, the prospect of the nation tiding over the present economic crisis largely depends on the PSUs becoming viable and surplus generating through stopping their continuous draft on the nation's surplus resources and in fact giving a return on the massive investment made by the nation. Even a 1 per cent improvement in efficiency in the public sector could yield about Rs 1,000 crores to the exchequer. Also, there has been little progress in freeing the PSUs from the stifling bureaucratic control exercised by Ministries on a day-to-day basis. The Navaratna scheme was announced in 1996-97 with much fanfare with the declared intention of making the reconstituted Boards (with non-official Directors) autonomous. But there has not been satisfactory progress in this direction.

## MOU

The MOU system introduced in 1988 on the model of the Contract de Programme of France, or a system of performance contract has now been introduced widely for performance improvement by the PSUs. MOU is a freely negotiated performance contract between the government and the public sector enterprises. It clearly outlines the rights, duties and tasks of the two parties. After a MOU has been signed, government is not expected to interfere in the day to day operations of the enterprise and will only review performance at the end of the year on the basis of the achievement by the enterprise of the targets clearly laid down and agreed upon in the MOU. MOU can be described as an attempt to move public sector management away from the government-style, procedure-oriented system on to the private sector norms of efficiency, accountability and results. If the MOU experiment succeeds, there may not be much more clamour for privatisation. Experience in countries like France, Pakistan and Korea attests to the success of the MOU system. There are two distinct types of MOUs viz. the 'French contracting system' and the 'signalling system'. Under the former, clear targets are laid down and one could judge the performance by enumerating whether or not a particular target was met. In the signalling system targets are indicated on a five point scale, the performance of the undertaking being judged with reference to whether it stands between 1 (Excellent) and 5 (Poor): Elaborate procedures have been drawn up combining the the Performance Evaluation System and the Performance Incentive System. MOUs are a sort of long-term corporate plan and annual targets are set within the context of the corporate plan. The entire relationship between public sector enterprises and the concerned administrative ministry is examined. A monitoring cell in the Department of Public Enterprises keeps the operation of the MOU under constant examination. There is also a high power official committee to review the draft MOU before the final draft is signed and to make an annual evaluation to judge how far the commitments made by both the parties through the MOU have been met. There is also an award system for MOU signing companies. It has also to take a final view about the assessment of the MOU scheme. The scheme is reported to have been operating successfully in most of the major industries.

## Disinvestment from P.S.Us.

Finally, we should note the accepted policy of the Central Government to sell a limited percentage of shares in selected Public Sector Units to the public sector financial institutions and Mutual Funds from 1991-92. This policy of partial disinvestment (from 20 per cent to a minimum of 0.27 per cent) announced in the central budget for 1991-92 was carried out in 31 selected PSUs. Their shares were grouped into bundles (comprising good and profitable companies with companies with lacklustre working results) for each of which a reserve price was fixed. Each bundle was sold to the public sector mutual fund which offered the highest price. The sale price amounting to Rs 3038 crores was used to reduce the central budget deficit. This has been criticised in some quarters on the ground that these sale proceeds should have been rather used for fresh investment by the PSUs. Also, the method of valuation of these shares and their disinvestment to only mutual funds have come in for adverse criticism. It has been said that the government could get a much higher price by following normal accepted methods of valuation and by consulting the stock exchange authorities and the PSU management concerned. According to a study by the Institute of Public Enterprises (IPE), See *Economic Times,* New Delhi of 13th November, 1992. the government could have raised more than 6356 crores from disinvestment in the public sector in 1991-92 by following alternative strategies. Instead it got less than 50 per cent of this. Following this line of criticism, the government changed the mode of disinvestment in 1992-93.

According to this study, while the government's decision to disinvest public sector shares to save itself from insolvency deserves approbation "our analysis points out that the government failed to realise not only the best value but also other objectives of the disinvestment programme." The study faults the government on the following considerations:

(i) The government launched the programme without creating the required conditions for its take off.

(ii) It did not get public enterprises listed on the stock market.

(iii) Enough efforts were not made to build up the much needed Profit Earning Capital Market linkages.

(iv) Opportunities were frittered away to sell these shares when favourable conditions existed in the market.

(v) Suitable organisations to oversee disinvestment of PSU shareholdings was not set up. The Department of Public Enterprises and the Finance Ministry adopted techniques and methods which resulted in lower than justified realisations.

(vi) Managements of public sector enterprises were not consulted.

(vii) There was no discussion with the stock market exchange authorities and experts on Capital Market.

The study is also critical of the fact that the government did not take lessons from similar disinvestment exercised in other countries particularly the U.K. and France.

There was no need to have a one shot deal with mutual funds, as the deals of the market could have been easily known by disinvestment of share holdings in 2 or 3 releases. "It is also unethical on the part of the government to have compelled mutual funds to buy public sector units' shares compulsorily, as they manage the money of small investors who are risk shy." The study suggests the appointment of a committee to oversee disinvestment of public sector shares. It also advises that there is no need to follow uniform methods of disinvestment of these shares as has been the practice in the past. The PSUs selected for disinvestment should be classified into various categories based on their subdivisions and the best price should then be arrived at by choosing one or a mix of share valuation methods.

The partial privatisation of the share capital of P.S.Us has now become a continuing annual ritual. The need for approaching the capital market should force these corporations to improve their dividend record and their profitability and financial performance in general. Also this process should slowly transform these PSUs into joint sector companies. However there is a continuing controversy as to whether the sale proceeds of these PSU shares should be used for shoring up the fiscal positions of the Central Government, or for expansion/diversification of these undertakings. A question that is still unresolved is what will be the resting point for government share-holding. Government appear to have decided that in generality of the cases. The Government's shareholding is PSEs will be brought down to 51 per cent. In case of the PSEs involving strategic considerations Government will continue to retain in majority holding 74 p.c. in PSUs in all areas, and 26 p.c. in some reserve areas. In pursuance of the Disinvestment Policy, the government equity in selected PSUs was offered to Mutual Funds.

A significant step in the year 2000 was the setting up of the Department of Disinvestment in the Finance Ministry to coordinate and speed up the process of disinvestment. But non-the-Iess progress has been tardy. A great event was the highly successful issue of the Coal India 2010 which turned this company as the most valued company in the Indians stock exchange. The recent issue of separate shares in the ONGC through public auction was a landmark event.

### 1991 Industrial Policy and After

The New Industrial Policy of July 1991 contains the following four major decisions in respect of the public sector:

(i) Reduction in the list of industries reserved for the Public Sector 3.

(ii) Disinvestment of shares of PSU's to raise resources and encourage wider participation of general public and workers in the ownership of the PSUs.

(iii) Policy for sick public enterprises to be same as that for the Private Sector; and

(iv) Improvement of performance through the performance contract or MOU system by which management are to be granted greater autonomy and held accountable for result.

That there is no reason for any pessimism among public sector employees should be clear from the various statements made by the government leaders, among them, the statement made by the Prime Minister in the Parliament on the 20th December 1991 which emphasised the following points:

(i) The mixed economy system will continue in the country.

(ii) There will be reduced budgetary support to sick or potentially sick Public Enterprises with a view to eliminate them as early as possible.

(iii) Nationalisation will normally not be resorted to in future.

(iv) While dealing with sickness, human hardship would be avoided to the extent possible through the National Renewal Fund.

There can be no doubt that turning the public sector enterprises into performing assets is an essential aspect of the economic reform programmes. This programme can never succeed unless these enterprises, which dominate our economy by virtue of the assets they command, the large number of people they employ the products they turn out and the huge finance they need, can be made to raise their own resources and give a fair return on the massive investment that the nation has made on them. Our nation cannot simply go on maintaining the public sector which as a whole gives a return of only 0.66 per cent on the capital employed and 1.9 per cent on the sales turnover. A public sector turn around is thus crucial to the success of the very structural adjustment programme. And yet the pathetic fact remains that nothing worthwhile has been done since July 1991 to make these undertakings truely independent and properly accountable or to reduce the bureaucratic stranglehold of the ministries over them. They are still required to refer to the government really all major strategic decisions or proposals which await month after month, sometimes year after year for the necessary clearance. Posts of the Chairman of Managing Director in an important undertaking are still kept unfilled for long stretches even when the exact date when the incumbents will retire is known years ahead. It is necessary to enable the enterprise management to take its own decision in all business matters when they are depending on their own resources and not ask for government budgetary support. Interestingly, the MOU was supposed to be an instrument for freeing enterprises from day-to-day bureaucratic control but the way this exercise has sometimes been carried out seems to bring about the opposite result. Infact the MOU appears to have a pretext for bringing about a new system of bureaucratic control by the ministry in addition to the existing ones.

Central Government has in general dithered on proposals for privatising chronically sick public enterprises when it is clear that government will in no way be able to master the massive resources that will be required to rehabilitate these sick undertakings. It has been decided to refer chronically sick PSUs to the Board for Industrial and Financial Reconstruction (BIFR) under the Sick Industrial Companies Act (SICA) 1985 (which is also applicable to the private sector) for the formulation of revival/rehabilitation schemes as SICA has since been amended so as to cover public sector as well. Offering such PSEs including some of the potentially sick ones, to workers cooperatives either directly or through the BIFR route could be a viable option. An important adjunct of this policy is a national safety net for workers for which a provision has been made in the budget. In order to protect the interest of the workers likely to be affected, the Government has already established a National Renewal Fund to take care of redundancies, retraining/redemployment and closures etc.

As on 31 March, 1999, 67 Industrial PSUs whose net worth had become negative and had become sick were registered with BIFR. Of these, 35 were the units taken over from private sector by the Government to safeguard the interest of workers. In the face of the governments resources constraint, the trade union opposition to any job cutting or restructuring, and the government's lack of political will to enforce privatisation, the BIFR is unlikely to achieve anything meaningful.

The National Renewal Fund has been brought in to existence, but so far it has not done anything worthwhile in the direction of retraining and re-employment or promoting self entrepreneurship. It has only been formulating and implementing Voluntary Retirement Scheme. Thus while performance improvement of the PSUs has been an avowed object of government policy, very little has been done concerted to bring it about.

Enhanced autonomy has been granted to 11 selected PSUs referred to as Navratnas in which non-official experts have been appointed as part time directors. Greater functional an operational autonomy has been granted to

39 other profit—making PSYs referred to as "Mini- Ratnas" making them more efficient and competitive. Recently in addition to Navratna and Miniratna companies a third category of CPSEs. Maharatna has been introduced. They have been delegated substantial auction.

All the performing enterprises can be very well grouped into two: those enterprises which are in a monopolistic position and those which are in competition with private sector units. The latter can again be divided between those who generate surplus and the losing ones. We should not, at this stage, think of privatising the monopolistic public sector enterprises, nor those which are in the nature of essential public utilities. This would leave us with enterprises such as cement, aluminium, hotels and airlines. One should think in terms of privatising most of the:;e units. As regards the erstwhile private sector units, efforts should be made to return them to the former owners leaving it to them to deal with the surplus workers as best as they deem fit.

Government can transfer these undertakings on an 'as is where is' basis with all the assets and liabilities"subject to an undertaking on the Sri Lanka model that there should not be any retrenchment within the first two years. In the worst scenario, government could take over the responsibility of paying the salary of all those found redundant till their superannuation from out of the National Renewal Fund. Regarding the enterprises which are run in competition with private sector parties, the same procedure can be followed. It is reasonably certain that there will be enough takers from amongst private, investors. Once this is pushed through government will be relieved of the substantial burden of budgetary support and subsidies. This leaves us only with the monopolistic enterprises and the government concerns run as public utilities. For the present those which are monopolies should, by and large, be kept under public control, but there should be no objection to selling off 49 per cent of the shares to private investors, thereby realising huge funds. As regards utilities, while there is every reason to privatise enterprises in the field of urban transportation, telecommunication and the like, and there is great scope for privatising electricity generation and transmission, we cannot think in terms of outright privatisation in these areas in the near future.

The major challenges for the public sector enterprises in the days ahead will consist in:

(i) Getting accustomed to loss of budgetary support and loss of special privileges such as purchase preferences and price preferences for purchase by the government or other public sector undertakings;
(ii) Restructuring and reforming the capital base involving conversion of huge loan amounts into equity and disinvestment of the government shareholding to public share holders and access to capital market;

(iii) Managing competition from both domestic competitors and foreign competitors;
(iv) Taking advantage of the ongoing globalisation process in sourcing raw materials from overseas at cheaper prices, in gaining access to cheaper off shore funds and building up an export base;
(v) Cutting down and controlling costs at every level;
(vi) Building up an overall culture of productivity and productive efficiency in the whole organisations;
(vii) Identifying redundant mar power and appropriately dealing with it through means such as retaining reemployment, encouraging self employment, and providing handsome termination packages through National Renewal Fund, etc.;
(viii) Changing over from the psyche of distribution of products to vigorous and aggressive selling and marketing involving consumer satisfaction and after sales service;
(ix) Giving due attention to the conditions on the shop-floor and production system, upgrading technology, whenever necessary, ensuring proper working conditions giving adequate incentives and ensuring adequate quality control and productivity; and above all
(x) Managing change as a collective effort involving management, trade union and the government.

In conclusion, public sector managers should not regard the 1991 industrial policy as a constraint, but as an opportunity to justify themselves in demonstrating their ability for diversification, entrepreneurship, quality control and export capability in competition with overseas competitors.

It is worth while mentioning that the public enterprises under the State Governments also suffer from the same constraints and disabilities as in the case of the C.P.S.Es. There are 849 operating public enterprises owned by the State Governments on the basis of information submitted by 579 of them to the Department of Public Enterprises. The total investment in these 579 SLPEs amounted to Rs.329079 crores in 2007-8 (Rs. 115588 crores as paid up capital and Rs. 183256 as long term loan). The total turnover of these 579 SLPEs aggregated to Rs. 239453 crores. The total subsidy received by these SLPEs during 2007-08 amounted to Rs. 14319 crores which work out to only 6% of the turn-over.

The over-all net profit for these 579 SLPEs stood at L 865 crores although as many as 190 amongst them (33 per cent) suffered losses during the year. In terms of employment these 579 SLPEs employed 1413646 employees during 2007-08. These figures are obtained from National Survey on State

Level Public Enterprises, 2007-08 Vol. 1 published by the Department of Public Enterprises.

## REFERENCES

1. Under the present policy of the Government the same person usually combines the posts of a Chairman and Managing Director in the majority of the companies. In very few of them there is a part-time Chairman.
2. Vide Bureau of Public Enterprises, NO.2 (56) 68-BPE (G.M.), dated 4 June, 1969.
3. *Economic and Political Weekly,* May 26, 1977.
4. The Bureau of Public Enterprises which was entrusted with the job of preparing this white paper containing the objectives of the public sector is said to have finalized it. But the 1977 elections and the political changes intervened to delay its publication. According to press reports (Economic Times, February 26, 1977) this draft white paper speaks of profit as an objective, but does not lay down any criteria or norms which can be used as a touchstone for unit's success or satisfactory performance It emphasizes the importance of the public sector in promoting economic development by way of creating employment potentialities and self-reliance, specially in strategic products, taking up projects in backward areas and projects with long gestation periods and investing in areas where profit cannot be the sole criterion.
5. *Op. cit.*

## CHAPTER 14

# New Economic Policy and its Implications for the Government Superstructure

The Indian governments on-going programme of economic reforms and structural adjustment since July 1991 have highlighted the visible inadequacies of the country's existing administrative structure as an effective change agent.

The new economic policies sought to restore government's fiscal balance move towards de-regulation of government's regulatory and administrative functions in economic administration vacating for the public sector huge chunks of industrial activity hitherto reserved for it, greater and greater reliance on private sector initiative for industrial and commercial development and, last but not the least, exposing Indian economy to the pulls and pushes from the global economy, in other words the process of globalization. These tasks are formidable and involve a complete change of the mind-set on the part of people in our administrative and political system who, for a whole generation, have been nurtured in a tradition of government's omnipresence in the economy, and also on India's traditional policy of self-reliance rather than an outward looking economy. This is not proving to be an easy transition. There are vested interests resisting having to part with power and authority. But more than these there are many not able to comprehend the significance of the breath-taking changes sweeping across our country.

Our administrative structure is essentially a survival from the colonial times when the entire emphasis was on regulation rather than growth, procedural perfection rather than achieving results. The assumption was that people in government know what is best for the country and, therefore, entrepreneurs, businessmen and managers should, by and large, follow the diktats from the government ministers and bureaucrats. This colonial tradition was further intensified as a result of the traditions of populism and socialistic intervention in economic matters which grew up in the year after independence. This essentially conservative machinery, when called upon to move with the mind-boggling policy changes which have taken place in the last two decades and to carry them forward naturally resists and is found to be an unwilling instrument.

The industrial, trade, fiscal and financial policy changes since June 1991 have brought about a complete metamorphosis in the business scenario in India. These changes have posed for Indian Industry both a great challenge and great opportunities. The challenge consists in the fact that, for the first time since the 1950s, Indian economy has been de-regulated both in respect of allowing domestic competition, and permitting liberal imports. The nature of their interface has thus change Indian industry needs to learn to operate in this de-regulated environment where it is required to compete not only with domestic competitors but also with foreign firms which could not hitherto send their goods to India on account of import barriers and prohibitive customs duties. To tackle this challenge, Indian industry needs to show all its competitive efficiency, marketing skills and quality improvement. Also Indian management needs to show its innovative potential. Those who have successfully tackled this challenge have not only reaped a rich harvest in the domestic economy, but have also become big global players in the world economy. The opportunity consists in the fact that entrepreneurial decision making which, for about four decades, was a close preserve of government authorities-ministers and bureaucrats has now been returned, by and large, to the entrepreneurs to whom it rightfully belongs. Except for a few industries, industrial licensing has been abolished and this puts up new horizons for industrial entrepreneurs. Also, government is giving utmost thrust on exports which have been given lot of incentives. Under the previous policy regime in a sheltered domestic economy, most of the industrial enterprises did not feel the need to go to the overseas market for selling their products as they were making enough profits from the huge and sheltered domestic market. In the changing context they need to build up a compulsive export culture, both in their own interest and the national interest.

## Major Changes

They key changes in the recent and on-going industrial policy are the following:

1. Reduction of the number of industries or activities reserved for the public sector under the 1956 Policy Resolution from 29 (17 industries in

Schedule A+ 12 industries in Schedule B) to only the 8 (vide appendix I of the Industrial Policy Statement June 24, 1991).

This means that a vast range of industries, which were closed to private sector initiative from 1956 onwards will now be open to it for setting up new projects or expanding existing enterprises. The significance of this vast change in sectors such as steel, power etc. cannot be over-estimated. Indeed this will have enormous implications for the future growth of the private sector industry.

2. The abolition of industrial licensing except for 18 industries listed in Annexure II of the Industrial Policy Statement of July 23, 1991.

Since this announcement, at least 4 of these areas have been further delicenced viz. Motor cars (entry 11), while goods like refrigerators for Airconditioners (october 18) mining of most of the minerals and molasses. Delicensing of several other items like sugar is also reported to be under consideration. As already stated, the policy of industrial !incensing for all practical purposes will transfer entrepreneurial decision-making from the lap of ministers and bureaucrats, with whom it rested since 1951, back to the entrepreneur himself. The entrepreneurs will no longer be required to visit Delhi for obtaining industrial licences and go through a very round-about administrative procedure which was time consuming, full of uncertainty and meant a lot of administrative and economic costs. They can straight away formulate their project on the basis of their assessment of the market, approach financial institutions for term loans or approach the capital market and go on implementing the projects. Needles to say that this will also mean much greater responsibility for entrepreneurs in term of alternative investment proposals and, eventually, taking correct investment decisions.

3. The new policy on small-scale industry, for the first time, allows SSI units access to overseas technology and also permits foreign equity investment upto 24 per cent. This policy change opens up new horizons for small scale industry units.

4. The new policy has openly welcomed foreign direct investment. It promises automatic approval to direct foreign investment upto 51 per cent foreign equity in a list of 34 high priority industries (Annexure III) of the Industrial Licensing Policy.

The significance of this announcement, both from the point of view of foreign companies seeking to come to establish joint ventures in India and Indian entrepreneurs seeking foreign collaborators in establishing joint ventures in India,.is not to be under-estimated. Also significant is the announcement that foreign equity proposals need not necessarily be accompanied in future by foreign technology agreement, and the announcement that majority foreign equity holding upto 51 per cent will be allowed to trading companies primarily engaged in export activities, and the formation of a specially empowered Foreign Investment Promotions Board for negotiating with large international firms and approving direct foreign investment proposals in selected already.

5. Along with a generally open foreign open investment policy, the procedure for foreign technology agreement has been made much simpler and easier. The policy announces automatic permission to foreign technology agreement in all the Annexure III industries upto a lumpsum payment of Rs 1 crore, 5 per cent royalty for domestic sales and 8 per cent for exports. Over a 10 year period from the date of agreement or 7 years from commencement of production. It also assures automatic permission to all foreign technology agreements in industries other than in Annexure III if there is no significant of free foreign exchange. It abolishes the need for government permission for hiring foreign technicians.

The abolition of Chapter III of th e MRJP Act, which bedevilled large industrial houses ever since its commencement in 1971. The 91 Policy announced this intention and suggested that in future the MRTP Act will only be concerned with controlling and regulating monopolistic restrictions, unfair trade practices. The required amendment in the MRTP Act has been carried out since then and Chapter III has been abolished for all practical purposes.

This frees corporate industry from an irksome restrictive system, almost an additional licensing system to which it has been subjected since 1971.

7. The introduction of partial convertibility of the rupee by the 1992 budge of full convertibility of rupees on trading account m the 1993 budget, and of full convertibility on current account in the 1994 budget also opened up new vistas for the future development of industry. Firms which are earning foreign exchange by export of their goods and services will be permitted to realize full value of their earning and use part of it to meet their own foreign exchange requirements. This is again for export-efficient units, although the units accustomed to full foreign exchange allocation from the government will no longer get this benefit and will be constrained. There were indications that convertibility on capital account would also come about soon. Unfortunately the series of global crises and financial crises in recent decades have foreclosed this.

8. The drastic changes in the Foreign Exchange Regulation Act in 1992 are of great significance for companies with more than 40 per cent foreign

share-holding. For all practical purposes all these irksome restriction imposed on them in 1973 e.g. prior permission of RBI for a whole range of business activities such as expansion, diversifying appointment of foreigners and even purchasing houses have been removed. The Act returns to its original form in 1947. Also 527 which prohibited Indians from accepting directorships etc. in foreign countries is removed. This was a great obstacle to internationalization of our business. The replacement of FERA by the Foreign Exchange Management Act (FEMA) signify this change.

9. Since the budget of 1991 there has been a general trend towards the lowering of customs duties and removal of blanket ban on imports. The 1994 budget has carried this process much further in its wide-spread customs duty reductions (from a general level of around 200 per cent to a general level of 65 per cent). While this is partly inevitable in the interest of meeting the MF loan conditionalities and in the interest of exposing Indian industry to external competition so as to raise its competitive efficiency, this has also brought about great difficulties for enterprises in a wide variety of industries. Indian Industry has been traditionally subjected to lots of quantitative controls and other difficulties such as prohibitive duty on capital goods import, and prohibitive cost of term loan and working capital loan. Industrial licensing has subjected Set enterprises to scale restrictions. Overseas competitors have not been suffering from these disabilities. If Indian market is suddenly thrown open to Overseas competitors it will be difficult for some of our industries to survive in open competition. After all competition has to be among equals and not among non-equals. This reduction or removal of customs duties and import barriers must therefore be not an event, but a process spread over three to four years during which time Indian Industry should be encouraged, persuaded and pressurized to improve its efficiency, to take advantage of the incentives being offered and to reach level of intèrnational competitive efficiency. Those enterprises who can do that will no doubt succeed. But many others, hitherto nurtured in a sheltered atmosphere free. from competitiol1 may have to close down. This aspect of globalization is therefore both a serious constraint and a great opportunity. But Indian Government must take care to see that globalization should not be at the cost of destroying our nationol industrial capabilities built up over a period of 4 decades without giving our industry a fighting chance.

10. The 1993 and 1994 budgets also broke new ground by seeking to create demand by substantial reduction of central excise duties on a very wide variety of goods. Indian industry must take advantage of this. The

benefit of this should be passed on to the consumers in full fledged manner so that they can feel encouraged to buy these products at substantially reduced prices. The Ministry of Finance should be congratulated for adopting this approach for demand regeneration through reduced levies. An aspect of this that should necessarily be borne in mind is that the substantial reduction of import duties will have a bearing on foreign direct investment, for the obvious reason that if multi-nationals can import their own final products into this country by paying a minimum duty or by not paying any duty at all, they will neither feel compelled to nor will have incentives to take the route of foreign direct investment and starting joint ventures in our country.

11. The launching of the 8th plan (1992-97) and subsequent plans also marked sea-change in the business scenario. They mark a switch from detailed physical planning to indicative planning, from predominant government percentage share in plan expenditure to a larger percentage share for the corporate private and household sectors, and from an emphasis on pure spending to emphasis on productive efficiency and return.

This will also provide fillip to further economic growth. The acceptance of a clear policy not to subsidies losses in industrial enterprises and the gradual withdrawal of budgetary support from public enterprises, mark a water-shed. Clearly, public enterprises must stand on their own feet and Substantially improve their performance, improving their goods and services and changing over from resource-guzzling enterprises to surplus generating units. This will call for tremendous degree of management capability, innovation, change and results. Also. the private sector has to learn to operate in a de-regulated and internationlising business environment.

### Need for Export Compulsive Culture in All Enterprises

Both the public sector and the private sector must give priority of emphasis on improving their export performance. If Indian economy has to get over the current impasse. there must be a spectacular improvement in exports. An export inhibition in our attitude needs to be replaced by a compulsive export culture. This again will mean full attention to quality control and assurance, product improvement, improved design and packaging. In short, a reorientation of our production management and shop floor culture which have been in general a dark area in our management system. In his book 'Out of the crisis' Edwards Deming shows that 85 per cent of defective products come from defective production process, and gives his famous 14 points by which managers can bring about substantial improvement in quality or productivity. To quote him "Innovation, the foundation of the future cannot thrive unless top management has a declared and unshakeable commitment to quality and productivity." Much of the performance of China in recent years has been on account of her spectacular increase of exports. Both China and India were exporting at roughly the same level around 1971-72 (China exported goods worth US$ 2.2 billion). While Indian exports have risen to the level of US$ 20/25 billion now, Chinese exports have already crossed US$ 100 billion. There is no reason why India's exports cannot also rise up proportionately. But we need to shed off our pessimism, adopt a bold vision and follow it up by energetic action in building up export surplus, improving the quality of our goods and their brand name, providing vigorous marketing and after-sales service and showing greater integration with emerging regional markets such as the Asia-Pacific Region, the Gulf countries, the European community and the North American free trade area.

The collapse of the former Soviet Union and, with it, of the pattern of bilateral Rupee trade are often mentioned as the major reasons for affecting India's current export performance. We should not any longer lamant the passing away of the old USSR but try to seek new opportunities in the future growth of Russia and the other successor republics. They have many things to give us 8g arms and armaments, petroleum and technology. We also have many things to give them e.g. foodgrains, processed agricultural and horticultural commodities, light engineering goods and consumer products of any variety. That satisfactory currency and institutional arrangements have not emerged for bilateral trading, is no reason why we cannot resort to barter trade or counter trade which should enable us to survive the transitional period of uncertainty and free-for-all. Surely, we have greater potential than the West has in fulfilling some at the needs of some of these countries. The entire situation should, therefore, be regarded more as an opportunity than as a constraint.

## On-going Constraints for Growth

Despite the sea changes in policies, these changes have not yet been reflected in procedural simplification and in bureaucratic attitudes. Many of the procedures from the old order still survive. Also, the old attitude of control, regulation and patronage still prevails among many politicians and bureaucrats, in particular among lower functionaries in the central and state governments who refuse to part with their power of patronage and, therefore still insist on following the old procedure and practices (eg. Motorola case). Industry must help the government in transforming the old attitudes at all levels and discarding the prevailing counter-productive and bureaucratic procedural bottlenecks. Unless this is done we cannot really show any visible and spectacular improvement in our production, exports, foreign investment promotion and import liberlisation.

## Public Sector Reform and Turn-Around

One of the major challenges facing India's economy today is how to turn the public sector enterprises from being non-performing assets to performing assests. If these enterprises would have given a return of even 10 per cent that itself would substantially improve the currently miserable state of public finance in our country. Only a handful of these enterprises are giving a reasonable return of the investment, most of them again, operating the oil sector or other monopoly areas. The great majority of them not only fail to give a return on the massive investment made, but go on drawing on budgetary support every year at considerable cost to other priority sectors which are starved of investment. According to the latest figures available their profitability works out to a disappointing percentage of 0.9 per cent on the capital employed and 1.6 per cent on the sales turnover. This non-performance of the public sector is one of the principal reasons for India's lack-luster growth record and prevalence of so many ills such as chronic budgetary and fiscal deficit inflationary pressure and steep price rise. Also, these public sector enterprises control many essential imports and raw materials in industry. On account of their inefficiency, the administered prices of these products have to go on increasing from time to time in order to cover their .... and this further aggravates the government's fiscal and financial situation and adds to spiralling inflation. Clearly, the successful turn-around of PSUs is one of the top priorities of our economy today. While utmost priority should be given to management improvement, cost cutting, aggressive marketing, quality control and after-sales service etc groups of professional managers and private sector industrialits should also come forward to take charge of management of some of these enterprises which have promise of return to profitability and performance with better management. There needs to be a total change of culture and acceptance of competition, ability to eventually stand on their own feet rather than continuing to rely on budgetary support from Government and an attitudinal transition from distribution of products, sometimes of patronage to marketing and at times have aggressive selling. There is a related question of redundancy. This should be solved by taking the trade unions into confidence and relying on the National Renewal Fund which could follow a vigorous programme of retraining, redeployment, golden handshake and, in general, a social safety net.

## Globalisation, An Irreversible Trend

Globalisation or internationalisation of our economy had become an irreversible phenomenon. In today's environment of super-fast communication and breaking down of geographical barriers, no country can live in splendid isolation from the rest of the world. Inter-dependence rather than self-reliance has become the key work. True self-reiiance which many people in the past confused with total avoidance of any import from outside and complete reliance on domestic market and domestic sources of supply can, in today's context, only mean concentrating on a country's own strengths and not hesitating to import whenever it is cheaper to do so than relying purely on supplies from domestic sources maintained at a high cost to the national economy.

The process of globalisation relies primarily on private sector initiative, aided by the evolution of the global information network. Government has a very important supportive or facilitating role in connection with macro adjustments, maintaining efficient infra-structure and, thirdly, promoting human development including anti-poverty programmes.

In the West there are many outstanding examples of corporations which have shaken up and changed their top management with a view to bringing about a "turn-around" e.g. General Motors, American Express, Westinghouse, IBM. All these companies and many others are feverishly engaged in identifying and working out key elements of turn-around, cost cutting, reengineering operations, laying off surplus people and entering into strategic alliances across the globe. Also, they are trying their best to close down all uneconomical operations and enter into new lines of business which promise growth and profit. There is a feverish surge for the best technology around the Globe, cheaper sources of finance and markets that promise higher selling prices. To quote- Peter Drucker: "The years ahead will be years of repeated changes in technology, in markets and market segmentation, consumer values and consumer behaviour, in finance, in political and geographical realities, in economic and trade policies. They will, therefore, steadily make existing theories of business obsolete. In fact, the most probable assumption is that no currently working business theory will be valid 10 years hence—at least not without major modifications. And yet, few executives accept that for a turn-around a company requires fundamental changes in the assumptions on which the business is being run. It requires a different business. It is not only businesses that will have to learn to turn themselves around, almost any large organisation will find itself in stagnation, frustrated, ailing none more than the government. Almost every large organisation will have to rethink its business theory" [Asian Wall Street Journal February 4, 1993 (page no. 8)]. If the first half of the current century witnessed the end of separate histories for separate countries and separate regions, the last decade witnessed another profound change, what someone has picturesquely called the end of geography – "Richard O' Brien – Global Financial Integration." The end of geography. The phenomenal inventions in the field of information technology, statellite communication and related fields have not only killed distances between various countries but have made it possible to shift strategic information and also funds across the globe at moment's notice. Also there is a breaking of the barriers between frontiers of communication, computer software, space satellites, TV and videos leading to the emergence of a powerful multimedial approach. These are aspects of globalisation our administration cannot afford not to take notice of. In fact, our administrators and managers, must familiaries themselves and become adapt at seeing themselves as parts of the global information network and to conducting their operations accordingly. Globalisation is essentially an attitudinal change that does not confuse markets or areas of operation with notional geographical boundaries and looks upon the whole world as the legitimate field of operations. Here money can be obtained from where it is the cheapest. raw materials should be procured from any source that promises the least price, the best technology should be obtained from wherever possible across the globe and, lastly, finished products are marketed wherever one gets the highest price. People in so called multinational enterprises should stop thinking in terms of a parent holding company and subsidiaries but look upon themselves as global players with no particular attachment to any single country. At the same time, they should get accustomed to working as a team of transnational managers recruited from all over the world. The end of geography paradigm is still psychologically a difficult concept to accept, but is fast becoming a reality.

The key areas for concentrated attention and concern in formulating a response strategy are: cost control and cost cutting at all levels; identification of redundant manpower and hiving it off from the enterprise strength through re-training. redeployment and good compensation packages for retirement and scheme self-employment/resettlement through the National Renewal Fund; close look at the existing product mix and willingness to shed off the chronically non-profitable activities and diversity into newer promise areas; close attention to the shop floor and production management with a view to improving the quality of products, the brand image and R&D;

technological upgrading and modernisation; attention to after-sales service and aggressive marketing strategy both in exports and for the internal market; and effective HRD strategy with a view to improving the work ethos, all round productivity and morale; taking full advantage of the convertibility of the rupee on trade account by sourcing of inputs from outside the country wherever it is obtainable the cheapest and selling finished products overseas markets wherever one gets the highest price; and taking advantage of the abolishing of the licencing system to attain economies of the scale through appropriate expansion with a view to meeting global competition. There has to be a corporate vision that includes strategic choices and organisation re-positioning wherever necessary. Private sector enterprises must evolve a strategy to fill the vacuum caused by the withdrawal of the public sector from a whole range of activities hitherto reserved for the public sector. For public sector enterprises there must be a strategy for converting the non-performing assets, wherever they are. into performing assets. When, after weighing the pros and cons, it is observed that a turn-around cannot be brought about in an enterprise on account of reasons beyond anybody's control, there should be no hesitation in closing down such enterprises without necessarily throwing people out of their jobs. Proper exploitation of the assets which area already there should give enough funds, for giving the employees appropriate compensation packages on retirement and suitable resettlement benefits. Trade Unions should be taken into confidence as partners in a turn-around strategy. Those politicians, bureaucrats and industrialists who had a vested interest in the licencing and permit regime of the last four decades and are still hoping that these reforms are a temporary phase and that we will soon return to the old order, must reconcile themselves to the fact that these reforms and adjustments are irreversible, no matter whichever be the government in power, and that the sooner they fall in line the better. A successful continuance of the same policy should ensure that India attains what can truly be a phenomenal technological and economic quantum jump by the time we step into the 21st century.

To understand this problem of interfacing between new tasks and the existing administrative apparatus, one has to analyse some of the features of the prevailing system:

1. Authority in the government is horizontally defused among large number of ministries and agencies and no single ministry or agency is competent enough to take the final decision in any important matter. Everybody needs to be consulted and there needs to be a broad agreement, even if not complete unanimity to get any policy change.

2. Authority is also structured vertically along a long line of hierarchy. In the Secretariat hierarchy starts with a lower level functionary called the Section Officer and moves along Under Secretary, Deputy Secretary, Joint Secretary, Additional Secretary, Secretary, Minister of State and Cabinet Minister. There is little of level jumping or a decision being taken at the same level where a reference from outside is received. Many important cases need to go to the Prime Minister's Office or even to the appropriate Cabinet Committee.
3. There is an overwhelming reliance on administrative controls implying individual decision on individual cases by the prescribed authority, rather than legislation or budgetary type of indirect control. This again means arbitrar decisions in individual cases and inevitable delay on account of the requirement of the prescribed application to be submitted in individual cases to the prescribed authority.
4. The Secretariat appeared to have appropriated a large proportion of decision-making power in individual cases which normally should have been left with authorities lower down or authorities locally available.
5. The system of Parliamentary control or supervision over executive action also means the requirement of lots of administrative work, paper work and discussion etc. which run directly contrary to the concept of high speed decisions.
6. The so-called principle of accountability or responsibility specially accentuated in the last 2-3 decades, induces a general tendency on the part of officials to avoid taking decisions and playing safe in general so that they are not eventually made accountable and subjected to inquisitorial action.
7. There are several other factors: Our administrative machinery is divided between the Secretariat and the Directorate, the former concerned with policy making and the latter concerned with implementation of decision. This itself is a reason for avoidable delay and procrastination whereas, in general, the distinction between policy making and implementation is increasingly getting fuzzed.

We therefore have to think seriously of drastic orientation:

(i) in organisation structure;

(ii) procedural simplication, and

(iii) in our manner and style of function.

The policy changes during the last two decades have brought about a complete metamorphosis in the administration-cum-business scenario in India. Gone are most of the administrative and quantitative government controls Which, for decades, dominated the commercial and industrial landscape of the country. But the procedural and bureaucratic hangover still persists. There is an imperative need to get away from the traditional control-oriented mind-set to the psychosis of promotion, assistance and motivating in general. People in administration need to shed off the traditions of colonial governor or socialist regulator and to move on to a new role of facilitator for industry and business. Also, we need to give up many of the old laws which still clutter our industrial and commercial landscape, but have by and large outlived their utility. Even some of the essential laws which need to remain must be drastically I overhauled, We need to ruthlessly axe a large number of ministries, government agencies and other offices which also have outlived their functions in this era of de-regulation, not necessarily by throwing people in these organisations out of employment, but by retraining them, re-deploying them in newer activities and in encouraging many of them to turn to self entrepreneurship. Examples of such organisations are: DGTD, DGS&D, Ministries of Electronics, Bio-technobgy, Textile Commissioner, Jute Commissioner, Iron and Steel Controller, Chief Controller of Import and Exports.

As State Government personnel are still unaware of the significance of the reform process and its inevitability, it is necessary to launch a mass communication movement to indoctrinate and motivate them and to help them transform themselves into their new role of facilitators rather than controllers.

We need to give up the present hierarchical, overmanned administrative organisation and turn to flat, cellular or modular organisations which can be flexible and, therefore, adjusted suitably with changing times. Many of the problems which come to administration today are without precedents in the sense that the problems which arose in the past and were dealt with in particular ways do not provide adequate guidance. There has to be, an end to the tyranny of government by precedents. Also there has to be less of the insistence on governance through written files and much more of governance through oral communication. The new information technology has speedily cut across hierarchical and geographical boundaries and has made the old type of levels and hierarchies largely redundant. It is thus no longer necessary, nor desirable, to mechanically adhere to old norms about prescribed channels, of communication such as from the Ministry to the Directorate or the Ministry to the Chief Secretary and the Chief Secretary to the concerned Secretary of the State Government, from the Secretary to the Head of Directorate, from the Head of the Directorate to the District Officer and from the District Officer to the subordinate authorities. The new multi-media information technology under which it is possible to send information or messages in seconds and minutes across the continent makes such outdated mechanisms superfluous and time-consuming. We have to accept that our procedures and practices are very often survivals from the 19th century, while the tasks and functions are of the 21st century. Can we not avoid having to deal with 21st century issues and problems with 19th century tools and apparatus?

There is a general lack of awareness among both politicians and state employees of the need for economic reforms and structural adjustments and of their inevitability and, for that matter, irreversibility. This ignorance pervades even in the minds of many officials in the central ministries. The State government officials are still living in oblivion. Schemes are being prepared, new demands for funds are being made and such demands are still being dealt with in the old style and old manner of functioning, blissfully unaware of the fact that our government, Centre and the States, are in the throes of unprecedented critical financial difficulties, and that government is not likely to have in the near future the kind of funds which are needed to meet the existing deficits or to meet the new demands being made. De-regulations, de-bureaucratisation and greater reliance on private initiative are, therefore, the prime needs of the hour. The sooner we all realise this and are willing to give up our authority and power of yester-years and reconcile ourselves to smaller government, and to a situation where control is reduced to the very minimum and promotional work will be given prime importance, the better for the nation. To quote from Machiavelli's Prince "Nothing is more difficult than initiating a new order of things.... If you will always be doing what you did in the past you will also be getting what you got in the past."

## CHAPTER 15

# An Overview

In India, as in the rest of the world there has been during the early 90's a strong revival of interest in utilising private sector initiative as a catalyst for dynamic economic growth as also, as a necessary corollary, in a visible reduction in the perceived role of the Government in economic development. No longer is the Government viewed as necessarily the dominant owner of the means of production and distribution and holding the private sector under a strong leash, but it is viewed instead as a facilitator of growth by the private sector under market conditions, as laying down and enforcing the rules of the economic game, as directly controlling only those sectors of the economy such as sections of the infrastructure and macro-economic management where it is not possible for the private sector to assume the major role. India's 8th Five Year Plan Document (1992-97) and the tidal wave of industrial policy, trade policy and other economic policies during the last, about two decades of economic reform fully reflect this growing concern for the State vacating those activities where it does not make any economic sense for it to stay and for progressively opening up these sectors not just industrial sectors like power and steel, but even infrastructure areas such as roads to private sector initiative. Also there is a growing recognition that wherever State enterprises operate they must do so with a view to generating a surplus and giving some degree of return to the State exchequer rather than being chronically dependent on Government's budgetary support for their existence.

This sea-change has arisen on account of a variety of factors. The most important of which are:

(i) The crippling budgetary and fiscal deficit to which most Governments have run and the imperative need to remove this by appropriate economic reform measures;

(ii) The eloquent evidence of the spectacular level of growth achieved in the 1980s by economies such as Korea, Taiwan, Malaysia, Indonesia and Thailand by relying on private sector as the main engine for economic growth and Government playing the role of a facilitator.

(iii) The galloping cost of Government intervention in trade and industry and other organisational and procedural difficulties.

(iv) Increased evidence of the inability of public sector enterprises in general to raise surplus revenue and consequently to ensure a return on the massive investment made and to eliminate dependence on Government's budgetary support for their· current operation.

(v) The cataclysmic collapse of the economies and the public sector systems of the former USSR and the Communist countries of Eastern Europe.

(vi) Other sweeping changes in the international environment including the example of China and Vietnam to re-create or revive the private sector based on competition and incentives, the dramatic experience China's phenomenal economic rise during the last two decades.

(vii) An increasing acceptance of the true public character of the so-called private sector in terms of the overwhelming public shareholding in most of the modern corporations the emergence of professional management and the actual separation between ownership and management.

Luckily, India never abandoned the private sector. During the early 50's, when she adopted her Five Year Plan on the model of the Soviet centralised plan, she modified the model to provide for the private sector in this model. The 1956 Industrial Policy Resolution sanctified this approach by accepting the concept of "mixed economy" where both public sector and private sector enterprises will co-exist. Agriculture by and large remained in the private sector. So did the bulk of the services sector. The 1956 Policy reserved whole range of activities, about 29 in number for almost exclusive development in the public sector in the future. All other industries were by and large left to the initiative enterprise of the private sector and even in these activities where private sector enterprises existed, these were by and large generally allowed to remain and also grow. Even when during the 70's, Indian policy makers made big advances in extending the area of public sector enterprises by nationalising some existing private sector industries such as Coal and Copper, setting up new public sector ventures and taking over large number of private enterprises which had become sick. Even in this scenario contrary to some impression outside, private sector maintained a very visible and perceived presence in the economy. Thus, it is easier for India to change into a market economy unlike the former socialist countries and many other developing countries which for all practical purposes extinguished the private sector and all traditions of private entrepreneurship and private corporate activities.

The dramatic policy changes since June, 1991 qualitatively changed the pattern of government-business relationship. Gone are the old suffocating physical and quantitative controls. These have been largely replaced by entrepreneurial freedom, greater reliance on the private sector and open policy to foreign investment. Government is withdrawing its pervasive presence and concentrating on macro-economic management and facilitating role.

During the 60s and the 70s the relationship between Government and business often tended to be not one of mutual understanding and trust, but of mutual suspicion and mud slinging. One section of businessmen developed a vested interest in the regime of controls and licences. The nexus between them and dishonest politicians and bureaucrats became the bane of public life in India, specially from the late 1960s when in presence of populist policies government's licensing regime reached its zenith. Even when a slow process of deregulation started during the 80s, these elements became the most vocal critics. Apprehensive of losing their preferential status with the advent of deregulation and competition they opposed these policies from the platforms such as self-reliance, protecting indigenous industry and preventing misdirection of investment to non-essential industries. They often formed alliances with leftist idealogues and also left-oriented parliamentarians to build up noisy campaigns against deregulation, liberalisation and decontrol.

The following are some of the key economic reforms which have been undertaken as parts of the breath-taking industrial and economic policy changes since July, 1991:

(i) Industrial Licensing has been abolished, except in 6 industries which are related to security and strategic concerns, social reasons, hazardous chemical and environmental reasons.

(ii) The industries reserved for the public sector has been reduced from 29 (Schedule A and B of the 1956 Policy) to 3(Annexure I attached to the chapter three).

(iii) Permitting automatic clearance of foreign investment with foreign equity investment up to 50/51/74/100 per cent in specific groups of industries. See Annexure IV to Chapter three. This has to be viewed in conjunction with the open and welcome attitude to direct foreign investment announced by government from time to time.

(iv) Abolition of all location restrictions other than in cities of more than 1 million population.

(v) Permitting foreign direct investment up to 100 per cent in export-oriented trading companies.

(vi) Automatic clearance for foreign technology agreement with payments not exceeding US$ 2 million and royalties up to 5 per cent on domestic sale and 8 per cent on export sold.

(vii) Repeal of the Monopolies and Restrictive Trade Practices Act thereby freeing companies from the crippling parallel license system introduced by the 1969 Act.

(viii) The small-scale industrial policy provides *inter alia* the small-scale industries among other things will have access to the capital market and to foreign equity participation up to 24 per cent.

(ix) The abolition of the system of capital issues control and transferring many of these functions to merchants bankers and other specialised bodies which are placed under the superintendence of the Security and Exchange Board of India.

(x) Introduction of convertibility of the rupee full on the current account and partial on the capital account. Many other sweeping changes in the banking and financial sectors, tariff and trade are also undertaken, many more are underway.

(xi) Securities Law (amendment) Act, 1999 incorporates derivative instruments in the definition of securities in the Securities Contract (Regulations) Act, 1956. Steps have also been taken to promote dematerialisation of stock in order to bring greater efficiency, transparency and lower cost and to serve the interest of small investors.

(xii) Enactment of Foreign Exchange Management Act (FEMA) from June 1, 2000 brings a paradigm shift in the manner in which foreign exchange is to be treated in India. The objective of FEMA is to switch from the regime of conservation of foreign exchange resources to facilitate external trade and payments and promote orderly maintenance of foreign exchange market.

The tidal wave of privatisation sweeping the whole world including the former socialist countries has not yet made substantial impact in India. A substantial section of public opinion including politicians and trade-unionists still remain unimpressed with all the claims made for privatisation and are still dogmatically tied to an old outdated philosophy which looks upon the State as the dominant player in the economy and as the main job-giver. Any attempt to weaken this role is fraught in their estimation with the possibility of large-scale retrenchment, lay-off and unemployment. It was on account of this difficulty that the attempt made in the late 1980's to privatise the Scooters India, a chronically sick undertaking was aborted. Same difficulty is faced even today when banks, power and other sectors are tried to bring under privatisation. But the factors which are working inexorably for a growing role for the private sector are the failure of the public sector enterprises in general to provide a surplus, a growing awareness that it is no longer possible for the Government to go on running enterprise by giving them funds from the general budget, a realisation that Government should not be tied down to the running of enterprise in too many fields where it is not necessary for the government to be and an acceptance of the growing capability of private sector initiative to take over from the Government in many areas and to that extent a general perception that privatisation of some of the enterprises will not only relieve the Government of substantial budgetary commitments, but will also enable it to redeploy funds so released in other essential areas. At the same time, under private management these enterprises will be subjected in a larger measure to the discipline of the balance sheet and the profit and loss statement and would therefore gradually move towards a turn-around which will eventually help the economy in many ways.

For many, privatisation is a magic wand, or an "open sesame" that can cure all the ills of the present day industrial economy, like redundancy and unemployment, technological obsolescence and falling demands. Others view privatisation as a kind of empty slogan, a temporary illusion or palliative, that may not, in the long run, solve the problem of unemployment and other economic ills to the workers. The real answer lies in between. Privatisation in the sense of a mere transfer of ownership from the State to private investors must be accompanied by a package of income distribution, unemployment insurance and economic participation by a larger number of common people. Where an industry is seriously suffering from ailments caused by technological, economic or sociological reasons, it would be puerile to expect privatisation by itself to lead to a turn-around unless these deep-seated reasons are cured, and feasible programmes of economic revival accepted as a concommitant of the privatisation programme. But where the transfer of ownership is backed by the induction of adequate professional management, investment by investors who feel attracted to a feasible programme of rehabilitation and the induction of private sector norms of efficiency including the discipline of balance sheet and profit and loss statement, privatisation can surely be a portent for economic revival. It also reduces political and bureaucratic interference and abuse of trade union rights. In such cases to the extent to which Government can recover a substantial amount of the funds which have so far been locked up and is at the same time freed from the constant worry of having to meet the budgetary deficits of loss-making public enterprises, a privatisation programme can be to some extent helpful in reducing Government expenditure and tax burden of the people and in enabling Government to divert resources to more productive sectors. In the Indian context, one has to tread this path rather cautiously, as there is always a political and ideological overtone, and any fanfare of publicity is likely to ensure that the programme is resisted wholeheartedly by political elements, trade unionists and even people at large. The result may, therefore, be counterproductive. Despite mounting public sector losses 'privatisation' is still a sort of anathema. What can be a pragmatic policy irrespective of a socialist or market economy is viewed by many as the touchstone of the country's socialism. Government's efforts to sell off the assets of Rs. 128 crore loss-maker Scooters India to the private sector Bajaj Auto was vehemently opposed by nearly all sections—trade unions, political parties and employees—and was eventually abandoned despite strong forces within the government backing up this proposal. But in sharp contrast the State Government of Andhra Pradesh privatised Allwyn-Nissan by selling its shares to Mahindra and Mahindra. Also, the U.P. State government has taken commendable initiatives in the direction of privatising its public enterprises. The tide has at last reached even die-hard West Bengal where the State owned Great Eastern Hotel has been privatised. We must make sure that any privatisation programme is accompanied by a degree of public education which will project the correct position, and remove from public mind apprehensions, such as unemployment or loss of jobs. We must try to take labour with us. This can be done by successfully putting the idea across that privatisation will indirectly create more job opportunities. Where a sick unit suffers from crippling redundancy, it cannot be nursed back to health until the extra wage bill is removed. Those who are identified as surplus must be given golden hand-shake or redeployment opportunities through training. Once the unit's wage-bill is reduced to a level that it can afford on the basis of its ongoing business, it has a good chance of survival and growth. Thereafter, it will again be in a position to create new jobs. Alternatively, it will continue to incur cash losses which will have to be met by budgetary support through higher incidence of taxation. Privatisation provides a fighting chance to get out of this industrial sickness syndrome. Privatisation in the United Kingdom owes its success in no small measure to the support that it received from the working class which got additionally enthused by the ownership stake it was encouraged to develop in the privatised enterprises through the sale of share to the workers.

In part the privatisation wave of the 1980's was an antithesis to the nationalisation wave of the previous decade. The general decline in macro-economic performance in most countries during the 70's led to increasing questioning of the efficiency and efficacy of large public ownership. They certainly proved Herbert Morrison, the father of British nationalisation wrong. Morrison had felt that competition would lead to unnecessary wastage of resources, and nationalised industry would alone bring about public good. Not only did the public sector fail to generate a surplus despite massive investment, but it continued to need huge budgetary support. Inevitably, people turned to privatisation not only to remove the strain on the Government budget, but also to bring about increased economic efficiency as well as allocative efficiency of resources.[2]

Narrowly interpreted, privatisation means the sale of State's equity holdings in an enterprise to private persons. But in a broader sense privatisation comprises many more developments some of which are:

(i) Transition to private sector business management principles and methods including an overwhelming concern for profit.
(ii) Closure or liquidation of state owned enterprises and the sale of assets.
(iii) Leasing of a state enterprise to a private party.
(iv) Management contract of an enterprise to a private party.
(v) Permitting private sector to enter into certain industries exclusively reserved for the government.

Traditionally, a public sector enterprise has been viewed as one in which the government has 100 per cent ownership. But there can also be enterprises where the government holds the majority shareholdings of the controlling block of shareholding, allowing the general public to subscribe to the balance. Such joint holdings are envisaged by the Companies Act, 1956, and the Industrial Policy Resolution, 1956. Such an enterprise need not be called an example of privatisation, but just a modern joint stock corporation with a mixture of both government and public shareholding. In fact, there are leading examples in India of such enterprises with mixed ownership, e.g. Indo-Burma Petroleum, Balmer-Lawrie, Andrew Yule, Hyderabad Allwyn, Gujarat State Fertilizers Corporation, Gujarat Narmada Fertilizer Corporation. These are all quoted on the stock exchanges. Even the State Bank of India has a small percentage of public shareholding.

The issue is whether as a measure of resource-gathering from the capital market through public subscription, or as a measure of making these enterprises more flexible and result-oriented, we should not encourage this mixed form of enterprise as a pervasive feature in our economy. In other words, more and more wholly owned government enterprises can be converted through partial subscription into joint sector corporations. This cannot be called privatisation or denationalisation, but simply a case of limited public shareholding in an otherwise government-owned corporation. Today, there are so many public enterprises which have established a steady record of profitability. As the general public will be interested in subscription to the share capital of only profitable concerns, a start could be made selectively.

Fixing a proper selling price for the share of an enterprise may pose some problems. The net assets value and profits earning value, as calculated according to the standard guidelines, should apply mutatis mutandis in such cases. Special factors such as a monopolistic position should also be given due credit. Initially, selling some shares in small lots so as to establish a trading price before they are offered in bulk for sale may be a workable starting point. In some cases, there will have to be an agreed price on a willing buyer-willing-seller basis. Interestingly, the JRD Tata planning group on civil aviation in the year 2000 recommended that partial public shareholding in both Air India and Indian Airlines be permitted. In this way, according to the group, not only can the two enterprises raise substantial funds, but also become less dependent on the government for future growth, more self-reliant and able to raise resources from the market on commercial terms, like Singapore Airlines and Thai Airlines. This will boost the capital market by increasing the floating stock. It will also give the public at large a sense of participation and partnership in the nation's public sector. Stock market quotations will also provide an independent criterion for a company's true worth and performance. Market quotation reflects the degree of the confidence of the public in a company's future, and is a true indication of a company's health. The substantial rise in the market value of shares such as Andrew Yule, Hyderabad Allwyn and Balmer Lawrie indicates that these companies, by recording vastly improved working results, regained investor's confidence. The corporate restructuring will not in any way dilute the government's overall control while at the same time making the company management responsive to shareholders from the public, some of whom are bound to ask difficult questions at the annual general meetings. The present pattern of wholly-owned government companies makes management bureaucratic, non-responsive and rigid. They often behave as if they were extensions of the administrative ministry. The reduction of government shareholding to 49 per cent or even 26 per cent will bring in a much-needed realism in the corporate management of these enterprises. According to court judgement any enterprise where government holds more than 50 per cent shares is an organ of the state and, therefore, subject to all the requirements of a state agency in matters such as recruitment, discipline, termination of service and various organisational standards. This puts PSUs in a handicap in relation to private sector competitors and also makes for inefficiency and sickness. Reduction of government's holdings below 50%, would, therefore, be all the more desirable.

It will also bring some key non-political, non-establishment criteria into play for evaluating and improving corporate efficiency—for example, raising finances from the national or international capital market. The advent of private shareholders brings about market quotation of share prices, and better preparedness for the annual general meetings. This will make for all-roun improvements in corporate discipline. Also, this will bring about a true partnership between the public and private sectors based on commonality of approach to issues and economic problems. As for the government, the budgetary benefits will be multiple—both directly through the release of funds and through the sale of large blocks of shares (which could be reinvested in other priority areas), and indirectly through better profitability and performance of the enterprises, higher tax receipts and less dependence on subsidies from the government. Eventually, the proposed restructuring wrongly described as privatization, will have to be reflected in the economic efficiency of the enterprises, this is the aim. Partial privatization is only the means to an end viz. economic growth with social justice. Despite persisting opposition the Indian Government has accepted a general policy of selling some percentage of shares in all CPSEs with a view to getting these companies quoted on the Stock Exchange. The Disinvestment Department in the Ministry of Finance handles this task.

It is also important to note that only a part of today's public sector consists of enterprises which need to be in the public sector even in terms of the Industrial Policy Resolution of 1956. Many enterprises which Government set up went beyond the parameters laid down by Schedules A and B of the 1956 Resolution. Public enterprises, such as Modern Food Industry or India Tourism Development Corporation or Scooter India, were never envisaged by Industrial Policy Resolution, 1956. Also Government have willingly taken over a large number of enterprises which were in the private sector, and went sick under private management. Among these, many units were beyond redemption under the normal efficiency criteria in business. Disinvestment of Government ownership and turning them to professional private management with emphasis on the criteria of private sector norms, offer a way out. This will not .really mean any dilution of socialism or even the Industrial Policy Resolution of 1956. On the other hand, Government will be relieved of a hefty financial burden arising out of the need for continuing budgetary support having to be given to such enterprises. Even when a taken-over enterprise is commercially doing well, there is no harm in selling it to private entrepreneurs at the market price provided it does not fall under Schedule A of the 1956 Resolution. This can bring to Government coffers considerable cash. There are a number of public enterprises which have established a record of profitability. In such cases, Government could easily sell upto 49 per cent of shares to the public at the market price. In this way, Government can raise substantial resources which can be invested in priority industries and activities which are now being starved of funds. This change will also encourage the induction of better efficiency and productivity norms in these enterprises while retaining the umbrella public sector character of these enterprises. Possible examples of such enterprises where minority public, share-holding of anything between 49 per cent and 25 per cent can be tried as an experiment are ONGC, IOC, Bharat Petroleum, Hindustan Petroleum, Cochin Refineries, Lubrizol India, Madras Refineries, Oil India, HMT, STC, MMTC, BHEL, Air India, ITDC, and nationalised commercial banks.

With regard to loss-making units, policy must make a clear choice between:

(i) a bold policy of outright sale to anyone who is willing to run an enterprise subject to his freedom to retrench surplus staff on payment of compensation, close down uneconomical activities and take on new profitable activities. OR

(ii) continuing to run the unit and suffer losses for only political reason, and also taxing people heavily only to meet these cash losses. This has to be *matter* of political judgement. Sending all such cases to the Board for Reconstruction of Public Enterprises is a clear option.

As regards the first alternative, there is the related question whether privatisation in itself will improve enterprise efficiency. If not, we may, first concentrate on those key factors which can bring back efficiency or remove those constraints which are responsible for the prevailing inefficiency. In that event, it may be relatively easier to find private sector buyers. An interesting straw in the wind is the unambiguous recommendation by the Planning Commission in the 8th Five Year Plan Document and continuation of same thrust in the subsequent Plan Document, for the closing down or sale of all unviable public sector units which should no longer be a burden on government's finances. The second alternative is the logical outcome of a prevailing political faith in India that equates socialism with state ownership of enterprises, or with a sort of pervasive statism from which even the avowed communist countries are now moving away. Privatisation can never be a panacea for all.

We must note that despite interesting straws in the wind such as the unsuccessful efforts to privatise Scooters India and the successful cases of transfer of Nissan-Allwyn, an Andhra Pradesh State Government project, to the Mahindras, of the Uttar Pradesh State Cement Corporation to the Dalmias, and Modern Foods to Hindustan Lever Ltd. the subject of privatisation is still a taboo in India. But there is a general view that Public sector needs to vacate those areas where it is not necessary in public interest for it to be and leave these activities to the private sector entrepreneurial ability and its capacity to mobilise financial resources on a large-scale. There is a general awareness in the country today that a policy of the public exchequer continuing to meet the cash loss of chronically unviable enterprises for all time to come and a policy of Government taking over private sector undertakings which in public interest. It is in this context that one has to view the policy announced in the 1991-92 and subsequent Central Budgets that the Central Government will sell 20 per cent of its shareholdings in selected public sector enterprises to financial institutions and Mutual Funds and the actual sale of shares in 31 public sector enterprises in pursuance of this discussion during the year 1992-93. The actual sale was affected initially in a somewhat hamhanded fashion by grouping private companies with loss-making companies into several bundles and selling those bundles to the highest bidders among mutual funds etc. In that process sometimes potentially very good marketable shares were sold at very low price e.g. Steel Authority of India, Indian Petrochemicals Corporation. This exposed the government to some public criticism. A public offer of sale in some of these companies with a reserve price calculated according to the government's own standard guidelines could perhaps have yielded substantially higher prices. Government has therefore changed the procedure for disinvestment in 1992-93 turning to the practice of auction and sale to the highest bidder. Also highly significant are the announcement by the 1998 review of the Industrial Policy of July, 1991, that areas reserved for the public sector will be reduced from 29 to 3 activities, the open welcome to private sector initiative to enter into the fields of power and steel, the announcement of a number of State Governments to denationalise road transport and tourism, the partial opening up of infrastructure areas such as roads and bridges to the private sector, the policy announcement that Government will progressively reduce and eliminate the present practice of continuing budgetary support to public enterprises and encourage them by and large to rely on their own internally generated or extra budgetary resources and the policy of enforcing the system of MOU for all public enterprises in order to make them efficient and the policy of referring the cases of chronically sick PSEs to the BIFR. While there is controversy over the so-called 'exit policy', there is no doubt that in the process of restructuring of the public enterprise system including partial privatisation of shareholding and management, Government will have to make adequate provision for a social safety net by which the redundent man-power in these enterprises will be treated with a mixture of measures like handsome compensation package, retraining and redeployment in the new enterprise and a system of unemployment insurance.

In conclusion, India cannot afford to put on an ostrich like appearance in relation to the quiet revolution of privatisation which is sweeping across the whole world covering nearly 100 countries which have accepted it in some form or other, e.g., selling of State enterprises outright, partial privatisation of the shareholding structure in public enterprises, deregulating industrial and agricultural sectors, contracting out Government services including collection of taxes to private agencies, merging of sick enterprises with healthy enterprises in the public or private sector, handing over operating public enterprises to foreign corporations which are expected to bring in new technology, new investable finance, new management and marketing skills, and export capability. In that process, the economies of the concerned countries have made remarkable progress.

In a way, the substantial reduction of the areas under Government ownership, the move towards selling of significant, although not yet very high proportion of shareholding, in public enterprise to Mutual Funds, Financial Institutions, Employees and eventually the public, the denial of budgetary support to public enterprises and compelling them to depend on their own internally generated or extra budgetary resources are all moves in the direction of privatisation in a larger sense. These larger developments will surely have considerable impact than the somewhat narrower aspects of privatisation in the sense of selling of public enterprises to private sector owners. The eventual treatment of the chronic loss-making central public sector enterprises will in the long run no doubt strengthen the move towards privatisation. Although there is considerable dithering even now, it seems inescapable in the long run, for the simple reason that Government does not have funds to continue to maintain them.

It has been keenly felt for quite some time that the existing apparatus or regulating investment and industry through a system of administrative and quantitative controls administered by the bureaucratic apparatus has outlived its utility and time. Our industrial structure has now become broader and much more diversified than in the past. Similarly, the need for Government's constant intervention in respect of specific investment and industrial activities is no longer them. In the sixties and the seventies Indian policy-makers devoted a great deal of attention to the need for controlling concentration of economic power to common detriment. That policy has been largely successful in the sense that today there has been a substantial degree of entrepreneurial diffusion in our industrial economy that we did not have in the past. On the other hand the need for our industry achieving competitive efficiency and quality control consistent with international standards means that it needs to be freed from the vexatious and costly administrative, bureaucratic and quantitative controls and should be allowed to grow or diversify according to economic logic and normal entrepreneurial impulses. Our systems of monetary, budgetary and fiscal instruments have also attained a certain degree of sophistication where they can easily replace the highly counter-productive quantitative types of control. It is in this context that a gradual shift from a system of quantitative import controls to a tariff-based system which the Indian Government initiated during 80s and intensified the late 90s (expected to end from April, 2001) will not impinge adversely on any single enterprise or groups of enterprises but would rather operate as a general impersonal influence. Also we have to initiate a move towards a progressive reduction in tariff protection so that domestic enterprises are compelled to rise up to international levels of efficiency and productivity rather than being forever sheltered under a protective umbrella of tariff barrier. However, WTO's pressure cannot be ignored in this regard. In the end our industry, whether in the public sector or in the private sector, must be efficient, productive and internationally competitive. It is in this context again that we have to address ourselves to the imperative need of reforming and restructuring our public sector enterprises. While it is not envisaged that India will, in the near future completely dispense with the avowed object of the primacy of public sector in her plan of socialist economy, and opt for full market economy, she will have to take lesson from recent examples from China and various countries of East Asia and South-East Asia following somewhat different routes in trying to attain industrial growth. However, giving serious considerations to the lessons learnt from the crises in economies, India should choose positive elements and reject negative ones so as to grow but without the experiences these turbulent countries are undergoing. Wherever public sector enterprises exist these should be encouraged to be managerially efficient and economically viable. We also have to learn from the massive collapse of the economies in East European countries largely on account of nonperformance of the state sector and the public sector enterprises, in particular their failure to give due return on the massive investments made and their propensity to go on drawing more and more investment resources from the Government's budgetary resources. Similarly they must learn from the Wall Street Collapse of 2008 and the recent collapse of the Euro system in Europe. China on the other hand has been a better manager of economic change as illustrated by the phenomenal growth in the non-state sector, in foreign direct investment and exports during the 90s and after. In 1992 she was behind India in GDP or per capita income. Today she is far ahead. We have to draw necessary lessons from all these actual developments. We have to improve the performance of our public sector and allow greater freedom to the private sector. It is imperative that our public sector enterprises are reformed and restructured in such a way that they function with productive efficiency wherever they function. Recent government policies have already vacated almost all areas except three for private sector initiative. In those areas where public sector continue all efforts should be made through appropriate managerial and financial reforms, through establishing proper systems of accounting and decentralization and through obtaining help from private sector parties wherever appropriate to make these enterprises return to the path of profitability and growth.

The central thrust in the move towards reform and reconstruction has been a quest for productive efficiency and a continuing attempt, first somewhat half-hearted and then becoming more and more determined, to remove various legal, procedural and attitudinal obstacles to foster economic growth. Irrespective of the political changes during the last few years, there has been this central phenomenon of a move towards change, reform and restructuring. Rajiv Gandhi as Prime Minister started a process of deregulation in 1985 with a bang, but slowed down after 1987 under political compulsions. Nevertheless the decade of the 1980s registered an impressive growth rate of 5.5 per cent of GDP, significantly higher than the so-called Hindu Rate of Growth of only 2 to 3 per cent during the 1960s and 1970s. The rate peaked up to 7 to 8 per cent during the latter half which corresponds to the 7th Five Year Plan. India's 8th Five Year Plan started on this foundation in 1992. The Industrial Policy of the Congress Government led by Narasimha Rao (1991) brought about a complete overhaul of policies which included abolition of industrial licensing except in 18 industries and an open-door policy for direct foreign investment with 51 per cent ownership in 34 groups of industries. Later on State monopoly has been reduced from 29 to 3 industries. This is the culmination of a decade long process of deregulation and greater reliance on private sector industry. The Eighth Five Year Plan of India (1992-97) and subsequent plans repeatedly have emphasised the States' role as a facilitator of economic activities, the need to do away with all schemes which do not make any economic sense and the need for concentrating the available resources on speedy completion of economically meaningful existing schemes rather than on spreading the resources thin over a very large number of half-baked and incomplete schemes. These have also underscored the need to open up vast segments of the economy to private initiative and private sector participation, and the need for state-owned enterprises vacating vast areas of economy where their presence is not necessary and their becoming lean, efficient and profit oriented in the remaining essential sectors of the economy. Not only is the private sector expected to fill the gap created by the withdrawal of the public sector monopoly from all except 3 broad fields but its participation is encouraged in infrastructure activities such as roads and power. Even higher education and medical care will be opened up to private sector initiative. Highly significant is the ongoing exercise for diversifying the share holding of PSEs by selling shares to mutual funds, employees and eventually the public and making these enterprises lean, efficient and profit oriented. The cases of so called 'unviable' enterprises will be referred to the BRPSE for surgical reconstruction including even closure, when inevitable, with compensation package for surplus employees. A National Renewal Fund was set up by the Central Government with a corpus of Rs 200 crore to facilitate retraining, redeployment and rehabilitation of surplus employees in public and private sector enterprises consequent on reconstruction, modernisation or closure.

The massive process of adjustment and restructuring that is going on is bound to create some apprehension of significant volume of retrenchment and unemployment. We must face this problem boldly and with determination. The legitimate apprehensions of working class and the trade unions must be met by providing a system of social safety net which will concentrate on avoiding retrenchment wherever possible, providing attractive compensation packages wherever retrenchment is unavoidable and training and redeployment in new enterprises being created with added focus of employment generation programmes. The recent developments have cast very wide responsibilities on the private sector. As we move more and more to the philosophy of private-sector-Ied economic development and the market forces as the primary determinants of investment, private sector will be increasingly expected to shoulder the main responsibility for development. The government will have to play the role of facilitator or macro-economic manager. Can India's private sector rise up to this task as its counterparts have done in the Pacific Rim countries? The outcome of all these changes have been certainly marked uncertainties in the labour market, necessitating a fresh look at the labour laws.

Slowly, but surely the movement towards deregulation and opening up of Indian economy seems to be getting general acceptance. The Government has now allowed automatic entry of enterprises with a foreign majority holding in a vast area. The Foreign Investment Promotion Board has been set up and also a unified machinery has been set in motion for clearing other investment proposals in a quick, hassle-free and less complicated manner. A Foreign Investment Implementation Authority (FIIA) has been set up for providing single point interface between foreign investors and the Government machinery. The FIIA is empowered to give composite/ comprehensive approvals. A project monitoring unit has also been set up for facilitating implementation of projects. India has also abolished industrial licensing and clearance requirements in respect of monopoly and restrictive trade practices which hitherto applied to all large business houses and foreign majority companies. Foreign businessmen are being assured that India had become a good and attractive field for foreign investors who would be given full protection of their interests by the Government, and ruled out nationalisation in future.

From the response of trade and business community in U.S., Britain, Japan, Germany and other countries, it is quite clear that these reforms have been widely appreciated abroad. Also, the multilateral institutions like World Bank, the IMF and the Asian Development Bank, have applauded India's economic reforms and restructuring. According to the U.N. India is the third most favorite destination preceded only by USA and China. The recent reports of the World Bank, the I.M.F. and the Asian Development Bank testify to the prospects of reform and significant improvement in the efficient use of resources in India. The Incremental Capital Output Ratio

(ICOR) which measures net output from the inputs of an extra unit of capital has come down from the peak of 10.5 in 1975 to 5.3 in 1987 and to 4.1 by 1989. A high ICOR is assumed to signify a low efficiency in the use of a country's savings. This improvement coincided with the initiation of the liberalisation process during the late 1970s and early 1980s. These Reports commended the Indian Government's recent policy initiatives. India is going through a rather traumatic process of economic adjustments since mid-1991 in order to tide over the twin dangers of high fiscal deficits and serious balance of payment difficulties and these no doubt created much dislocation and turbulence in the short run, clearly making long term prospects are bright. The lowering of government spending, the deceleration of industrial production on account of the import compression and 'dear-money' policy, the closure of a number of enterprises in the public and the private sectors and the resultant loss of jobs no doubt hurt the nation. But in the long run, these difficulties are much more than made up by the recovery of the economy which mean creation of many new enterprises in the private sector and the creation of many more jobs in the new sun-rise industries. Although, external position has been brought under almost complete check, fiscal deficit problem is still one of the major problems. When the government eventually regains its fiscal balance, this will have an immense impact in reducing the inflationary pressure and in putting the economy back on the rails for future progress.

The three ongoing process of deregulation of government functioning, the opening up of the economy to private sector initiatives including foreign investment, and integrating Indian economy with the global economy are irreversible in many respects. The sooner India falls in. step with these processes, the better for her economic growth and welfare. Clearly, the country is on the right track and the future for the private sector in a deregulated economy moving under market impulses can only be bright.

Given this pragmatic policy environment and the recent. G.D.P. growth trends (around 8 per cent to 9 per cent per annum) India is today on the threshold of what can be a phenomenal technological-industrial quantum jump in the present millennium which should be. accompanied by substantial and visible improvements in the standards of living. This is inevitable, provided the ongoing process of debureaucratisation of the economy is continued and the national goal of pushing India up to the level of the most advanced countries in the world is pursued as a giant collaborative effort by government, industry, professional managers and the trade unions.

We can cross the threshold if the genuinely productive elements of the society whether in the private or public sector are allowed to grow and diversify according to economic logic and unfeltered by day-to-day bureaucratic controls. There must be greater involvement of our managers and industrialists in the country's planning process. We need pragmatic non-doctrinaire and production-oriented policies.

The impact of the destruction of the World Trade Centre on the 11th September 200 I and the attack on the Pentagon by fundamentalist terrorists on international business has been profound. Not only has it sent shivers down all sections of international business, but it has also led to unprecedented demand recession spells in a few industries like aviation, tourism and hotels and international business in general. In a way, such incidents have a much larger impact on today's world than in the past on account of the galloping pace at which globalisation is overtaking us. In the same way the impact of the Enron collapse could not be as large in the past as in the globalised world in which we live today. As globalisation has become an irreversible unstoppable process, business management must necessarily come to terms with it. There are no doubt constraints which have to be anticipated and contained in time. Also there are opportunities which have to be seized. Managers should stop thinking in terms of operating within the national frontier to which they were accustomed during the, last 2 or 3 centuries. The phenomenal growth of information technology, the ATMS, E-mails, telefax systems, space technology-aided telecom system will simply not tolerate national frontiers any more. Management must be aware of all , these developments.

The world is in a state of unprecedented change. Not only has it changed beyond recognition since the second world war, but it is also changing fast at an accelerated pace. This change should be seen as an oppourtunity to be seized rather than as a constraint. As cross border trade of goods and services enters the liberalised Indian economy, Indian managers must learn to master the change brought out by delicensing, liberalisation and advent of competition and globalisation. In the global market-place boundaries between industries, nations and cultures have lost their meaning. Today's competitor can be tomorrow's ally. Today's associate may be tomorrow's rival. Thus there is no permanent alliance, nor any permanent business rivalry. The only thing which is certain is the principle of uncertainty. In the context of globalisation, a border-less world, accelerating competition and the fast pace at which knowledge is being generated, the ability to minimise uncertainties and anticipate change could substantially determine the extent of a company's success in the market place. To what extent organisations can adopt themselves to new conditions will determine who will perish, who will survive and who will prosper. Only those who can complete the process of change to their advantage will survive and grow. The best way to understand the future is to grasp the accelerating changes which will transform the world that we know, analyse the process of change, anticipate trends and act on them taking advantage of the opportunities and eliminating or at least minimising the constraints, and understanding the patterns that mark our repeatedly changing national and global environment. In order to make the right moves at the right time we have to introduce the "business approach," a cost benefit analysis of every event, and an all-pervasive productive culture in the corporate sector as well as in the government. Our administrative tools and procedures are often survivals from the 19th century while the tasks that we face are of the 21st century. We have therefore to scrap a lot, refashion and innovate a great deal and introduce new organisational forms and procedures consistent with the new information technology. As Jack Welch says in his autobiography "Take charge of your destiny, otherwise someone else will." To quote the well-known medieval Italian strategtist, Machiavelli "Nothing ever is more difficult than initiating the new order of things. If you are going to do the same things again and again you will also get the same results." In fact Information Technology has become crucial not only in und strategy management but also even in day-to-day operations. CEOs have no choice but to understand it and make use of it in this digital age. Knowledgeable people talk about "the end of geography" or "the death of distance" to forcefully press how the communication revolution is changing our lives and our life styles. The key buz words are globalisation, interdependence, technology orientation, a border-less world, integration of time zones, freedom to obtain inputs from anywhere in the world wherever they are the cheapest and of the best quality and also sell products anywhere in the world where the best prices are available. The integration is between what is known as the old economy, i.e. manufacturing industry and the new economy. There are pronounced trends towards the dispersal of the factory and the office systems under the impact of the new information technology and the increasing trend of more and more people working from home through a whole network of computer terminals. The experience of European Union could be the foretaste of the emerging pattern in the future where the boundaries among nations gradually get blurred. From the perspective of a historian this remarkable transformation is taking place at an incredibly fast pace, giving rise to what Alvin Toffler described three decades ago as the "premature arrival of the future." For most companies—even global multinationals—"global strategy" will increasingly mean not just trying to gain market share outside "home" countries. But that is going to change, even in industries that are local today. Our objective is to help managers think clearly about how to take on the challenges of operating in a transition economy whose pace of integration will at times seem very slow and then remarkably fast—an economy that will be confusing and uncertain.

The process of globalisation, not the end state, is the focus of our inquiry. We try to show how changes in industry structures will be caused by active economic agents (i.e., aggressive companies) and the enormous opportunities to raise market capitalisations that will result. Critical to success will be pace and timing—knowing not just what to do but when to do it. The answers will come as much from action as from analysis.

Indian economy, for about five decades, i.e. from 1950s to 1990s, was a highly government controlled economy, as also a highly sheltered economy. One needed to understand and make use of the government's formidable industrial regulations mechanism to set up new industries or to expand on existing lines. Also, it was by and large a competition-free economy where those who were lucky to get licences had a promised monopoly of their products. Other domestic competitors were not easily permitted to come. Also international competition was precluded as the country was protected by a high tariff and quantitative barrier. All this started changing from 1991 and today India is by and large a free economy where all entry barriers in industrial production as also any barriers for foreign investors have by and large been removed, if not 100 per cent eliminated. This also means that strategic managers and corporate planners have to adjust their thinking and ways completely. They have to be ready to make investment in accordance with normal business prospects, growth impulses and economic logic with a world view. They need not mind competition from overseas. Indeed, they have to take advantage of the opportunities offered by competition, deregulation and globalisation, confidently fight the constraints which are imposed and some times learn to turn the constraints into opportunities. In recent years there are several leading examples, where companies have turned constraints into opportunities.

# Index